# Kölner Schriften zu Recht und Staat

Herausgegeben von
Prof. Dr. Hartmut Schiedermair und
Prof. Dr. Bernhard Kempen

Band 40

PETER LANG
Frankfurt am Main · Berlin · Bern · Bruxelles · New York · Oxford · Wien

Zan He

# The ICJ's Practice on Provisional Measures

PETER LANG
Internationaler Verlag der Wissenschaften

**Bibliographic Information published by the Deutsche Nationalbibliothek**
The Deutsche Nationalbibliothek lists this publication in the Deutsche Nationalbibliografie; detailed bibliographic data is available in the internet at http://dnb.d-nb.de.

Zugl.: Köln, Univ., Diss., 2009

Cover illustration
Historisches Universitätssiegel der Universität zu Köln.

D 38
ISSN 1433-0253
ISBN 978-3-631-60010-8



www.peterlang.de

**Acknowledgements**

This study was carried out from June 2008 to October 2009 at the Institute for International Law and Comparative Public law, University of Cologne.

I would like to express my sincere gratitude to my supervisor, Professor Dr. Bernhard Kempen for his essential guidance, endless enthusiasm and kind encouragement throughout my study. At the same time I am thankful to Dr. Andreas Funke, Mr. Robin Lengelsen and Miss Jannika Jahn for their inspiring suggestions.

Warm thanks are given to the whole group for the friendly working atmosphere.

Thanks to the Institute for International Law and Comparative Public law, University of Cologne for the financial support.

Finally I am grateful to my parents and to my husband for their support.

Cologne, October 2009 Zan He

**Table of Contents**

## Introduction

Since the first appearance of the provisional measures before the INTERNATIONAL COURT OF JUSTICE in 1951,[1] the development of the practice on provisional measures in the Court has had a long history. The binding force of provisional measures was finally recognized in 2001 (in the *LAGRAND*[2] case). Since then, a trend of more frequent requests for provisional measures appeared before the Court. The jurisprudence of the ICJ on provisional measures has risen to prominence in the past several decades. This has provoked great interest in the academic field. Some authors believe that its jurisprudence also has the greatest impact on the development of international law because the INTERNATIONAL COURT OF JUSTICE is the only international judicial instance which is accessible to practically all States and whose jurisdiction *ratione materiae* extends at the same time to the whole field of international law.[3]

It is a matter of common knowledge that "provisional measures" are one of the important procedural instruments before the INTERNATIONAL COURT OF JUSTICE.[4] The origin of this procedure might also be a commonplace. Professor *Rosenne* put it as "the rights and obligations of the parties to a dispute shall be determined by reference to the situation that existed at the date on which the proceedings were instituted when a dispute is submitted to a court or tribunal for judicial decision."[5] The PERMANENT COURT OF INTERNATIONAL JUSTICE defined provisional measures as: "the parties to a case must abstain from any measures capable of exercising a prejudicial effect in regard to the execution of the decision to be given, and in general not allow any step of any kind to be taken which might aggravate or extend the dispute."[6] The present Court confirmed its predecessor's ruling in the *Passage through the Great Belt* case: No action taken *pendente lite* by a State engaged in litigation before the Court with another State "can have any effect whatsoever as regards the legal situation which the Court is called upon to define".[7]

---

1 *Anglo-Iranian Oil Co.* (UK v. IRAN), (Provisional Measures), Order of 13 July 1951, ICJ Reports 1951, p.89-95.

2 *LAGRAND* (GERMANY v. USA), (Merits), Judgment of 27 June 2001, ICJ Reports 2001, p.506, para. 109.

3 *Sztucki*, Interim Measures in The Hague Court, (1983), preface.

4 *Eg. Elkind* observed: "this is potentially one of the most important and actually one of the most controversial functions of the Court.", *Elkind*, Interim Protection: A Functional Approach, (1981), Foreword, p.XI.

5 *Rosenne*, Provisional Measures in International Law, (2005), p.1.

6 *Electricity Company of Sofia and Bulgaria* case (BELGIUM v. BULGARIA), (Interim Measures), Order of 5 December 1939, PCIJ Series A/B, No.79, p.199.

7 *Passage through the Great Be*lt case (FINLAND v. DENMARK), (Provisional Measures), Order of 29 July 1991, ICJ Reports 1991, p.19, para. 32. The Court cited and adapted a passage from the Judgment of the Permanent Court in the *Case Concerning the Legal Status of the South-Eastern Territory of Greenland*, (NORWAY v. DENMARK), (Interim Measures), Order of 3

## A. The legal basis for the indication of provisional measures

To begin with the discussion on the legal basis for the indication of provisional measures, it is necessary to analyze the relationship between the present Court and the PERMANENT COURT OF INTERNATIONAL JUSTICE. As the successor of the PERMANENT COURT OF INTERNATIONAL JUSTICE, the INTERNATIONAL COURT OF JUSTICE was established in April 1946. Although the INTERNATIONAL COURT OF JUSTICE is an entirely new international court as concerns the institutional structure, its Statute was mainly based upon that of the PCIJ. In April 1945, a meeting of a committee of jurists representing 44 States was convened in WASHINGTON. This Committee, under the chairmanship of G. H. *Hackworth* (UNITED STATES), was entrusted with the preparation of a draft Statute for the future international court of justice, for submission to the SAN FRANCISCO CONFERENCE, which during the months of April to June 1945 was to draw up the UNITED NATIONS CHARTER. The draft Statute prepared by the Committee was based on the Statute of the PCIJ and was thus not a completely new text. The SAN FRANCISCO CONFERENCE nevertheless showed some concern that all continuity with the past should not be broken, particularly as the Statute of the PCIJ had itself been drawn up on the basis of past experience, and it was felt better not to change something that had seemed to work well. The Charter therefore plainly stated that the STATUTE OF THE INTERNATIONAL COURT OF JUSTICE was based upon that of the PCIJ. At the same time, the necessary steps were taken for a transfer of the jurisdiction of the PCIJ so far as was possible to the INTERNATIONAL COURT OF JUSTICE.[10] Furthermore, as the predecessor of the present Court, the jurisprudence of PCIJ is significant for the study of provisional measures in the present Court. Therefore, although the dissertation will focus on the study of the present Court, the statute of PCIJ and the cases concerning provisional measures before the PCIJ will also be referred to in this dissertation.

### I. The Statute of the INTERNATIONAL COURT OF JUSTICE

Article 41 of the Statute of the Court is the only source of the Court's power to indicate provisional measures. Article 41(1) provides that the Court has the power "to indicate, if it considers that circumstances so require, any provisional measures which ought to be taken to preserve the respective rights of either party." Article

10 History of the Court, www.icj-cij.org

41(2) provides that notice must be given to the UN SECURITY COUNCIL. However, the article does little more than that and leaves it to the Court to develop the law. As professor *Rosenne* wrote, "in fact, it can be said that the whole of the substantive law of the International Court on provisional measures of protection and its procedure is judge-made law, with the minimum of outside interference".[11]

This article has gone through a long development process. The question of provisional measures was presented for the first time in the history of the PICJ, at the fifth meeting of the ADVISORY COMMITTEE OF JURISTS,[12] on 3 July 1920. On that meeting, the ADVISORY COMMITTEE established a Drafting committee to draw up rules for procedure. In the memorandum presented by the LEAGUE SECRETARIAT, the question of provisional measures was put under the heading: *Is the Court competent to decree, as regards the subject-matter of the dispute, the fixation of the status quo pending its decision?* In that context the memorandum described the experience of the CENTRAL AMERICAN COURT OF JUSTICE quoting Article 18 of the 1907 WASHINGTON CONVENTION[13] and the BRYAN TREATIES,[14] Article 12 of the PHILLIMORE PLAN of March 1918,[15] and one new proposal by the German Government to empower the tribunal to settle by provisional arrangement the relations arising from the dispute for the duration of the proceedings (Article 34).[16]

---

11 *Rosenne*, *supra* note 5, p. 33.

12 At its second session in February 1920, the COUNCIL OF THE LEAGUE OF NATIONS decided to convene an ADVISORY COMMITTEE OF JURISTS to prepare plans for the establishment of the Court.

13 CENTRAL AMERICAN COURT was established on the basis of 1907 WASHINGTON CONVENTION. Article XVIII of the Convention provided that "From the moment in which any suit is instituted against any one or more governments up to that in which a final decision has been pronounced, the court may at the solicitation of any one of the parties fix the situation in which the contending parties must remain, to the end that the difficulty shall not be aggravated and that things shall be conserved in *status quo* pending a final decision."

14 On 23 April 1913 the UNITED STATES SECRETARY OF THE STATE W.J. *Bryan* laid before the SENATE COMMITTEE ON FOREIGN RELATIONS a proposition to create commissions of enquiry for the advancement of international peace. A series of treaties were concluded following the proposal. These treaties provided for recourse to a PERMANENT INTERNATIONAL COMMISSION when ordinary diplomatic proceedings had failed and the parties did not have recourse to arbitration. Each of the treaties with CHINA, FRANCE and Sweden contained a clause regarding provisional measures, reading: In case the cause of the dispute should consist of certain acts already committed or about to be committed, the Commission shall as soon as possible indicate what measures to preserve the rights of each party ought in its opinion to be taken provisionally and pending the delivery of its report. These provisions served as a basis for Article 41 of the PERMANENT COURT OF INTERNATIONAL JUSTICE.

15 For the PHILLIMORE PLAN, see *Miller*, The Drafting of the Covenant, 2 doc.1, (1928), p. 3-6.

16 PCIJ, ADVISORY COMMITTEE OF JURISTS, Documents presented to the Committee relating to existing plans for the establishment of a PERMANENT COURT OF INTERNATIONAL JUSTICE (1920), Documents 127.

This DRAFTING COMMITTEE presented its text at the twenty-fifth meeting, on 19 July 1920.[17] At the Committee's twenty-eighth meeting on 20 July, M. Raoul *Fernandes* of Brazil proposed a revised text.[18] This text version was adopted in principle and finally turned to be Article 39 of the draft Statute.[19] When the draft Article 39 was examined by the Sub-Committee of the Third Committee of the first Assembly of the LEAGUE OF NATIONS, a number of amendments were considered. *Fernandes* advised again to use the word "ordonner" in the French version. The Sub-Committee decided to stay with the word "indiquer", the Chairman of the Sub-Committee observing that the Court lacked the means to execute its decisions. The language of the first paragraph of the English version was then made to conform to the French text: thus the word "suggest" was replaced by "indicate", and "should" by "ought to". However, in the second paragraph of the English version the phrase "measures suggested" remained unchanged.[20] Another amendment was made in the Third Committee. The representative of Panama proposed a stipulation to ensure that all Members of the League are notified of the provisional measures to be taken. This proposal was rejected. In reply to questions, it was explained that this article covered cases where an omission to act, and not an act which had already been committed or was imminent, threatened the rights of one of the parties. But the representative of the British Empire protested against the extended interpretation of the word *act*. That led the suggestion to delete the initial words "if the disputes arises out of an act which has already taken place or is

---

17 PCIJ, ADVISORY COMMITTEE OF JURISTS -Procès-Verbaux of the Proceedings of the Committee, June 16th-July 24th (1920), the 25th meeting held on 19 July, 1920, p. 567-568.
It reads: If the dispute arises out of an act which has already taken place or which is imminent, the Court shall have the power to suggest, if it considers that circumstances so require, the provisional measures that should be taken to preserve the respective rights of either party.
Pending the final decision, notice of the measures suggested shall forthwith be given to the parties and the Council.

18 PCIJ, ADVISORY COMMITTEE OF JURISTS -Procès-Verbaux of the Proceedings of the Committee, June 16th - July 24th (1920), the 28th meeting held on 20 July 1920, p.609.
It reads: In case the cause of the dispute should consist of certain acts already committed or about to be committed, the Court may, provisionally and with the least possible delay, order adequate provisional measures to be taken, pending the final judgment of the Court.

19 It reads: If the dispute arises out of acts which have already taken place or which are imminent, the Court shall have the power to suggest, if it considers that circumstances require it, the measures that must be taken provisionally to ensure that the respective rights be not prejudiced.
Pending the decision, notice of the measures suggested shall forthwith be given to the parties and the Council.

20 *LAGRAND*, (GERMANY v. USA), (Merits), Judgment of 27 June 2001, ICJ Reports 2001, p.466, p.501, para.106. For the original discussion in the Sub-committee, *see* LEAGUE OF NATIONS, PCIJ, *Documents concerning the action taken by the Council of the League of Nations under Art.14 of the Covenant and the Adoption of the Statute of the Permanent Court* (GENEVA, 1921), p.134.

matter connected with the implementation of any provisional measure it has indicated.[31]

---

SECURITY COUNCIL in pursuance of Article 41, paragraph 2, of the Statute.

31 Article 78
The Court may request information from the parties on any matter connected with the implementation of any provisional measures it has indicated.

## B. A brief survey of the decisions

### I. The requests presented before the Court

The requests for provisional measures and the Court's decisions on provisional measures will be discussed in the following chapters in detail. However, a brief summary of the major cases will facilitate an overall view of the Court's jurisprudence on provisional measures.

During the jurisprudence of the PERMANENT INTERNATIONAL COURT OF JUSTICE, there were 6 requests for provisional measures brought before it. Among them, 2 were granted. From 1947 to October 2009, 40 requests for provisional measures[32] were raised before the INTERNATIONAL COURT OF JUSTICE. Among them, 16 were granted, 20 were rejected, 1 was withdrawn by the Applicant, 1 was lapsed and 2 were removed from the GENERAL LIST.

19 requests were raised from 1999 (after the *LAGRAND* case) to October 2009, comparing with 21 requests from 1947 to March 1999 (including the *LAGRAND* case). It can be observed that the procedure has been much more frequently triggered since 1999. This is partly because more states have become willing to accept the legal approach of settlement of disputes and have acceded to the jurisdiction of the Court. On the other hand, it is due to the encouraging effects of provisional measures on the requesting parties. However, only 4 requests were granted since 1999 despite of the greatly increased number of the requests before the Court. [33] This might reflect the Court's even more prudential attitude on the indication of provisional measures due to the risk of bringing more inappropriate restraint on the Respondent's rights after the recognition of the binding force of provisional measures.

---

32 There are forty cases before the INTERNATIONAL COURT OF JUSTICE involving requests of provisional measures. However, six cases are related to three single disputes: the *Fisheries Jurisdiction* cases (FEDERAL REPUBLIC OF GERMANY v. ICELAND), (UK v. ICELAND); the *Nuclear Test* cases (AUSTRALIA v. FRANCE), (NEW ZEALAND v. FRANCE), and the Cases Concerning Interpretation and Application of the Montreal Convention of 1971 arising out of the Aerial Incident at Lockerbie (LIBYA v. UK), (LIBYA v. USA) (abbreviated as the *Lockerbie* case in the following). These cases are formulated in six separate but linked cases. Besides, the *Legality of Use of Force* cases cover ten requests for provisional measures.

33 From 1947 to 1999 (including the *LAGRAND* case), 12 requests were granted, 7 requests were rejected, 1 was withdrawn, 1 was lapsed. From 1999 (after the *LAGRAND* case) to October 2009, 4 requests were granted, 13 requests were rejected, 2 were removed from the General List.

## II. The rejections and their basis

When observing the basis of the Court's rejection to indicate provisional measures in the specific case, it is found that the most frequently invoked ground is the "lack of urgency"(as in the *Interhandel* case[34], the *Passage through the Great Belt* case[35] and the Case Concerning *Certain Criminal Proceedings in FRANCE* case[36]). Besides, "the lack of *prima facie* jurisdiction over the merits" is also one of the reasons for rejection. Although it is widely accepted that "the establishment of a *prima facie* jurisdiction over the merits" is a relatively low threshold comparing to the high threshold of urgency, this basis has been raised in the *Legality of Use of Force* cases[37] and the Case Concerning *Armed Activities on the Territory of the CONGO.*[38] In the Case Concerning *the Arbitral Award of 31 July 1989*, the request for provisional measures was rejected on the ground that "the alleged rights sought to be made the subject of provisional measures were not the subject of the proceedings

---

34 *Interhandel* (SWITZERLAND v. USA), (Provisional Measures), Order of 24 October 1957, ICJ Reports 1957, p.105-114.

35 *Passage through the Great Belt* (GREECE v. DENMARK), (Provisional Measures), Order of 29 July 1991, ICJ Reports 1991, p. 12-21.

36 Case concerning *Certain Criminal Proceedings in FRANCE* (DEMOCRATIC REPUBLIC OF THE CONGO v. FRANCE), (Provisional Measures), Order of 17 June 2003, ICJ Reports 2003, p. 102-112.

37 *Legality of Use of Force* (YUGOSLAVIA v. USA), (Provisional Measures), Order of 2 June 1999, ICJ Reports 1999, p. 916-926.
*Legality of Use of Force* (SERBIA and MONTENEGRO v. UK), (Provisional Measures), Order of 2 June 1999, ICJ Reports 1999, p. 826-841.
*Legality of Use of Force* (YUGOSLAVIA v. SPAIN), (Provisional Measures), Order of 2 June 1999, ICJ Reports 1999, p. 761-774.
*Legality of Use of Force* (SERBIA and MONTENEGRO v. PORTUGAL), (Provisional Measures), Order of 2 June 1999, ICJ Reports 1999, p. 656-673.
*Legality of Use of Force* (SERBIA and MONTENEGRO v. NETHERLANDS), (Provisional Measures), Order of 2 June 1999, ICJ Reports 1999, p. 542-559.
*Legality of Use of Force* (SERBIA and MONTENEGRO v. ITALY), (Provisional Measures), Order of 2 June 1999, ICJ Reports 1999, p. 481-494.
*Legality of Use of Force* (SERBIA and MONTENEGRO v. GERMANY), (Provisional Measures), Order of 2 June 1999, ICJ Reports 1999, p. 422-434.
*Legality of Use of Force* (SERBIA and MONTENEGRO v. FRANCE), (Provisional Measures), Order of 2 June 1999, ICJ Reports 1999, p. 363-375.
*Legality of Use of Force* (SERBIA and MONTENEGRO v. CANADA), (Provisional Measures), Order of 2 June 1999, ICJ Reports 1999, p. 259 -275.
*Legality of Use of Force* (SERBIA and MONTENEGRO v. BELGIUM), (Provisional Measures), Order of 2 June 1999, ICJ Reports 1999, p. 124 -141.

38 Case Concerning *Armed Activities on the Territory of the Congo*, (New Application: 2002), (DEMOCRATIC REPUBLIC OF THE CONGO v. RWANDA), (Provisional Measures), Order of 10 July 2002, ICJ Reports 2002, p. 219-251.

before the Court on the merits of the case".[39] In the *Aegean Sea Continental Shelf*[40] case, the Court rejected to indicate provisional measures in view of two circumstances, one is the lack of "irreparable prejudice to the rights of either party" due to the existence of appropriate means of reparation or satisfaction, and the other is the adoption of the SECURITY COUNCIL RESOLUTION which could in fact meet the ends of GREECE's request for provisional measures. The *Lockerbie* case[41] is one of the most important cases in the Court's jurisprudence. The Court believed that the rights claimed by LIBYA under the Montreal Convention could not be regarded as appropriate for protection by provisional measures because in accordance with Article 103 of the UNITED NATIONS CHARTER, the obligations of the parties in Resolution 748 (1992) prevail over their obligations under any other international agreement, including the Montreal Convention. Due to its unique characteristic as concerning the relationship between the SECURITY COUNCIL RESOLUTION and the Court's exercise of power to indicate provisional measure, this dissertation will continue the study in Chapter E. In the *case concerning the request for an examination of the situation in accordance with paragraph 61 of the Court's judgment of 20 December 1974 in the Nuclear Tests* (NEW ZEALAND v. FRANCE) case,[42] the "further request for the indication of provisional measures" was dismissed because of the removal of the request from the General List in the main dispute. This general sketch of the rejected requests for provisional measures can probably shed some light on the issue we are discussing. Nevertheless, it is necessary to go further to the details of these cases and find out the circumstances, which the Court might take into consideration when it is in confrontation with a request for provisional measures.

---

39 Case concerning *the Arbitral Award of 31 July 1989*, (GUINEA- BISSAU v. SENEGAL), (Provisional Measures), Order of 2 March 1990, ICJ Reports 1990, p. 64 -71.

40 *Aegean Sea Continental Shelf*, (GREECE v. TURKEY), (Provisional Measures), Order of 11 September 1976, ICJ Reports 1976, p.3-15.

41 *Lockerbie* (LIBYA v. USA), (Provisional Measures), Order of 14 April 1992, ICJ Reports 1992, p.114 -128.
*Lockerbie* (LIBYA v. UK), (Provisional Measures), Order of 14 April 1992, ICJ Reports 1992, p.4 -17.

42 Case concerning *the Request for an Examination of the Situation in Accordance with Paragraph 61 of the Court's Judgment of 20 December 1974 in the Nuclear Tests* (NEWZEALAND v. FRANCE), (Provisional Measures), Order of 22 September 1995, ICJ Reports 1995, p.288 -308.

## C. The purpose of provisional measures

Beginning the discussion on the interpretation and application of Article 41 of the Statute, it is necessary to put close examination on the statutory purpose of it. Article 41 of the Statute states: "the Court shall have the power to indicate, if it considers that circumstances so require, any provisional measures which ought to be taken to *preserve the respective rights of either party*". "Preserve the respective rights of either party pending the ICJ's final decision" might be the only express statement of the purpose of provisional measures in the Statute and Rules of the Court.

However, the other documents of the Court show more details of the Court's opinion. In the Orders in the *Fisheries Jurisdiction* cases, there is a paragraph, which could be regarded as the Court's detailed interpretation of this issue. This paragraph has been frequently adopted in the Orders ever since 1972. It reads:

> "whereas the right of the Court to indicate provisional measures as provided for in Article 41 of the Statute has its object to preserve the respective rights of the Parties pending the decision of the Court, and presupposes that irreparable prejudice should not be caused to rights which are the subject of dispute in judicial proceedings, and that the Court's judgment should not be anticipated by reason of any initiative regarding the measures which are in issue".[43]

Three elements are mentioned in the paragraph:

i) the indication is intended to preserve the respective rights of the parties
ii) irreparable prejudice should not be caused to disputed rights
iii) the Court's judgment should not be anticipated by reason of any initiative regarding the rights, which it sought to protect.

"To preserve the respective rights of the parties" could be regarded as the statutory purpose of provisional measures because of the word "object". However, the expression of the relationship between these three elements has not always been very consistent in the Court's Orders.[44] In some cases, the last two elements were not mentioned. In my view, "to preserve the respective rights of the parties" is the

---

43 *Fisheries Jurisdiction* (FEDERAL REPUBLIC OF GERMANY v. ICELAND), (Provisional Measures), Order of 17 August 1972, ICJ Reports 1972, p.34, para. 22.
*Fisheries Jurisdiction* (UK and NORTHERN IRELAND v. ICELAND), (Provisional Measures), Order of 17 August 1972, ICJ Reports 1972, p.16, para. 21.

44 *Thirlway*, The Indication of Provisional Measures by the INTERNATIONAL COURT OF JUSTICE in: *Bernhardt* (ed.), Interim Measures Indicated by International Court, (1994), p.6.

general expression of the basic purpose of provisional measures. "Irreparable prejudice should not be caused to disputed rights" and "non-anticipation of the judgment" is put in a negative sense, tending to restrict the purpose of the provisional measures. The last two elements are stated in a contrary and complementary manner. They are the derivative and specific purposes of provisional measures.

### I. Preservation of rights

What does the expression "to preserve the respective rights of either party" mean in Article 41 of the Statue? It is quite a general term and there are no explanatory or supplementary articles in the Statute or the Rules of the Court. Nevertheless, the drafting history of Article 41 of the Statute of the Court and the Court's practice on the interpretation of Article 41 provide some reference. In the memorandum presented by the League Secretariat to the drafting committee in 1920, the 1907 Washington Convention and the Bryan Treaties were taken as examples. However, the 1907 Convention adopted a different term "non-aggravation of the dispute" instead of the term "to preserve the respective rights of either party". The concept of preservation of rights was found in connection with the Arbitration Commission contemplated by the Bryan Treaties. It is quite reasonable to infer that it was a delicate choice of "preservation of rights" rather than "non-aggravation of the dispute".[45]

"Preserve the respective rights of either party" does not have a meaning as broad as "prevent the rights from infringement or breach". Otherwise, the threshold of the indication of provisional measures would be too low. That would be against the intention of the drafters of the Statute. As an incidental procedure to assure the ultimate justice of the decision on the merits, provisional measures shall keep a balance between the rights of the Applicant State and the sovereignty of the Respondent State. If proceedings are brought claiming that State A has a right and State B is breaching it, while State B believes that it is not breaching State A's right, the effect of provisional measures is to presume that State B is breaching State A's right and ask State B to take some measures to "freeze" the state of rights and obligations between the two states without any proceedings on the merits of the case. Too wide open the door for the indication of provisional measures might cause unfair and inappropriate risks to the sovereignty of the Respondent State. Therefore, provisional measures shall not be indicated on the sole ground that the rights are under infringement or breach. Take the Case Concerning *the Legal Status of the South-Eastern Territory of Greenland* in the Permanent Court as an example,[46] the

45 *Thirlway*, *ibid.*, p.7.

46 Case concerning *the Legal Status of the South-Eastern Territory of Greenland* (NORWAY V.

Court refused to indicate provisional measures, stating the reasons as follows: "whereas, having regard to the character of the alleged rights in question, considered in relation to the natural characteristics of the territory in issue, even 'measures calculated to change the legal status of the territory' could not, according to the information now at the Court's disposal, affect the value of such alleged rights, once the Court in its judgment on the merits had recognized them as appertaining to one or other of the Parties, and as, in any case, the consequences of such measures would not, in point of fact, be irreparable." In the *Interhandel* case, the Court refused to grant the provisional measures, stating the reasons as follows:

> "whereas in the light of information furnished to the Court, it appears that, according to the law of the United States, the sale of those shares can only be effected after termination of a judicial proceeding which is at present pending in that country in respect of which there in no indication as to its speedy conclusion, and whereas such a sale is therefore conditional upon a judicial decision rejecting the claims of Interhandel ..."[47]

Then, what should the scope of "preserve" be? When should the Court grant the provisional measures to preserve the respective rights of the parties? The jurisprudence of the Court shows that it tends to grant the provisional measures to preserve the respective rights of parties if the circumstances show that the rights are going to disappear, or conceivably that the subject-matter of the right is going to be non-existent totally, or the rights will be without any virtual value to the other party when the final judgment renders if the provisional measures are not granted.[48] A good example to interpret the expression "to preserve the respective rights of parties" is afforded by the *Case Concerning UNITED STATES Diplomatic and Consular Staff in Tehran.*[49] The UNITED STATES OF AMERICA instituted proceedings against IRAN, alleging that the Government of IRAN tolerated, encouraged, and failed to prevent and punish the conduct of seizure and holding as hostages of members of the UNITED STATES diplomatic and consular staff in the UNITED STATES Embassy in Tehran. Here, the rights which the UNITED STATES OF AMERICA was requesting to preserve are "the rights of its nationals to life, liberty, protection and security; the rights of inviolability, immunity and protection for its diplomatic and consular officials; and the rights of inviolability and protection for its diplomatic and consular premises" and "the right of the United States to maintain a working and effective embassy in Tehran, the right to have its diplomatic and consular

---

DENMARK), (Provisional Measures), Order of 3 August 1932, PCIJ, Series A/B, No. 48, p.288.

47 *Interhandel* (SWITZERLAND v. USA), (Provisional Measures), Order of 24 October 1957, ICJ Reports 1957, p.105-114.

48 *Thirlway, supra* note 44, p.7-8.

49 Case concerning *United States Diplomatic and Consular Staff in Tehran*, (UNITED STATES v. IRAN), (Provisional Measures), Order of 15 December 1979, ICJ Reports 1979, p.7-21.

personnel protected in their lives and persons from every form of interference and abuse, and the right to have its nationals protected and secured."[50] The Court stated in the paragraph 42 of the Order as follows: "whereas continuance of the situation the subject of the present request exposes the human beings concerned to privation, hardship, anguish and even danger to life and health and thus to a serious possibility of irreparable harm." The Court found that the circumstances required it to indicate provisional measures in order to preserve the rights claimed.

The Court was inclined to indicate provisional measures in the cases concerning the rights to human life, health and liberty. These rights in nature are more likely to disappear, or turn to be non-existent totally, or will be without any virtual value to the applicant party at the final judgment if the provisional measures are not granted. However, this is only a specific case, it does not cover all. The Court takes all the relevant circumstances into consideration. Usually, the Court considers whether there exists "imminent risk of irreparable prejudice to the rights". Only if all the circumstances convince the Court that immediate action is necessary to protect the right as claimed, could the Court conclude that it is the right moment for it to "preserve the respective rights of the parties".

## II. Prevention of irreparable prejudice

What is the exact meaning of the "irreparable prejudice" in the *Fisheries Jurisdiction* dictum? In the context of provisional measures, "irreparable prejudice" points to the future rather than the past. Infringement to the rights which has already happened might not be regarded as the "irreparable prejudice" that justifies provisional measures. Only the rights which might to a great degree of possibility be harmed pending the decision of the Court if no provisional measures are granted could be described as "irreparable prejudice". As observed by *Dumbauld*, "an order on interim measures is not designed to impose redress for wrong already and irreversibly inflicted but, on the contrary, it is designed to prevent a prejudice, which would probably happen in the future. If this has already occurred, interim measures will not be granted".[51] In reality, it is sometimes impossible to draw a clear dividing line between the rights that have been infringed and those that might be irreparably prejudiced in the future. Most of the time, the rights sought to be protected are being infringed and are in deteriorating situation. Take the *Case Concerning UNITED STATES Diplomatic and Consular Staff in Tehran* as an example, the rights of the UNITED STATES OF AMERICA of its nationals "to life, liberty, protection and security...and the right of inviolability and protection for its

50 Case concerning *United States Diplomatic and Consular Staff in Tehran*, *ibid.*, p.19, para. 37.

51 *Dumbauld*, Interim Measures of Protection in International Controversies, (1932), p. 164.

diplomatic and consular premises" had already been greatly infringed. Although there is no doubt that the infringement should be ceased, the already existed injury would not be regarded as "irreparable prejudice". However, in this case, the provisional measures were nevertheless appropriately granted because it was necessary to take some measures to prevent the continuing or future injury to the rights above mentioned. Dr. *Thirlway* raised a good metaphor that I would like to quote here to illustrate the point. He stated that "it is not impossible to imagine an irreparable injury in this context; if the Iranian intruders had not already gained access to the secret files in the Embassy vaults, to prevent them doing so would be to forestall an injury which would be irreparable; once the cat is out of the bag, no monetary compensation will make up for the impossibility of putting it back in again."[52]

Provisional measures are indicated to protect certain recognized rights or keep a certain recognized legal status. The legal status that the UNITED STATES was requesting to keep has already been well recognized in the applicable rules of international law. However, it is possible that the Court grants provisional measures even when there is necessity to preserve the rights claimed by the requesting state which are uncertain under the current frame of international law. The two *Nuclear Test* cases are good examples on this point. AUSTRALIA and NEW ZEALAND respectively instituted proceedings against French asking the Court to declare that the carrying out of further atmospheric nuclear weapons tests in the South Pacific Ocean was inconsistent with the rules of international law. They then requested the Court to order FRANCE not to carry out any further such tests. The Court was satisfied that AUSTRALIA/NEW ZEALAND's allegations had proved that there was an immediate possibility of a further atmospheric nuclear test. It stated that "for the purpose of the present proceedings it suffices to observe that the information submitted to the Court...does not exclude the possibility that damage to AUSTRALIA/NEW ZEALAND might be shown to be caused by the deposit on their territory of radioactive fallout resulting from such tests and to be irreparable."[53] The Court was satisfied that "it should indicate interim measures of protection in order to preserve the right claimed by AUSTRALIA/NEW ZEALAND in the present litigation in respect of the deposit of radioactive fallout on their territory but not in respect of other rights claimed by the applicants."[54] Professor *Rosenne* commented that "here the purpose of the provisional measures was not to preserve any *status quo* or a specific object, but the applicant's claimed rights, concerning which at the

---

52 *Thirlway*, *supra* note 44, p. 8, *footnote* 21.

53 *Nuclear Test* (AUSTRALIA v. FRANCE), (Provisional Measures), ICJ Reports 1973, p.105, para.29, *Nuclear Test* (NEW ZEALAND v. FRANCE), (Provisional Measures), ICJ Reports 1973, p.141, para.30.

54 *Nuclear Test* (AUSTRALIA v. FRANCE), *ibid.*, p.105, para.30, *Nuclear Test* (NEW ZEALAND v. FRANCE), *ibid.*, p.141, para.31.

time international law had no clear rule. This is an important extension of the purpose for which provisional measures can be claimed."[55]

### III. Non-anticipation of the Court's decision

Hence the idea of "non-anticipation of the Court's decision" comes into picture, which is the third element mentioned in the *Fisheries Jurisdiction* dictum. "The Court's judgment should not be anticipated by reason of any initiative regarding the measures which are in issue."

In the paragraph following the above-quoted dictum, the Court applied it to the facts. It stated that "whereas the immediate implementation by ICELAND of its Fishery Regulations would, by anticipating the Court's judgment, prejudice the rights claimed by the United Kingdom and affect the possibility of their full restoration in the event of a judgment of its favor".[56] It can be inferred that the immediate implementation by ICELAND of its Fishery Regulations, which would extend unilaterally its exclusive fishery jurisdiction, would anticipate the Court's judgment. What is the exact meaning of "anticipate" here? *Dumbauld* defined it as follows:

> "until it has been approved and established by a judicial decision having force of *res judicata*, no party is obliged to accept his opponent's view of the law as correct. Is he free to act upon his own view as correct, or must he act upon the assumption that his opponent may possibly be right? The former alternative applies in the absence of provisions authorizing interim protection; the latter if the law has introduced such remedies."[57]

In a case which the Respondent State is claiming that he is entitled to do something, while the Applicant State considers that he is not entitled to do, if the Respondent State ignores the Applicant State's opinion and acts upon the assumption that his view is correct, without waiting for the final judgment, he is anticipating the Court's decision. One of the purposes of provisional measures is to ensure that no initiative is taken by either party on his own assumption of the judgment. In the *Fisheries Jurisdiction* cases, the UNITED KINGDOM and NORTHERN IRELAND instituted proceedings respectively against ICELAND, asking

---

55 *Rosenne, supra* note 5, p. 209.

56 *Fisheries Jurisdiction* (UK and NORTHERN IRELAND v. ICELAND), (Provisional Measures), ICJ Reports 1972, p.16, para.21; *Fisheries Jurisdiction* (FEDERAL REPUBLIC OF GERMANY v. ICELAND), (Provisional Measures), ICJ Reports 1972, p.34, para.22.

57 *Dumbauld, supra* note 51, p. 28.

the Court to declare that ICELAND's claim to extend its exclusive fisheries jurisdiction to a zone of 50 nautical miles around ICELAND was without foundation in international law. They also requested the interim measures preventing the Government of ICELAND to enforce the Fishery Regulations and take any measures against the vessels registered in UNITED KINGDOM or NORTHERN IRELAND. ICELAND was not permitted to take any actions on his assumption that the claim of extended fisheries jurisdiction was well founded in international law until the delivery of the final judgment. This demonstrates the proposition that one of the purposes of provisional measures is to ensure that the parties not do anything on his own anticipation or assumption of the result of the case until the final judgment is rendered. "Non-anticipation of the Court's decision" requires both parties to mind the possibility that the other party's view might be right. In other words, "non-anticipation of the Court's decision" means that neither party is permitted to act on his own assumption of the result of the case until the final judgment is rendered.

The readers might remind the expression that "the indication of provisional measures should not in any way prejudge the rights which the Court may subsequently adjudge to belong either to the Applicant or to the Respondent". This statement has been adopted in the Court's Orders. At the provisional measures stage, the parties have not had any opportunity to plead the merits of a case. Thus, the provisional measures that have the effect of prejudging the Court's final judgment are against the "provisional" nature of provisional measures. Therefore, it is incontestably correct that provisional measures shall not prejudge the merits of the case, or in other words, the indication of provisional measures shall not function as an interim judgment.

However, it might be a misunderstanding of the term "non-anticipation of the Court's decision" as "non-prejudgment of the merits of the case" here. "Non-prejudgment of the merits of the case at the stage of provisional measures" is a statement in the respective of the contents of provisional measures rather than its purpose. It is the necessary requirement for the contents of the provisional measures. The Court might not grant the provisional measures as claimed if the contents of the provisional measures possess the effect of a prejudgment of the merits. We are now discussing the issue under the heading of "the purpose of provisional measures". It seems to be better to interpret the paragraph in the *Fisheries Jurisdiction* dictum as "one of the objects of provisional measures is to ensure that no initiative is taken by either party to anticipate the judgment" than "provisional measures should not in any way prejudge the rights which the Court may subsequently adjudge to belong either to the Applicant or to the Respondent". More support can be found from the language of the paragraph above quoted: "whereas the immediate implementation by ICELAND of its Regulations would, by anticipating the Court's judgment, prejudice the rights..." It is the action of ICELAND that would anticipate the Court's judgment, not the provisional measures. Therefore, it is inappropriate to understand "non-anticipation of the Court's decision" as another expression of the proposition that "the indication of provisional measures should not in any way prejudge the rights which the Court may subsequently adjudge to belong either to the Applicant or to the Respondent". These two terms are closely related, but totally different.

### IV. Preservation of the *status quo*

Besides the Statute and the Orders of the Court, there are other documents mentioning the purpose of provisional measures. In the individual opinions of judges, in the pleadings of the parties and in some authoritative works, the purpose of provisional measures is sometime described as the preservation of the *status quo.*[58]

Preservation of the *status quo* then gives rise to a problem. What is the *status quo* in a certain case? In other words, what status shall the provisional measures re-establish or safeguard?[59] To what extent shall the provisional measures have effect?

*Dumbauld* observed that the *status quo* sanctioned was not that at the time of the judgment, or at the date suit is brought, but the last uncontested status prior to the controversy.[60] Considering the object of provisional measures, it might be appropriate to understand controversy as the disputed state of rights and obligations in the case. Viewing the jurisprudence of the Court, the cases concerning the issue of provisional measures could be divided into two categories according to the time when the actual interference of rights occurs. In some cases, the alleged interference of rights is going to happen in the near future if no provisional measures are granted. Here provisional measures are designed to prevent the happening of some events that would cause interference of rights. In the cases of *Fisheries Jurisdiction*, the infringement of the rights would happen only when the ICELAND's Fisheries Regulations were implemented. Since the Regulations had not been implemented until the request for provisional measures, *status quo* here could mean preservation of the status existing at the date of the order. It's similar also in the *Nuclear Tests*

58 *Request for Interpretation of the Judgment of 31 March 2004 in the Case Concerning Avena and Other Mexican Nationals* case (MEXICO *v.* UNITED STATES OF AMERICA) , (Provisional Measures), Order of 16 July 2008, ICJ Reports 2008, p. 2;
During the discussion on then Rules in 1931, Judge *Negulesco* observed that provisional measures "sometimes...were regarded as designed to preserve rights claimed in an action at law, sometimes their object was to re-establish or safeguard the *status quo ante.*", PCIJ, Series D, No.2, Add.2, p.192.

59 The term of "re-establish or safeguard" is quoted from Judge *Negulesco*'s observation during the discussion on the Rules in 1931, *ibid.*

60 *Dumbauld, supra* note 51, p.187.

cases where the actual irreparable prejudice to the rights would only happen when any future atmospheric nuclear tests were taken. In some other cases, the actual interference of rights has already existed and is continuing. Here provisional measures are designed to restore the status prior to the events causing the alleged interference of rights. Most of the cases belong to the latter category. One of the good examples might be the *Case Concerning UNITED STATES Diplomatic and Consular Staff in Tehran.* In the case, the provisional measures were requested to restore the state prior to the seizure and holding of staffs and interference of the prestige. No matter prevention or restoration, the object of provisional measures can be summarized as keeping the last uncontested status existing prior to the alleged interference of rights, to simply put it, prior to the controversy.

Professor *Sztucki* proposed a different view on this point.[61] He believed that it could not be regarded as a general rule because provisional measures were motivated by certain circumstances of a case, not by the dispute. Accordingly, the conservatory effect was related to those circumstances rather than to the controversy as a whole. He compared the *Fisheries Jurisdiction* cases with the *Electricity Company* case. In the *Fisheries Jurisdiction* cases, interim measures were designed to prevent the enforcement that were to come into force at a date subsequent to the Court's orders, thus, *status quo* can mean the preservation of the status existing at the date of an order. However, in the *Electricity Company* case, the object of interim measures was to restore the *status quo* prior to the petitory action instituted against the Company in Bulgaria, but not the status prior to the institution of proceedings before the Court. It appears to me that *Sztucki* regarded controversy as the proceedings before the Court. Thus, he believed that *Dumbauld*'s rule of "the last uncontested status prior to the controversy" was not applicable here. Instead, *status quo* meant the restoration of the last status prior to the events, which gave rise to the request for provisional measures. However, it might be better to understand controversy as the disputed property right of the Company, not the institution of proceedings before the Court in my view. To be more general, *Dumbauld*'s term of "controversy" can be interpreted as "the contested status of rights and obligations" at a specific point, rather than the beginning of the whole controversy. There is only different understanding of the "controversy" and no substantial difference exists between these two opinions. Provisional measures are called for by the urgent events that might lead to irreparable prejudice. Therefore, provisional measures shall be designed pointing to these events. The occurring of the events is the dividing point for the effect of provisional measures. *Status quo* is the last uncontested status prior to the interference of the rights. To this extent, it is quite similar to the term of "non-anticipation of the Court's decision" discussed above.

The *Passage through the Great Belt* case is a typical case which reflects the practical significance of discussing "*status quo*". In that case, DENMARK intended

61 *Sztucki*, *supra* note 3, p.73.

to construct a bridge over the Great Belt strait that was its own internal waters. FINLAND claimed that the construction of the bridge would prevent FINLAND from exercising a right of passage through the Great Belt for the vessels, especially the oil drilling rigs, which required much more than the designed clearance of the bridge. FINLAND therefore asked for a judgment that DENMARK was not entitled to interfere with FINLAND's right of passage and for provisional measures to stop the bridge construction works. FINLAND argued that the mere continuation of the project was creating a situation in which it would be too late for DENMARK to turn back and therefore the *status quo* was a status in which DENMARK was not planning a bridge, or was at least not proceeding with construction works of the project. On that basis FINLAND sought to stop the works long before they were going to reach the stage when the Great Belt would be actually blocked. The Court rejected the request for provisional measures because it found that the actual interference was not going to happen until after the Court would have given judgment on the merits.[62] It could be inferred that the Court understood the *status quo* as the last uncontested status prior to the blockage of Great Belt. The blockage of the Great Belt would not happen until the judgment on the merits. Therefore, there was no necessity to grant provisional measures to preserve the *status quo*.

## V. Non-aggravation or extension of the dispute

There is no expression of "non-aggravation or extension of dispute" in the above mentioned explicit statement of the purpose of provisional measures, neither in Article 41 of the Statute nor in the *Fisheries Jurisdiction* dictum. However, it is an element appeared in all the Orders ever since the *Electricity Company of Sofia and Bulgaria* case. After regarding "non-aggravation or extension of dispute" as the sole ground for the indication of provisional measures in the *Electricity Company of Sofia and Bulgaria* case, it seems to be an inconsistent practice to what extent the Court considers the element of "non-aggravation or extension of dispute". This apparent disharmony raises some ambiguity as to whether "non-aggravation or extension of dispute" could be regarded as one of the purposes of provisional measures or not. If it could be, then it will lead to a conclusion that "non-aggravation" could be the legal basis of indication of provisional measures. To go even further, to what extent could the Court take it as the basis of indication of provisional measures? Although the term of "non-aggravation or extension of dispute" has been organized under the heading of "the purpose (object) of

62 *Passage through the Great Belt* case (FINLAND V. DENMARK), (Provisional Measures), Order of 29 July 1991, ICJ Reports 1991, p.18, para.27.

provisional measures" in some authoritative literature,[63] its relation to the indication of provisional measures is not so clear.

### 1. Cases prior to the Pulp Mills case

"Non-aggravation or extension of dispute" appeared for the first time in the Order of 5 December 1939 in the *Electricity Company of Sofia and Bulgaria* case before the PERMANENT COURT OF INTERNATIONAL JUSTICE.[64] The PERMANENT COURT, in the operative part of its Order, stated that "the State of Bulgaria should ensure that no step of any kind is taken capable of prejudicing the rights claimed by the Belgian Government or of aggravating or extending the dispute submitted to the Court". In the reasoning part of the Order, the PERMANENT COURT also mentioned the element of "aggravation or extension of the dispute". It seems to be that the PERMANENT COURT clearly expressed its intention to broadly interpret Article 41 of the Statute. However, the diction of the Court might imply its prior purpose to preserve the respective rights of the parties and the ancillary nature of the "non-aggravation" measures. The PERMANENT COURT stated that the parties should refrain from "any measures capable of exercising a prejudicial effect in regard to the execution of the decision to be given *and, in general,* not to allow any step of any kind to be taken which might aggravate or extend the dispute."[65] (emphasis added)

Moreover, it is worth noting that the Order was rendered in quite short time and in a quite harsh and brief way. It did not indicate any specific measures. And the reasoning was made in a quite simple and general way. It mentioned Article 41 of the Statute and Article 61 of the Rule first, then it stated that "whereas the above quoted provision of the Statute applies the principle universally accepted by international tribunals and likewise laid down in many conventions to which Bulgaria has been a party - to the effect that the parties to a case must abstain from any measure capable of exercising a prejudicial effect in regard to the execution of the decision to be given and, in general, not allow any step of any kind to be taken which might aggravate or extend the dispute;" Then the PERMANENT COURT summarized simply that "the present conditions and the successive postponements and resulting delays and, finally, the action as demandant above mentioned, justify in view of the Court the indication of interim measures ... " It is difficult to infer from these paragraphs the actual reasons that induced the Court to indicate such a general interim measure. *Stzucki* also observed that to some extent both the general

63 *Thirlway, supra* note 44, p.13.
*Sztucki, supra* note 3, p. 74.

64 *Electricity Company of Sofia and Bulgaria* (BELGIUM v. BULGARIA), (Provisional Measures), Order of 5 December 1939, PCIJ, Series A/B, No.79, p.199.

65 *Ibid.*

formula of its operative part and the motives of that general indication presented themselves rather as a pragmatic way out of a situation in which the Court: (i) was not quite certain as to the legally relevant facts and therefore could not engage its authority in invoking such specific facts which might prove to be simply incorrect; (ii) at the same time apparently considered that, under the circumstances of the case (war condition, discontinued Bulgarian cooperation and ensuing uncertainty as to the prospects of further proceedings on the merits), it was more appropriate to indicate interim measures in general terms than to refuse interim protection which the requesting party might really need. He therefore believed that the function of the "non-aggravation" measure in the *Electricity Company of Sofia and Bulgaria* case was rather occasional.[66]

Indeed, in the other three cases concerning provisional measures presented before the PERMANENT COURT, the PERMANENT COURT had not ever adopted the "non-aggravation" measures approach. In the *Sino-Belgian Treaty* Case, the Court explicitly limited the object of provisional measures to the preservation of "the respective rights of the Parties, pending the decision of the Court".[67] In the *Polish Agrarian Reform* case, the Court stated that "the essential condition" that provisional measures "must necessarily" fulfill was that they "should have the effect of protecting the rights forming the subject of the dispute submitted to the Court".[68] In the *South-Eastern Greenland* case, the Court observed as follows: "it has been argued that, under Article 41 of the Statute, the Court is also competent to indicate interim measures of protection *for the sole purpose of preventing regrettable events and unfortunate incidents* … In the present case, there is no occasion for the Court to take a final stand upon this controversy as to interpretation …"[69] (emphasis added)

Therefore, neither from the diction and the background of the Permanent Court's Order in the *Electricity Company of Bulgaria and Sofia* case, nor from its uniqueness in the jurisprudence of the PERMANENT COURT, could it be possible for us to conclude that the PERMANENT COURT had established a consistent practice to regard "non-aggravation of dispute" as the purpose of provisional measures.

It can be found that the Orders granting provisional measures usually begin with the following paragraph: "each Party shall refrain from any action which might prejudice the rights of the other Party in respect of whatever judgment the Court may render in the case, or which might aggravate or extend the dispute before the

---

66 *Sztucki, supra* note 3, p.75.

67 *Sino-Belgian Treaty* (BELGIUM v. CHINA), (Provisional Measures), Order of 8 January 1927, PCIJ, Ser. A, No.8, p.6.

68 *Polish Agrarian Reform and German Minority* case (GERMANY v. POLAND), (Provisional Measures), Order of 29 July 1933, PCIJ, Ser. A/B, No.58, p.177.

69 *South-Eastern Greenland* (NORWAY v. DENMARK), (Provisional Measures), Order of 3 August 1933, PCIJ, Ser. A/B, No.48, p.284.

Court or make it more difficult to resolve;"[70] Then the specific preservative measures follow.

*Anglo-Iranian Oil Co.* case[71] is the first time the present Court faced the request for measures to prevent the aggravation of the dispute. It is also a representative of the cases in which the Court indicated non-aggravation measures along with the preservative measures. The UNITED KINGDOM and NORTHERN IRELAND filed a request for interim measures with three main parts. The first part consisted of five specific points ensuring the Anglo-Iranian Oil Company from interference by the Iranian government. Then there came two general clauses, one was to ensure that no further steps of any kind are taken capable of prejudicing the right of the UK to have a decision of the Court in its favor on the merits of the case executed, should the Court render such a decision. The other was to ensure that both governments take no step of any kind capable of aggravating or extending the dispute. The Court provided little reasoning and had a rather quick conclusion that the provisional measures shall be granted as UNITED KINGDOM and NORTHERN IRELAND requested. In the operative clause of the Order, the Court firstly indicated that both parties should "ensure that no action is taken which might prejudice the rights of the other Party in respect of the carrying out of any decision on the merits which the Court may subsequently render", both parties should each "ensure that no action of any kind is taken which might aggravate or extend the dispute submitted to the Court". Then the Court listed the specific preservative measures. A series of cases seemed to follow the *Anglo-Iranian Oil Co.* case approach, such as the *Fisheries Jurisdiction* cases,[72] the *Nuclear Tests* cases, also the Case Concerning *Military and*

70 In a few cases, the specific preservative measures come before the general non-aggravation clause, see the *Case Concerning United States Diplomatic and Consular Staff in Tehran*, (USA v. IRAN), (Provisional Measures), Order of 15 December 1979, ICJ Reports 1979, p. 21; Case Concerning *Military and Paramilitary Activities in and against NICARAGUA* (NICARAGUA v. USA), Order of 10 May 1984, ICJ Reports 1984, p.187, p. 24;
Case concerning *Application of the Convention on the Prevention and Punishment of the Crime of Genocide* (BOSNIA and HERZEGOVINA v. YUGOSLAVIA (SERBIA and MONTENEGRO)), (Provisional Measures), ICJ Reports 1993, p.25. (abbreviated as *Bosnian Genocide* case in the following). I do not regard this is significant difference concerning the issue under discussion.

71 *Anglo-Iranian Oil Co.* (UK v. IRAN), (Provisional Measures), Order of 5 July 1951, ICJ Reports 1951, p. 93.

72 *Fisheries Jurisdiction* (FEDERAL REPUBLIC OF GERMANY v. ICELAND), (Provisional Measures), Order of 17 August 1972, ICJ Reports 1972, p. 35.
*Fisheries Jurisdiction* (UNITED KINGDOM and NORTHERN IRELAND v. ICELAND), (Provisional Measures), Order of 17 August 1972, ICJ Reports 1972, p. 17.
*Nuclear Tests* (NEW ZEALAND v. FRANCE), (Provisional Measures), Order of 22 June 1973, ICJ Reports 1973, p. 142.
*Nuclear Tests* (AUSTRALIA v. FRANCE), (Provisional Measures), Order of 22 June 1973, ICJ Reports 1973, p. 106.

*Paramilitary Activities in and against NICARAGUA,*[73] the Case Concerning *Application of the Convention on the Prevention and Punishment of the Crime of Genocide.*[74]

However, in the *Aegean Sea Continental Shelf* case, GREECE had requested the provisional measures "in order to prevent the aggravation or extension of the dispute", along with its request for measures to protect its rights. The Court rejected the request and observed the issue of "non-aggravation" measures as follows: "before this request could be entertained, the Court would have to determine whether, under Article 41 of the Statute, the Court has such an *independent* power to indicate interim measures having that object; whereas, however, for the reasons now to be explained, the Court does not find it necessary to examine the point."[75] (emphasis added)

Here the Court explicitly raised the question of the position of the "non-aggravation" measures for the first time. The Court used the word "independent" which confirm the above assertion that it was indeed a "circumstance" which had been taken into consideration under Article 41 of the Statute. The problem that the Court was considering is just whether it was a circumstance that could be regarded as the sole basis for indication of provisional measures. If the answer is yes, then the Court will have the power to indicate non-aggravation measures when there is no need to indicate measures to ensure no irreparable prejudice. However, the Court found it unnecessary to probe into this question in this case because of the recommendations by the SECURITY COUNCIL and the willingness of the parties to accept them.[76]

There are two cases that draw attention. One is the *Frontier Dispute* case. The Chamber seemed to be ready to answer the above-mentioned question in the case. It found that the incidents asserted by the parties could not affect the existence or value of the rights claimed and rejected to indicate any measures to preserve the specific rights. After recognizing the rights in issue in the proceedings were "the sovereign rights of the Parties over their respective territories on either side of the frontier as eventually defined by the judgment which the Chamber is called upon to give", the Chamber invoked the principle established in the *Case Concerning Legal Status of South-Eastern Greenland*[77] and stated that the incidents likely to aggravate the dispute in the *Frontier Dispute* case could not "in any event, or to any

73 Case concerning *Military and Paramilitary Activities in and against NICARAGUA*, (NICARAGUA v. USA), (Provisional Measures), Order of 10 May 1984, ICJ Reports 1984, p.186-187, para.41.

74 *Bosnian Genocide* (BOSNIA and HERZEGOVINA v. YUGOSLAVIA (SERBIA and MONTENEGRO)), (Provisional Measures), Order of 8 April 1993, ICJ Reports 1993, p.24, para.52 (B).

75 *Aegean Sea Continental Shelf* (GREECE v. TURKEY), (Provisional Measures), Order of 11 September 1976, ICJ Reports 1976, p.12, para.36.

76 *Ibid.* p. 14, para. 41.

77 *Case Concerning Legal Status of South-Eastern Greenland* (NORWAY v. DENMARK), (Interim Measures), Order of 3 August 1932, PCIJ, Series A/B, No.48, p.285.

degree, affect the existence or value of the sovereign rights claimed by either of the Parties over the territory in question". That meant the incidents that gave rise to the request did not cause any risks of irreparable prejudice to the rights of either party, and the traditional basis for provisional measures seemed not to exist. However, the Chamber believed that these incidents that were likely to aggravate the dispute would nevertheless justify the provisional measures. The Chamber indicated provisional measures seemingly on another basis. It stated as follows: "considering that, *independently* of the requests submitted by the Parties for the indication of provisional measures, the Court or, accordingly, the chamber possesses by virtue of Article 41 of the Statute the power to indicate provisional measures with a view to preventing the aggravation or extension of the dispute whenever it considers that the circumstances so require."[78]

Here the Chamber appeared to assure the power under Article 41 to indicate provisional measures to avoid the aggravation of the dispute, regardless whether the necessity to indicate provisional measures to preserve the specific rights existed or not. Then the Chamber tried to support this standing on the basis of provision of the Charter of the UNITED NATIONS and its function of peaceful settlement of disputes:

> "whereas, in particular, when two States jointly decide to have recourse to a chamber of the Court, *the principal judicial organ of the United Nations*, with a view to the *peaceful settlement of a dispute*, in accordance with *Article 2, paragraph 3, and Article 33 of the Charter of the United Nations*, and incidents subsequently occur which not merely are likely to extend or aggravate the dispute but comprise a resort to force which is *irreconcilable with the principle of the peaceful settlement of international disputes*, there can be no doubt of the Chamber's power and duty to indicate, if need be, such provisional measures as may conduce to the due administration of justice;"[79]

The Court adopted this approach again ten years later in the case concerning the *Land and Maritime Boundary between CAMEROON and NIGERIA.*[80] The Court also cited the *South-Eastern Greenland* principle to state that the incidents likely to aggravate or extend the dispute could not affect the "existence or value of the sovereign rights claimed", and then stated that it possessed the power to indicate provisional measures "with a view to preventing the aggravation or extension of the dispute independently of the requests for the indication of provisional measures submitted by the Parties to *preserve specific rights*". Here the Court had made some

78 *Frontier Dispute* (BURKINO FASO/REPUBLIC OF MALI), (Provisional Measures), Order of 10 January 1986, ICJ Reports 1986, p. 9, para. 18.

79 *Ibid.*, p. 10, para. 19.

80 Case concerning the *Land and Maritime Boundary between CAMEROON and NIGERIA* (CAMEROON v. NIGERIA), (Provisional Measures), Order of 15 March 1996, ICJ Reports 1996, p. 22.

adjustments to the 1986 dictum. It added the phrase of "to preserve specific rights". It is quite possible that the Court was intending to clarify the ambiguity of 1986 dictum by excluding the interpretation of the word "independently" as *pripro motu*.[81] And it is reasonable to regard the 1996 dictum as the maintenance and reinforcement of the 1986 dictum. Different from the practice of indicating "non-aggravation" measures along with the specific preservative measures as in the above listed cases, the Court appeared to indicate "non-aggravation" measures when there was no need to preserve the irreparable prejudice. In fact, there was an opinion to affirm this assertion, not only within the Court, but also in the contemporary literature. Judge *Ranjeva* and Judge *Ajibola* expressed their positive opinions on the issue.[82] Some commentaries also held that the *Frontier Dispute* case appeared to show a tendency towards attaching more relevance to the issue of aggravation in the Court's jurisprudence.[83]

Some authors believed that the 1996 dictum, namely the power to indicate measures independently of the requests for measures "to preserve specific rights" was again employed by the Court in the Order of 1 July 2000 in the case concerning *Armed Activities on the Territory of the CONGO* (CONGO v. UGANDA).[84] However, it was still arguable that the measures were indicated on the basis of the risk of irreparable prejudice to the rights, instead of solely on the basis of risk of aggravation. Different from finding the subject of the dispute as the sovereignty

81 *Thirlway* observed: "there is still some confusion here, as what is clearly meant is that the power to indicate non-aggravation measures exists whether or not preservative measures are indicated, not independently of whether they are *asked for*." *Thirlway,* The Law and Procedure of the INTERNATIONAL COURT OF JUSTICE 1960-1989 (Part Twelve), British Year Book of International Law (2001), Vol. LXXII, p.103.

82 Judge *Ranjeva* recognized that the Order "does not confine itself to the indication of measures preserving rights in the traditional sense". He regarded the decision as "a contribution by the Court to ensuring the observance of one of the principal obligations of the UNITED NATIONS and of all its organs in relation to the maintenance of international peace and security.", Declaration of Judge *Ranjeva* appending to the Order of 15 March 1996, case concerning *Land and Maritime Boundary between CAMEROON and NIGERIA*, ICJ Reports 1996, p. 29;
Judge *Ajibola* considered that "the purpose and content of Article 41 of the Statute is not and cannot be restricted only to the preservation of the rights of the parties in a matter like the one before the Court", Separate Opinion of Judge *Ajibola* appending to the Order of 15 March 1996, case concerning *Land and Maritime Boundary between CAMEROON and NIGERIA*, ICJ Reports 1996, p. 53.

83 *Sztucki* observed: "it appears that in the recent decades in general, and in the present case in particular, the Court, using Article 41, is embarking on exercising just these powers – powers of *general prevention*", *Sztucki*, case concerning *Land and Maritime Boundary between CAMEROON and NIGERIA* (CAMEROON v. NIGERIA): Provisional Measures, Order of 15 March 1996, Leiden Journal of International Law (1997), Vol. 10, p.357;
*Thirlway* observed: "recent developments in the practice of indication of provisional measures suggest that there has been some shift of thinking within the Court away from the intentions of the Statute in this respect.", *Thirlway, supra* note 81, p.99.

84 *Thirlway, supra* note 81, p. 104.

rights on the territory in the 1986 and 1996 cases, the Court found that the subject of the dispute were essentially the rights to sovereignty, territorial integrity, the integrity of its assets and natural resources and the rights to respect for the rules of international humanitarian law and for the instruments relating to the protection of human rights.[85] Then the Court stated that the rights that were the subject matter of the dispute in issue, as persons, assets and resources present on the territory of CONGO might suffer irreparable prejudice. Therefore the Court considered that the provisional measures to protect these rights should be indicated.[86] Then the Court stated as follows:

> "whereas, independently of requests for the indication of provisional measures submitted by the parties to preserve specific rights, the Court possesses by virtue of Article 41 of the Statute the power to indicate provisional measures with a view to preventing the aggravation or extension of the dispute whenever it considers that circumstances so require ... whereas, having regard to the information at its disposal, and in particular the fact that the Security Council has determined, in its resolution 1304 (2000), that the situation in Congo 'continues to constitute a threat to international peace and security in the region', the Court was of the opinion that there exists a serious risk of events occurring which might aggravate or extend the dispute or make it more difficult to resolve;"[87]

Therefore, it still remained unclear whether "non-aggravation" had been regarded as the basis for the indication of provisional measures. Because the subject of the dispute was a series of rights which particularly covered the rights to respect for the rules of international humanitarian law and for the instruments relating to the protection of human rights, it is reasonable to understand that the provisional measures were indicated on the basis of the risk of irreparable prejudice to the rights, not solely of the risk of aggravation of the dispute. Moreover, the Order did explain the risk of events occurring which might aggravate the dispute, while it did not explain why the risk of aggravation could trigger the necessity to indicate provisional measures. In other words, the question whether "non-aggravation" could be regarded as the basis for provisional measures was not settled. It might still be argued that the "non-aggravation" paragraph was more likely a standard clause that the Court added into the operative clause for some pragmatic and occasional purposes, just as in the *Electricity Company* case,[88] rather than the implication that

---

85 Case concerning *Armed Activities on the Territory of Congo* (CONGO V. UGANDA), (Provisional Measures), Order of 1 July 2000, ICJ Reports 2000, p. 127, para. 40.

86 *Ibid.*, p. 128, para. 43.

87 *Ibid.*, p. 128, para. 44.

88 *Stzucki*, *supra* note 83.

the Court considered the "non-aggravation" element as one of the purposes of provisional measures.

### 2. the *Pulp Mills* case

The decision of the Court in the Order of 23 January 2007 in the case concerning *Pulp Mills on the River URUGUAY*[89] (abbreviated as the *Pulp Mills* case in the following) seemed to make the above-mentioned ambiguity even more complicated. The Court's restricted view on the position of the non-aggravation measures in this case seemed to contradict the tendency established ever since the *Frontier Dispute* case. ARGENTINA and URUGUAY shared part of the River URUGUAY and had signed the Statute of the River URUGUAY to "establish the joint machinery necessary for the optimum and rational utilization" of the shared part. In October 2003, URUGUAY authorized the Company ENCE to build a pulp mill in the shared part. In February 2005, URUGUAY issued a second authorization to another company to construct another pulp mill and to build a port for the exclusive use of this mill. The construction of the mills had a significant employment and economic impact for URUGUAY. ARGENTINA complained about "the amount of effluent which these mills are expected to discharge into the River URUGUAY, the proximity to major urban populations centers ... and the inadequacy of the measures proposed for the prevention and reduction of the potential impact of liquid effluent, gas emissions and solid waste." URUGUAY requested the Court to indicate three provisional measures, the first being a specific measure directing ARGENTINA to take all steps at its disposal to prevent or end the interruption of transit between URUGUAY and ARGENTINA. The other two were general measures directing ARGENTINA to abstain from any measures that might aggravate the dispute and to refrain from any other measures that might prejudice the rights of URUGUAY in issue. The Court refused to grant the first measure on the basis that there was no threat of irreparable prejudice to the rights of URUGUAY in issue. As for the second measure requested, the Court observed that, in all cases in which it issued provisional measures directing the parties not to take any conduct that would aggravate or extend the dispute, other measures were also indicated. Therefore it stated that since it had not found any necessity to grant provisional measures to preserve the respective rights of the parties in issue, it could not indicate the "non-aggravation" measures either. The Court refused to grant the third measure requested for the same reason.

89 *Pulp Mills* (ARGENTINA *v.* URUGUAY), (Provisional Measures), Order of 23 January 2007, ICJ Reports 2007, p. 1-14.

### 3. Necessity of the "non-aggravation" measures

The Order of 23 January 2007 did not state expressly the reasons for its restrictive view. The cases prior to the *Pulp Mills* case showed a practice that the Court was taking "non-aggravation" as one of the "circumstances" under Article 41 of the Statute. A tendency to make the "non-aggravation" consideration even stronger was showed in the *Frontier Dispute* case and the case concerning *Land and Maritime Boundary between CAMEROON and NIGERIA*. Then how could it be explained the *Pulp Mills* case's inconsistency with the past practice?

Judge *Buergenthal* in his declaration found that the Court's findings were based on the conclusion that the Court lacked the power under Article 41 to indicate any provisional measures in a case in which there had been no showing of an imminent risk of irreparable prejudice to the subject matter in dispute between the parties.[90]

He criticized the Court's restrictive interpretation of Article 41, arguing that, "by taking this position, the Court did not adequately address the problem of how to deal with situations in which one party to the case resort to extrajudicial coercive measures, unrelated to the subject matter in dispute, that aggravate a dispute by seeking to undermine or interfere with the rights of the other party in defending its case before the Court."[91]

The general "non-aggravation" measures are indeed necessary under some circumstances. As observed by *Sztucki*, although the function of the general prevention clause appeared in an order indicating provisional measures in the *Electricity Company* case was rather "occasional", "it was not difficult to realize that they also could fulfill more general and broader functions". When addressed to both parties, "general clauses offer the possibility of achieving better balance in the Court's action by making some indications - be they unspecific ones- to the requesting parties as well". Furthermore, the Court was not "in a position to foresee with exhaustive precision all conceivable actions which may turn out to be prejudicial to the rights at issue".[92] This statement appropriately addressed the character of the "non-aggravation" measures as secondary, subsidiary and complementary. They were firstly brought into practice to make up the inexhaustibility of the preservative measures. That might be the initial intention of the Court to make such an attempt to indicate the "non-aggravation" measures in the prior cases.

90 Declaration of Judge *Buergenthal* appending to the Order of 23 January 2007, *Pulp Mills*, (Provisional Measures), ICJ Reports 2006, p.2, para. 8.

91 Declaration of Judge *Buergenthal* appending to the Order of 23 January 2007, *ibid.*, p.3, *para.* 11.

92 *Sztucki*, *supra* note 3, p.76.

### 4. The position of the "non-aggravation" measures

In my view, the power to indicate the "non-aggravation" measures is far from being independent of the power to indicate preservative measures. Judging from its origin as a subsidiary and complementary instrument of the preservative measures and its being adopted along with the preservative measures in the majority of the cases, the "non-aggravation" measures could only be indicated along with the preservative measures. Its function is rather limited.

From the perspective of the Court's role and the purpose of provisional measures, it is necessary to restrictively interpret the Court's power under Article 41. In the *Frontier Dispute* case, the Chamber's reasoning gave rise to some doubts on the question whether it was within the border of the power under Article 41 to indicate measures to prevent extension or aggravation of disputes. The Chamber based its opinion on Article 2, paragraph 3, Article 33 of the Charter of the UNITED NATIONS and the Court's position as the principal judicial organ of the organization.[93] This reasoning is to some extent difficult to agree. Considering the fact that the Court is a judicial organ and the arrangement of Article 41 under the title of "procedure" in the Statute, it might be more plausible to interpret Article 41 as an article that serves the judicial purposes rather than the general purpose of preventing dispute aggravation. I suppose that the drafters of Article 41 were intending to deal with the specific rights under the imminent risk of irreparable prejudice within its jurisdiction rather than regrettable incidents within a broader scope. *Thirlway*'s observed on the essential purpose of provisional measures as: "the essential purpose... is to preserve the respective rights of either party. This is a matter of justice, not of peace-keeping; neither the intensity of a dispute, nor even the risk that it may escalate into the use of force, is a consideration which necessarily enters into the equation, as so defined, unless of course such escalation threatens to cause irreparable prejudice to the rights of either party."[94] It is interesting to note that in the case concerning the *Land and Maritime Boundary*, although the facts were quite similar to that of the *Frontier Dispute* case, the Court abandoned the above reasoning on the UNITED NATIONS CHARTER in the Order. This might be some suggestion of the Court's hesitation on the point.

Furthermore, regarding to the Court's practice in the above-mentioned cases, the Court did draw some attention on the links between the "non-aggravation" measures and the specific rights although it was asserting to independently indicate the "non-aggravation" measures. In other words, the Court indeed did not indicate provisional measures for the sole purpose of preventing the aggravation, but

93 *Frontier Dispute* (BURKINO FASO/REPUBLIC OF MALI), (Provisional Measures), Order of 10 January 1986, ICJ Reports 1986, p.9, para.19.

94 *Thirlway*, *supra* note 81, p.99.

focused on those incidents that would aggravate the dispute while at the same time create a risk of irreparable prejudice to the rights in issue.

In its Order of 10 January 1986 in the *Frontier Dispute* case, the Chamber quoted the *Legal Status of the South-Eastern Territory of Greenland* principle and explicitly stated that the incidents likely to aggravate the dispute could not affect the existence or value of the sovereign rights claimed over the territory in question.[95] Therefore, the provisional measures were indicated on the sole basis of the risk of aggravation of the dispute rather than the irreparable prejudice to the respective rights of the parties. However, the Chamber nevertheless mentioned the links between the "non-aggravation" measures and the specific rights in issue. It stated that the armed actions that gave rise to the requests for the indication of provisional measures submitted to the Chamber took place within or near the disputed area as defined by the Special Agreement.[96]

In the Order in the case concerning the *Land and Maritime Boundary* case, the Court recognized that "the rights in issue in these proceedings are sovereign rights which the Parties claim over territory". It also quoted the *Legal Status of the South-Eastern Territory of Greenland* principle and stated that the incidents likely to aggravate the dispute could not affect the existence or value of the sovereign rights claimed over the territory in question.[97] However, the Court also stated that "these rights also *concern* persons".[98] (emphasis added) It observed that "the events that have given rise to the request, and more especially the killing of persons, have caused irreparable damage to the rights that the parties may have over the Peninsula; whereas the persons in the disputed area and, as a consequences, the rights of the Parties within that area are exposed to serious risk of further irreparable damage ... the Court takes the view that there is a risk that events likely to aggravate or extend the dispute may occur again, thus rendering any settlement of that dispute more difficult". Judging from these statements, the Court seemed to be trying to argue that the incidents that might aggravate the dispute, namely the military aggression, had caused irreparable prejudice damage to the rights in issue. This was contradictory with its prior statement that the incidents likely to aggravate the dispute could not affect the existence or value of the sovereign rights claimed over the territory in question. Judge *Oda*, in his declaration appending to the Order of 15 March 1996, disagreed the Court's mentioning of the concept "irreparable damage". He commented that the loss of life in the disputed area did not constitute the real subject matter of the present case.

---

95 *Frontier Dispute, supra* note 93, p.10, para.17.

96 *Frontier Dispute, supra* note 93, p.10, para.16.

97 Case concerning the *Land and Maritime Boundary between CAMEROON and NIGERIA* case (CAMEROON v. NIGERIA), (Provisional Measures), Order of 15 March 1996, ICJ Reports 1996, p. 10, para. 17.

98 *Ibid.*, p. 22, para. 39.

Judging from the Court's practice in these two cases, although it might be an acceptable assertion that the Court was tending to indicate the general "non-aggravation" measures, the Court was taking a quite prudential or even reluctant attitude. It was arguing to take "non-aggravation" as the independent basis for provisional measures, while at the same time embarrassedly grounding the decision on the establishment of "irreparable prejudice".

To go a step further, the recognition of the Court's power to indicate provisional measures on the sole basis of "non-aggravation" would raise some difficulties. The first problem is: what is the content of the "non-aggravation" measures if they are independently indicated when there are no preservative measures? How could the parties comply with these measures? Although the Court listed some specific measures under the general "non-aggravation" measures, such as the withdrawal of troops, in the *Frontier Disputes* case and the case concerning *the Land and Maritime Boundary*. There still remained some difficulty. What is the exact scope of the actions that might aggravate or extend the dispute? Some authors held that the "non-aggravation" measures were mainly subject to military actions. Some others emphasized the extrajudicial coercive action such as economic coercion.[99] The scope seemed to be too subtle and too general to define. In the history of the Court, the controversy on the scope of the "non-aggravation" measures between the parties once occurred. After the indication of the provisional measures in the case concerning *the UNITED STATES Diplomatic and Consular Staff in Tehran*, Judge *Morozov* criticized the UNITED STATES rescue operation in his partial dissent in the merits phase of the case.[100] He also suggested that the UNITED STATES had violated the Order of Interim Protection[101] since paragraph 47, 1B of that Order[102] indicated that no action was to be taken by either party "which might aggravate the tension between the two countries".

*Elkind* commented the issue as:

> "once a respondent has made it clear that it does not abide by the Court's Order, some limited self-help cannot be avoided. To deny this would put the Applicant in a worse position than it would have occupied had it not submitted the dispute to the Court. The Applicant would thereby be compelled to risk the irreparable or to endure the unendurable until the Court had concluded consideration of the case."[103]

---

99 Declaration of Judge *Buergenthal* appending to the Order of 23 January 2007, *Pulp Mills*, (Provisional Measures), ICJ Reports 2007, p.2, para.7.

100 Dissenting Opinion of Judge *Morozov* appending to the Judgment of 24 May 1980, case concerning *the United States Diplomatic and Consular Staff in Tehran*, (Merits), ICJ Reports 1980, p. 54-55.

101 *Ibid.*

102 Case concerning *the United States Diplomatic and Consular Staff in Tehran*, (USA v. IRAN), (Provisional Measures), Order of 15 December 1979, ICJ Reports 1979, para. 47.

103 *Elkind*, *supra* note 4, p. 229.

The UNITED STATES therefore had the right to undertake to some extent self-help to compel the protection of rights in issue where an Order of provisional measures had been granted. However, the UNITED STATES was not permitted to take any action that might aggravate or extend the dispute as indicated in the Court's Order. UNITED STATES' power to self-help was limited by the "non-aggravation" Order. The difficulty was how to define the scope of "action which might aggravate or extend the dispute". *Elkind* continued his reasoning as: "it would seem therefore that a limited raid, aimed specifically at securing the release of the hostages, was not a violation of the Court's Order because it was aimed only and specifically at securing the rights sought to be preserved. On the other hand, a more general military action such as an invasion, general bombing of installations or a blockade would have been a violation..."[104] In this specific case, "invasion, general bombing of installations or a blockade" were good examples for aggravation. However, there existed some situations that were not easy to be divided into the category of the plausible "self-help" or the opposite, the "aggravation". Then the question how the provisional measures shall be complied with remained to be unsolved.

The purpose of provisional measures is to preserve the imminent risk of irreparable prejudice. It is motivated by urgency and it in turn calls for prompt compliance. However, an Order of general "non-aggravation" measures as stated above might bring even more uncertainty and adverse effects, rather than achieving that goal.

Provisional measures on the sole basis of "non-aggravation" would also lead to another problem: does the Court have to satisfy itself that there is some *prima facie* jurisdiction over the merits when it indicates "non-aggravation" measures? It is an established practice that the Court indicates provisional measures only when there is *prima facie* jurisdiction over the merits.[105] If the answer is affirmative, another question arises. What is the jurisdiction on the merits here?

Some individual judges in the *Legality of use of Force* case asserted that the Court had the power to indicate "non-aggravation" measures regardless of whether the Court had *prima facie* jurisdiction over the merits. They believed that due to the Court's important role to play in the maintenance of international peace, a less stringent standard on *prima facie* jurisdiction could be possible.[106] An even stronger view was raised as: "when the Court seeks to prevent the aggravation, it is empowered to protect rights other than those already in issue in the case, provided that there is an instrument that confers on the Court *prima facie* jurisdiction to deal with those rights."[107]

---

104 *Ibid.*

105 The issue of "*prima facie* jurisdiction over the merits" will be elaborated in Chapter D, Part I, point 1.

106 *Legality of the Use of Force* (YUGOSLAVIA v. BELGIUM), (Provisional Measures), Order of 2 June 1999, ICJ Reports 1999, p.140, para.49.

107 *Greig*, The Balancing of Interests and the Granting of Interim Protection by the

The examination on jurisdiction over the merits aims to avoid the embarrassment that the Court finds that it has no jurisdiction over the merits of the case after the indication of provisional measures. That provides reasonable protection to the sovereign rights of the Respondent. If the "non-aggravation" measures were granted without satisfying the *prima facie* jurisdiction requirement, then the jurisdiction of the Court would be improperly broadened, not because of the wills of the parties, but because of the Court's indication of the "non-aggravation" measures. *Palchetti* argued that it was for the parties to delimit the object of the dispute over which the Court was called upon to exercise its jurisdiction and the Court did not have the power to protect *proprio motu* rights of the parties that were not in dispute in the case before it; this would constitute an *ultra petita.*[108] If no examination of jurisdiction over the merits were required, one would arrive at a conclusion that the Court may require two states to refrain from aggravating the dispute even when it has no jurisdiction to entertain that dispute at all.

Therefore, it is theoretically ungrounded for the Court to ignore the examination of *prima facie* jurisdiction when it indicates the "non-aggravation" measures. It is well-established jurisprudence that *prima facie* jurisdiction on the merits is the precondition for the Court to indicate provisional measures. The Court has never taken into consideration the possibility of indicating the "non-aggravation" measures in the absence of a basis for *prima facie* jurisdiction despite of the fact that the Court sometimes incorporates in its reasoning a statement recommending the parties not to take any actions that might aggravate the dispute.[109] The Court's practices in the two cases concerning *Armed Activities on the Territory of the CONGO (CONGO v. RWANDA), (CONGO v. UGANDA)* are good examples. The two cases were quite similar. Both involved the armed aggression in the territory of the CONGO. CONGO requested respectively in both cases to refrain UGANDA and RWANDA from violating the sovereignty, the territorial integrity, the human rights and international humanitarian law. In the case concerning *Armed Activities on the Territory of the CONGO (CONGO v. UGANDA)*, the Court indicated measures to refrain both parties from any action, and in particular the armed action that might aggravate or extend the dispute. However, the Court rejected to indicate any measures because of the lack of *prima facie* jurisdiction in the case concerning *Armed Activities on the Territory of the CONGO (CONGO v. RWANDA).*

In the case of the preservative measures, the measures are requested to protect the rights of the parties that are in issue before the Court. Therefore it is clear that the jurisdiction over the merits is the jurisdiction to settle the dispute over those rights. But if we recognize that the "non-aggravation" measures could be granted even

---

International Court, Australian Year Book of International Law, (1991), Vol.11, p. 127.

108 *Palchetti*, The Power of the INTERNATIONAL COURT OF JUSTICE to Indicate Provisional Measures to Prevent the Aggravation of a Dispute, Leiden Journal of International Law, (2008), Vol.21, p. 632-633.

109 *Palchetti, ibid.*, p. 631-632.

when no preservative measures are granted, it would be difficult to identify the jurisdiction over the merits because the provisional measures on the sole basis of "non-aggravation" are by the nature too general to define.

## 5. Summary

Developing from the pragmatic and occasional function in the *Electricity Company* case, the "non-aggravation" measures were firstly designed to preserve the respective rights in issue when not enough facts had yet been achieved by the Court and specific preservative measures were inappropriate because they might turn out to be improper when more facts were covered. Its general nature was expected to make up the inexhaustibility of the preservative measures. In the majority of the cases before the present Court, the "non-aggravation" measures functioned in such a modest and unnoticeable way indeed, as in the *Anglo-Iranian Oil Company* case, case concerning *Military and Paramilitary Activities in and against NICARAGUA* and the *Bosnian Genocide* case. They were incorporated in the Operative part of the Orders, along with some more specific preservative measures.

However, the "non-aggravation" measures once seemed to be more independently adopted in the *Frontier Dispute* case and the case concerning the *Land and Maritime Boundary between CAMEROON and NIGERIA.* In the two cases, the rights in issue were sovereignty rights on the respective territory of the parties. The Court (Chamber) found that although it was unnecessary to indicate provisional measures to preserve the sovereignty rights on the territory because of the lack of irreparable prejudice, there was nevertheless very urgent need to refrain both parties from any actions that might aggravate the dispute. The respective rights in issue in the proceedings were sovereignty on territorial integrity. However, the dispute of territorial sovereignty would escalate into military conflicts because of its special character. The Court seemed to break through the traditional approach and indicated provisional measures independently to refrain both parties from any actions that might aggravate the dispute. In my view, the Court (Chamber) has broadened the original scope of the application of "non-aggravation" measures in these two cases. Although the Court (the Chamber) did not explicitly state the reasons for the "non-aggravation" measures, the reasoning of the Order and the statement on the Court's role in the maintenance of international peace reveals that the Court was stressing the necessity to refrain the parties from military actions. Although the Court's concern on international peace is quite understandable, I am wondering whether it is proper for the Court to indicate measures, mainly aiming to maintain international peace while the subject matter of the dispute, namely the sovereignty on territory, is to some extent irrelevant to that aim. Second, it is also a shift from the Court's authority under Article 41 and the original function of the general "non-aggravation" measures as justified by its early jurisprudence.

Furthermore, the Court will confront some practical difficulties if it is empowered to independently indicate "non-aggravation" measures the preservative measures are unnecessary. It might cause uncertainty to the case and difficulty to the examination of the jurisdiction over the merits. Examining the two Orders, it is observed that the Court seemed to let the issue of jurisdiction untouched. For the question of jurisdiction in the *Frontier Dispute* case, *Thirlway* provided a thorough comment:

> "the whole emphasis of, in particular, the reasoning in the *Frontier Dispute* case is on the restraint of escalation; the actual nature of the dispute, the identification of the rights claimed and denied, is secondary. In that case the issue may have been obscured by the fact that there was no dispute as to jurisdiction, and consequently the condition requiring the establishment of probable jurisdiction was evidently satisfied, and the question therefore never raised."[110]

Presumably, the Court will face the difficulties on jurisdiction if it continues this sole "non-aggravation" approach. Moreover, the "non-aggravation" measures might not be effective as expected, due to the uncertainty they cause.

In the *Pulp Mill* case, the Court refused to indicate any "non-aggravation" measures because there was no basis for the indication of preservative measures. It stated that, "in all cases in which it issued provisional measures directing the parties not to take any conduct which would aggravate or extend the dispute, other measures were also indicated ...". Although the Court did not explain in detail the reasons for its opinion, the consideration on the Court's judicial functions, its jurisdiction basis, the scope of its power under Article 41, the origin and practice of the "non-aggravation" measures and the possible difficulties might arise as above discussed might make the Court reconsider this issue in the future. The Court's restrictive attitude in the *Pulp Mills* case seemed to be a turning-back to the prior case law after its shift in its 1986 and 1996 dicta. And the 1 July 2000 Order in the case concerning *the Armed Activities on the Territory of the CONGO* could be regarded as the reflection of the Court's transitional attitude on this issue.

Considering the role of the Court, the function of the Article 41 and the jurisprudence of the Court on this issue, it might be reasonable to assert that "non-aggravation" is one of the circumstances that the Court should take into consideration when it is deciding whether to indicate provisional measures or not. The risk of aggravation of the dispute on the respective rights in issue would be an important weighing element. However, the "non-aggravation" element could not be

110 *Thirlway, supra* note 81, p. 106.

regarded as one of the purposes of provisional measures or an independent basis of the indication of provisional measures. The Court may only consider the aggravation along with the irreparable prejudice to the rights in issue. Considering the necessity to prevent military action or other serious international crisis, a more reasonable approach might be that the Court makes some unbinding recommendations that advocate the non-aggravation of the dispute. *Palchetti*'s observation on the *Pulp Mills* Order thoroughly summarized this point: "a more plausible reading of the Court's Order would suggest that, in the Court's view, "non-aggravation" measures can be granted only if the circumstances of a case are such as to require the indication of measures aimed at preventing irreparable harm to the rights of the parties. Thus "non-aggravation" measures would merely be ancillary to measures directed at preserving specific rights."[111]

## VI. Purely procedural interests

A less complicated and controversial point is whether the purely procedural interests could be regarded as the purpose of provisional measures. The concept of "promotion of the satisfactory conduct of the proceedings" was raised for the first time in the Order of 15 February 1927 before the PERMANENT COURT in the *Sino-Belgian* case. After pointing out that the new fact had removed the circumstances which required the indication of measures of protection, the Order stated that there were "no other circumstances independent of the legal situation created by the Parties, … which would point to the indication of measures of protection in the interest of procedure alone".[112] Therefore, the PERMANENT COURT found that the invocation of the prior provisional measures was justifiable. It is reasonable to infer that the PERMANENT COURT was trying to exclude both the factual and procedural necessity to indicate provisional measures. The "interest of procedure" was one of the circumstances which the PERMANENT COURT took into consideration. However, it does not mean that the PERMANENT COURT could indicate provisional measures for the "interest of procedure alone".

A similar concept was raised in TURKEY's observation responding to GREECE's request for provisional measures in the *Aegean Sea Continental Shelf* case. TURKEY invoked Article 48 of the Statute, under which the Court shall make all arrangements connected with the taking of evidence and asserted: "that means that interim measures should be designed to promote the satisfactory conduct of the proceedings before the Court and particularly to ensure that the parties are enabled

111 *Palchetti, supra* note 108, p. 636.

112 *Denunciation of the Treaty of 2 November 1865 between CHINA and BELGIUM* case, (BELGIUM v. CHINA), (Interim Measures), Order of 15 February 1927, PCIJ, Series A, No. 8, p. 11.

to present all relevant evidence. In the present instance, the exploration activities undertaken by TURKEY will serve to gather evidence that might be relevant to the case..."[113] This assertion was not accepted by the Court.

This element was indeed mentioned once in the Court's Order in the *Frontier Dispute* case.[114] However, as was discussed in the last part, the deciding factor of the Court's decision to indicate provisional measures was the risk of aggravation of the dispute, despite that the Chamber mentioned the risk of destruction of evidence as a supplementary reason for its decision.

Therefore, it might be safe to draw the conclusion that "the interest of procedure" is a circumstance which adds some strength to the influencing element (the imminent risk of the irreparable prejudice to the rights) when the Court is considering to indicate provisional measures. However, it still lacks theoretical and practical evidence to assert that "promotion of the satisfactory conduct of the proceedings" could be taken as the purpose of provisional measures and as the basis of the indication of provisional measures.

113 *Aegean Sea Continental Shelf* (GREECE v. TURKEY), (Provisional Measures), Order of 11 September 1976, ICJ Reports 1976, p.3.

114 *Frontier Dispute* (BURKINO FASO/REPUBLIC OF MALI), (Provisional Measures), Order of 10 January 1986, ICJ Reports 1986, p.9, para. 20.

## D. The "circumstances" for the indication of provisional measures

As Article 41 of the Statute states, the Court has the power "to indicate, if it considers that circumstances so require, any provisional measures which ought to be taken to preserve the respective rights of either party." What does the word "circumstances" exactly mean? This article leaves much room for the Court to interpret in practice. This is also the most ambiguous and difficult point the Court is facing when it is about to exercise the power under Article 41.

## I. the conditions for the indication of provisional measures

### 1. The jurisdiction to indicate provisional measures

a) the basis of the Court's jurisdiction to indicate provisional measures

What is the jurisdictional basis for provisional measures? This is an issue causing much controversy. One view is to regard the power to indicate provisional measures as an inherent part of the Court's judicial function, namely the incidental jurisdiction. Judge Sir Gerald *Fitzmaurice* proposed this point. On this basis, the Court could be able to deal with the requests for provisional measures, "independently at that stage of whether it has substantive jurisdiction to determine the merits".[115] Another view is represented by *Thirlway*. He regarded the Court's

115 Judge *Fitzmaurice* stated: "For the whole purpose of the eventual exercise of substantive jurisdiction in the case would be defeated - or at any rate might be prejudiced - if interim measures necessary to preserve the rights of the parties, as ultimately found by the Court, could not (when necessary) be indicated in advance of the determination by the Court of its substantive jurisdiction in the case. It is therefore essential that the Court should be able to deal with the matter, independently at that stage of whether it has substantive jurisdiction to determine the merits, and without as yet having to form any definite view on the question of its substantive jurisdiction in the case…" Developing on this premise, he believed that substantive jurisdiction should nevertheless be examined at this stage to ensure the propriety of entertaining the requests. He seemed to be holding that the jurisdiction to indicate provisional measures existed as a form of incidental jurisdiction. But the Court still needs to examine the substantive jurisdiction before it reaches the merits of the requests. It seemed that he was intending to divide the Court's operation into two stages. Firstly the Court examines the substantive jurisdiction to ensure that it is proper to entertain the request. Then it goes on to the merits of the requests, namely to consider indicate or reject

jurisdiction on provisional measures as a form of statutory jurisdiction. He believed that the jurisdiction on provisional measures derived directly from the Statute, like the jurisdiction to revise or interpret a judgment, or the jurisdiction to give an advisory opinion, was not exposed to jurisdictional objections designed to show that an asserted jurisdiction over the merits was non-existent or did not extend to the case brought.[116] These two views share one point. They both regard Article 41 as the independent jurisdictional basis for provisional measures and substantive jurisdiction as irrelevant here. However, it seems to be too much a degrading of the States' consent underlying jurisdiction. Moreover, the view to regard the jurisdiction for provisional measures as statutory jurisdiction is to some extent doubtable. It is indeed the general character of statutory jurisdiction that it arises from the existence of the express provision of the Statute and is allowed to be exercised independently of the specific consent of the parties. However, it might be reluctant to regard the Court's jurisdiction to indicate provisional measures as a form of jurisdiction derived directly from the Statute. Unlike the jurisdiction to revise or interpret a judgment, or the jurisdiction to give an advisory opinion, the Court's power to indicate provisional measures to some extent touches on the substantive rights of the parties as revealed by the Court's practice. It would probably lead to a situation that a state has to constrain the rights that she believes to exist pending the proceedings when it is apparent that she has not even consented to the substantive jurisdiction of the Court. That might be overreaching or even misconstruction of the scope of the states' consent. It would probably exert potential risks on the Respondent's sovereignty. This would even encourage the Applicant to abuse provisional measures in a case where a lack of substantive jurisdiction is manifest.

It is without doubt that Article 41 is the direct source of the Court's power to indicate provisional measures. To take it even further, it can be stated that the states' consent to the jurisdiction of the Court is the source of the Court's power to indicate provisional measures. Article 35 of the Statute of the Court provides that "the Court shall be open to the States Parties to the present Statute". The Statute of the Court is a part of the UNITED NATIONS CHARTER. Article 93 of the UNITED NATIONS CHARTER further provides what constitutes a State Party to the Statute.[117] When a state accepts the Statute of the Court and becomes a party to the Statue, she has consents to the operation of Article 41. In other words, any States Party could be regarded as having consented to Article 41 by consenting to be a State Party to the

---

the request. *Fitzmaurice*, The Law and Procedure of the INTERNATIONAL COURT OF JUSTICE, (1986), p. 534, p.774-777.

116 *Thirlway*, *supra* note 44, p. 18.

117 Article 93 of the UNITED NATIONS CHARTER provides that:

(1) All Members of the UNITED NATIONS are *ipso facto* parties to the Statute of the INTERNATIONAL COURT OF JUSTICE;

(2) A State which is not a Member of the UNITED NATIONS may become a party to the Statute of the INTERNATIONAL COURT OF JUSTICE on conditions to be determined in each case by the GENERAL ASSEMBLY upon the recommendation of the SECURITY COUNCIL.

Statute. To this extent, the parties' consent to the Statute is the Court's jurisdictional basis to indicate provisional measures. In my view, this is the ground on which the Court's jurisdiction on the merits of the case is relevant to its jurisdiction to indicate provisional measures.

This theoretical study is again well illustrated by the Court's practice. Since the first case involving provisional measures, the Court examines the jurisdiction over the merits. However, its attitude remained to be somewhat unstable as was shown in the *Interhandel* case and the *Aegean Sea Continental Shelf* case. In the *Interhandel* case, the Court's reasoning of rejecting the provisional measures was mainly based on the non-existence of risk of imminent prejudice. In the *Aegean Sea Continental Shelf* case, the Court simply stated that "in order to pronounce on the present request for interim measures of protection, the Court is not called upon to decide the question of its jurisdiction to entertain the merits of the case". This reasoning was opposed to by several judges in their separate opinions and widely criticized by the commentators on failing to firstly examine the jurisdiction over the merits.[118] Nevertheless, the Court to some extent recognized the necessity to examine the jurisdiction over the merits but disregarded it for the sake of procedural economy. After decades of controversial discussion within and outside the Court, it was until the case concerning the *Military and Paramilitary Activities in and against NICARAGUA* (NICARAGUA v. UNITED STATES) that the Court abandoned its unstable attitude on this issue and expressly required the jurisdictional examination. The Court stated in the Order that jurisdiction over the merits was a point which was given "fullest consideration compatible with the requirement of urgency".[119] The practice to examine the jurisdiction on the merits before it indicates provisional measures has been affirmed and consistently followed nowadays.

---

118 Although the Court indeed examined this issue in the early cases, its less attention and unclear attitude on this issue as showed in the *Interhandel* and *Aegean Sea Continental Shelf* case lead to warmly discussion within the Court. President Jiménez de *Aréchaga* took the position that Article 41 is an autonomous grant of jurisdiction and that jurisdiction to entertain the merits of the dispute was "but ...one among the circumstances which the Court has to take into account in deciding whether to grant the interim measures". This opinion was disagreed by Judge *Mosler*, who held that it was a precondition to "examination of whether such circumstances exist". Judge *Tarazi* also opposed the "autonomous grant" theory. He believed that the Court was required "to show vigilance in the appraisal of various elements in the Application". Separate Opinion of President Jiménez de *Aréchaga* appending to the Order of 11 September 1976, *Aegean Sea Continental Shelf*, (Provisional Measures), ICJ Reports 1976, p.16; Separate Opinion of Judge *Mosler* appending to the Order of 11 September 1976, *Aegean Sea Continental Shelf* (Provisional Measures), ICJ Reports 1976, p.26; Separate Opinion of Judge *Tarazi* appending to the Order of 11 September 1976, *Aegean Sea Continental Shelf*, (Provisional Measures), ICJ Reports 1976, p.33.

119 Case concerning *Military and Paramilitary Activities in and against NICARAGUA* (NICARAGUA v. UNITED STATES), (Provisional Measures), Order of 10 May 1984, ICJ Reports 1984, p. 179, para. 25.

Based on this premise, it can be inferred that the jurisdiction over the merits is the precondition to indicate provisional measures, rather than one of the circumstances the Court considers. The authors are divided on this issue. Judge *Hudson* and Jiménez de *Aréchaga* regarded the possibility of the existence of the jurisdiction over the merits as one of the "circumstances" which the Court considered, along with other circumstances.[120] *Mendelson* in his paradigm also supported this solution.[121] *Thirlway* believed that this opinion inappropriately recognized that the existence of jurisdiction required the indication of measures and it downgraded jurisdiction to the same level as the other circumstances.[122] It is not difficult to find that "the existence of the jurisdiction over the merits" is in character different from the other circumstances. It might be more plausible to differentiate the position of the first element from the other two. Assuming that "the possibility of the existence of the jurisdiction over the merits" is a precondition of examining whether the "circumstances" exist, the Court needs to make sure that it is competent to entertain the request (Sir Gerald *Fitzmaurice* described it as the "jurisdictional aspect"[123]) before probing into the request for provisional measures, namely whether to reject or grant the request (which Sir Gerald *Fitzmaurice* regarded as the "substantive aspect"[124]). *Fitzmaurice* defined that the exercise of jurisdiction on provisional measures involved both a question of merits and a preliminary question of jurisdiction.[125] According to his statement, the exercise of jurisdiction on provisional measures is virtually divided into two steps. The first step is to make sure it is proper to entertain the request. The second step is to consider the substantive elements of the request and then decide whether to grant the request. That means, no matter whether the other circumstances in the request justifies the provisional measures or not, the Court needs to find the affirmative assumption on the jurisdiction on the merits before it touches on the other circumstances in the request. If the standard of jurisdiction over the merits is not achieved (the standard will be discussed later), it is not necessary to go on to consider the other circumstances. If it is achieved, while the Court later finds that one or more of the other necessary circumstances do not exist, the request shall be rejected. The *Interhandel* case is a good example to illustrate the different outcomes the different opinions lead to. In that case, the Court simply rejected the request for interim measures on its merits without expressly mentioning the jurisdictional issue. (The Court believed that the sale of the shares could only be affected after termination of a judicial proceeding that was then pending in respect of which there was no

120 Declaration of Judge Jiménez de *Aréchaga* appending to the Order of 22 June 1973, *Nuclear Tests*, (Provisional Measures), ICJ Reports 1973, p. 107.

121 *Elkind*, *supra* note 4, p. 180-181.

122 *Thirlway*, *supra* note 44, p. 20.

123 *Fitzmaurice*, *supra* note 115, p. 777.

124 *Ibid.*

125 *Fitzmaurice*, *ibid.*, p. 775.

indication as to its speedy conclusion. On the other hand, it was believed that the USA government was not taking action at present time to fix a time schedule for the sale of such shares. Therefore, the request was rejected on the ground of lack of imminent risk of irreparable prejudice.) Judge *Lauterpacht* expressed in his Separate Opinion that *prima facie* the Court had no jurisdiction, thus the rejection of provisional measures should be based on this ground instead of any considerations on the merits. It was believed that the Court had "by necessary implication ... left open the possibility of indicating such measures at a renewed request ... at a future date if circumstances should so require".[126]

Therefore, it might be safe to draw the conclusion that the existence of *prima facie* jurisdiction over the merits is the precondition for the Court to touch on the merits and examine whether the "circumstances" justify provisional measures, rather than one of the "circumstances".

b) How does the Court examine the jurisdiction over the merits?

Accordingly it can be concluded that the affirmative assumption on the jurisdiction over the merits shall be established before the Court indicates provisional measures. The issue that really matters might be to what degree the assumption on jurisdiction over the merits should be established. *Sztucki* explained the nature of the problem as follows: "The question at stake is not whether or not the Court may act under Article 41 when it (at least for the moment) has no jurisdiction over the merits; nor is the question at stake whether or not that jurisdiction must be definitely established before the Court may act under Article 41 - although occasionally the problem was posed in these ways."

He then continued that "the real issue, as it presents itself against the background of the Court's practice is ... the question of how much regard must be paid to the prospects of substantive jurisdiction if that jurisdiction is yet to be finally established at the moment when the Court has to decide on interim protection."[127]

The Court for the first time in its history presented its attitude on the "jurisdiction over the merits" in the *Anglo-Iranian Oil Company* case. Although it did not expressly invoke any term as "*prima facie*" which was frequently quoted in the Orders of the later cases, the diction of "cannot be accepted a *priori*" and "completely" showed its inclination on the low threshold of the requirement of jurisdiction. The Iranian Government contested the title of jurisdiction that was invoked in the application. At the same time, it refused to appear before the Court. Its challenge of the Court's jurisdiction over the merits was based on three grounds. Firstly, the dispute was arising between the Anglo-Iranian Oil Company and the Iranian government, the UK government was therefore incompetent as the

126 Separate Opinion of Judge *Lauterpacht* appending to the Order of 24 October 1957, *Interhandel*, (Interim Measures), ICJ Report 1957, p. 117.

127 *Sztucki*, *supra* note 3, p. 221-222.

complainant. Secondly, the agreement of 1933 was not a treaty and therefore the nationalization of the Anglo-Iranian Oil Company was within its domestic jurisdiction. Thirdly, the Iranian Declaration accepting the compulsory jurisdiction of the Court excluded those treaties that were concluded before the deposit of the Declaration and most of the treaties relied on by the UK Government were concluded prior to that time. Besides, some of the treaties relied on by the UK Government could only be invoked through most-favored-nation clauses. Therefore, these treaties could not be regarded as the basis for the title of jurisdiction. The UK Government argued that it had adopted the cause of the British company and was proceeding with the right of diplomatic protection. Therefore the complaint could not be excluded from the scope of the international jurisdiction. The Court seemed to recognize that the complaint was one of an alleged violation of international law by the breach of the agreement and also constituted a denial of justice that would follow from the IRAN's refusal to accept arbitration under that agreement. The Court therefore recognized that it could not be accepted a *priori* that a claim based on such a complaint fell completely outside the scope of international jurisdiction.[128] Then it followed that the considerations stated in the preceding paragraph sufficed to empower the Court to entertain the Request for interim measures. It can be concluded that the examination of jurisdiction over the merits at the provisional measures stage covers both *ratione personae* and *ratione materiae*. This observation has been frequently demonstrated by the Court's decisions on the jurisdictional grounds alleged by the Applicant and the challenges raised by the unwilling Respondents in the following cases. It was expressly stated by the Court in its Order to indicate provisional measures in the *Bosnian Genocide* case (BOSNIA and HERZEGOVINA v. YUGOSLAVIA (SERBIA and MONTENEGRO)).[129]

(1) The advent of the notion - "*prima facie* jurisdiction over the merits"

The Court faced this question in the *Anglo-Iranian Oil Co.* case. To what extent should the jurisdiction over the merits be established for the Court to indicate provisional measures? The Government of the UK based its claim to the jurisdiction of the Court on Article 36(2) and (5) of the Court's Statute. The Iranian Government

128 *Anglo-Iranian Oil Co.*, (UK v. IRAN), (Provisional Measures), ICJ Reports 1951, p. 93.

129 The Court stated: " whereas on a request for provisional measures the Court need not, before deciding whether or not to indicate them, finally satisfy itself that it has jurisdiction on the merits of the case, yet it ought not to indicate such measures unless the provisions invoked by the Applicant or found in the Statute appear, prima facie, to afford a basis on which the jurisdiction of the Court might be established; whereas this consideration embraces jurisdiction both *ratione personae* and *ratione materiae*, even though, inasmuch as almost all States are today parties to the Statute of the Court, it is in general only the latter which requires to be considered;", *Bosnian Genocide* ((BOSNIA and HERZEGOVINA v. YUGOSLAVIA (SERBIA and MONTENEGRO)), (Provisional Measures), Order of 13 September 1993, ICJ Reports 1993, p. 12, para. 14.

made a declaration accepting the compulsory jurisdiction of the PCIJ with reservations and the UK Government also made a declaration. The Iranian Government claimed that the nationalization of the Iranian Oil Company was an internal matter and was therefore excluded by its reservations. Without taking account of the reservations, the Court shifted its attention to the fact that "the Government of UK had adopted the cause of the British company and was proceeding in virtue of the right of diplomatic protection". The Court concluded that the complaint was an alleged violation of international law by the breach of the agreement and by a denial of justice and it could not be accepted a *priori* that a claim based on such a complaint fell completely outside the scope of international jurisdiction. Therefore the Court believed that these considerations sufficed to empower it to entertain the request for provisional measures. However, Judges *Winiarski* and Badawi *Pasha* held different opinions. They stated: "We find it difficult to accept the view that if *prima facie* the total lack of jurisdiction of the Court is not patent, that is, if there is a possibility, however remote, that the Court may be competent, then it may indicate interim measures of protection." They believed that the approach which the Court applied in this case appeared to be "based on a presumption in favor of the competence of the Court which is not in consonance with the principle of international law". On the other hand, the judges found that interim measures were "exceptional in character, and in derogation of general rights, they may easily be considered as a scarcely tolerable interference in the affairs of a sovereign State", therefore they suggested a test of "reasonably probable" instead: "If there exist weighty arguments in favor of the challenged jurisdiction, the Court may indicate interim measures of protection; if there exist serious doubts or weighty arguments against this jurisdiction such measures cannot be indicated".[130] Judge Sir Hersch *Lauterpacht* criticized the dissenting opinions of Judges *Winiarski* and Badawi *Pasha*. He held that for the Court to find at this stage that it probably had jurisdiction on the merits would have the effects of interim judgment, which was against the aim of this procedural instrument.[131] Weighing and balancing the facts all the relevant facts is also unrealistic due to the expeditiousness that provisional measures require.

---

130 Dissenting Opinions of Judge *Winiarski* and Badawi *Pasha* appending the Order of 5 July 1951, *Anglo-Iranian Oil Co.*, ICJ Reports 1951, p. 96-97.

131 Judge *Lauterpacht* stated that: "Any such finding [i.e. that the Court probably has jurisdiction] would, at least to some extent, commit the Court as to its final decision – a result which the Court has repeatedly and expressly disclaimed". In a footnote (n. 42 to p. 255) he continued: "The Court would be committing itself to some extent for it would be naturally disinclined to find in the end that its assessment of the probability of its jurisdiction was incorrect. Moreover, any finding based on the assumption that its jurisdiction on the merits is probable presupposes a measure of investigation, in connection with an application for interim measures, which the Court cannot properly undertake at this stage ..." , *Lauterpacht* , *supra* note 8, p. 255-256.

The issue of "jurisdiction over the merits" was not considered by the Court in the *Interhandel* case, which was widely criticized by the commentators for its failure to examine the jurisdiction over the merits before it entertained the request.[132]

It was until in the *Fisheries Jurisdiction* cases that the issue was raised again. This case arose from a long-standing conflict on the limits of ICELAND's territorial waters. The Government of ICELAND extended the limit of its territorial waters from 3 miles to 12 miles by a decree in 1958. The FEDERAL REPUBLIC OF GERMANY and the UNITED KINGDOM regarded this decree as invalid and continued to fish within the 12-mile limit. The Icelandic Parliament declared that it had an indisputable right to a fishing limit of 12 miles in a Resolution of 5 May 1959. The Icelandic Parliament approved an Exchange of Notes between the UK and ICELAND on 9 March 1961. Under this agreement, the UK lifted its objections to the 12-mile limit. The parties agreed on a transitional period of 3 years in which the British fishing vessels would continue to be entitled to fish in certain specified areas within the outer 6 miles of the 12-mile zone. The Government of ICELAND would continue to work for the implementation of the 1959 Resolution, but would be obliged to give the Government of the UK six months notice of any exclusion from any part of the 6-mile outer zone. The parties also agreed that in the event of any dispute in relation to such extension, the matter would, at the request of either party, be referred to the INTERNATIONAL COURT OF JUSTICE. A similar agreement was concluded with the FEDERAL REPUBLIC OF GERMANY on 19 July 1961. On 14 July 1971, the Government of ICELAND issued a policy statement announcing that the agreement with the UK and the FEDERAL REPUBLIC OF GERMANY were to be terminated and the Icelandic fishing limit would be extended to 50 nautical miles. At the same time a zone of 100 nautical miles would be created for protection against pollution. The Government of UK instituted proceedings, asking the Court to adjudge and declare that the ICELAND's claim of 50 nautical miles fishing limit was without any foundation in international law and the question was not susceptible in international law to regulation by the unilateral extension but by agreement. Then the Government of ICELAND issued regulations purporting to carry out the extension of its fishing limit on 14 July 1972. Therefore the UK and the FEDERAL REPUBLIC OF GERMANY filed requests for provisional measures, asking the Government of ICELAND to refrain from enforcing the regulation and taking any measures against the freedom of British vessels to fish outside the said 12-mile limit.

The Government of the UK and the FEDERAL REPUBLIC OF GERMANY based their claim to jurisdiction on the 1961 Agreement, while the Government of ICELAND cited its denunciation of the Agreements to challenge the jurisdiction. Concerning the issue of jurisdiction, the Court stated that: "on a request for provisional measures the Court need not, before indicating them, finally satisfy itself that it has

132 See *eg. Lauterpacht, Greenwood*, International Law Reports, (1994), Vol. 94, p.468-469.

jurisdiction on the merits of the case, yet it ought not to act under Article 41 of the Statute if the absence of jurisdiction on the merits is manifest;"[133]

This statement apparently followed its liberal attitude on the requirement of the certainty of jurisdiction in the *Anglo-Iranian Oil Co.* case. However, some authors believed that the Court actually adopted a somewhat less liberal criterion because the 1961 Agreement was a definite consent to the jurisdiction of the Court.[134] Citing the Exchange of Notes between ICELAND and the UK, the Court concluded that the above-cited provision appeared, *prima facie*, to afford a possible basis on which the jurisdiction of the Court might be founded.[135]

The Court tried to clarify its attitude on the extent to which the jurisdiction on the merits should be established in the 22 June 1973 Orders in the *Nuclear Tests* cases: "on a request for provisional measures the Court need not, before deciding whether or not to indicate them, finally satisfy itself that it has jurisdiction on the merits of the case, yet it ought not to indicate such measures unless the provisions invoked by the applicant appear, prima facie, to afford a basis on which the jurisdiction of the Court might be established."[136]

This *Nuclear Test* criterion is less liberal than the *Anglo-Iranian Oil Co.* test - "not clearly and a *priori* fall completely outside the scope of the Court's jurisdiction". The Court reaffirmed this attitude in the later cases and the term of "*prima facie* jurisdiction on the merits" has been followed to the most recent cases.

(2) What constitutes *prima facie* jurisdiction under Article 41?

It is an interesting question how the Court weighs the facts and finds out whether they satisfy the "*prima facie* jurisdiction" standard in a specific case. In the *Nuclear Tests* cases, the majority judges of the Court held that the General Act of 1928 and the French Declaration under Article 36(2) appeared, *prima facie*, to afford a basis on which the jurisdiction of the Court might be founded. Judge *Forster* opposed the *prima facie* doctrine, in the light of the "exceptional" nature of the *Nuclear Test* cases. From his point of view, doubt existed on the efficacy of the 1928 General Act as it was revised in 1949 and FRANCE did not accede to that revised General Act. Moreover, it remained as an open question whether the continuance of nuclear tests was within FRANCE's sovereignty rights to national defense. Therefore, he felt

---

133 *Fisheries Jurisdiction* (UNITED KINGDOM and NORTHERN IRELAND v. ICELAND), (Provisional Measures), Order of 17 August 1972, ICJ Reports 1972, p.15, para. 15.

134 *Elkind*, *supra* note 4, p. 117.

135 *Fisheries Jurisdiction* (UNITED KINGDOM and NORTHERN IRELAND v. ICELAND), (Provisional Measures), Order of 17 August 1972, ICJ Reports 1972, p. 16, para. 17.

136 *Nuclear Tests* (AUSTRALIA v. FRANCE), (Provisional Measures), Order of 22 June 1973, ICJ Reports 1973, p.101, para.13.

personally unable to attain the degree of certainty on jurisdiction as required to indicate provisional measures.[137]

Similarly, Judge *Pinto* believed that the situation in the present case could not satisfy the jurisdictional requirement because it lacked any instrument as showed in the *Fisheries Jurisdiction* cases, which could definitely afford a *prima facie* basis for jurisdiction.[138]

The issue was raised again and the debate turned to be even warmer in the *Aegean Sea Continental Shelf* case. Holding that "in order to pronounce on the present request for interim measures of protection, the Court is not called upon to decide any question of its jurisdiction to entertain the merits of the case", the Court rejected the request on the basis of the lack of risk of irreparable prejudice without examining whether the jurisdiction over the merits existed. The Court's lessened attention on the issue of jurisdiction might be due to its consideration concerning the economy of proceedings. It is open to criticism, both within and outside the Court, on whether the Court still needs to examine the jurisdiction when the other conditions of the indication of provisional measures are not satisfied. (This point has been discussed in the last part. This part will focus on the dissenting opinions concerning the extent to which the Court needs to be content on the jurisdiction over the merits only.) The issue of jurisdiction caused some dissenting opinions. Vice-President Nagendra *Singh* followed Judge *Gros*' opinion and believed that, in the event of the nonappearance of one of the parties, Article 53 placed a special burden on the Court to satisfy itself as to its jurisdiction. Citing the *Anglo-Iranian Oil* case, he felt that it was necessary for the Court to reach "a higher degree of satisfaction than can be derived from the positive but cursory test of '*prima facie*' jurisdiction or the negative test of 'no manifest lack of jurisdiction'".[139] Judge *Ruda* expressed his satisfaction with the *prima facie* test but was unable to find, *prima facie*, that the provisions and instruments invoked by the applicant afforded a basis for jurisdiction.[140] Judge *Mosler* also held that he was unable to form a conclusion that there was a *prima facie* basis for jurisdiction.[141] Judge *Tarazi* believed that a more thorough examination was needed.[142]

---

137 Dissenting Opinion of Judge *Forster* appending to the Order of 22 June 1973, *Nuclear Tests*, ICJ Reports 1973, p. 112-113.

138 Dissenting Opinion of Judge Ignacio-*Pinto* appending to the Order of 22 June 1973, *Nuclear Tests*, (Provisional Measures), ICJ Reports 1973, p. 128-129.

139 Separate Opinion of Vice-President Nagendra *Singh* appending to the Order of 11 September 1976, *Aegean Sea Continental Shelf*, (Interim Measures), ICJ Reports 1976, p.18-19.

140 Separate Opinion of Judge *Ruda* appending to the Order of 11 September 1976, *Aegean Sea Continental Shelf*, (Interim Measures), ICJ Reports 1976, p.24.

141 Separate Opinion of Judge *Mosler* appending to the Order of 11 September 1976, *Aegean Sea Continental Shelf*, (Interim Measures), ICJ Reports 1976, p. 25-27.

142 Separate Opinion of Judge *Tarazi* appending to the Order of 11 September 1976, *Aegean Sea Continental Shelf*, (Interim Measures), ICJ Reports 1976, p. 32-34.

(3) Judge *Lauterpacht*'s instrumental test

Along with the fierce debate on this point, great endeavor has been made to draw a specific test on the certainty of jurisdiction as required to indicate provisional measures. Judge Sir Hersch *Lauterpacht* represented one of the proposed tests, namely "the documentary or instrumental test". He stated in his separate opinion in the *Interhandel* case: "The correct principle which emerges from these apparently conflicting considerations and which has been uniformly adopted in international arbitral or judicial practice is as follows: The Court may properly act under the terms of Article 41 provided that there is in existence an instrument such as *a Declaration of Acceptance of the Optional Clause*, emanating from the Parties to the dispute, which *prima facie* confers jurisdiction upon the Court and which *incorporates no reservations obviously excluding its jurisdiction.*[143] (emphasis added )

This test might probably originate from his restrictive view on the Court's power to indicate provisional measures. He drew attention to the dangers of too great a freedom to indicate provisional measures, believing that to indicate provisional measures "in all cases in which … jurisdiction is merely possible" would be "…to open the door to abuse by enabling States with no more than a flimsy claim to the jurisdiction of the Court to obtain an interim Order limiting severely and for a relatively prolonged period the freedom of action of the State concerned."[144] Therefore, the requests for provisional measures shall be rejected not only on the basis of manifest lack of jurisdiction, but also when the possibility of the jurisdiction is too remote or hypothetical to justify the indication of provisional measures.

This test indeed provides a certain and easily applied standard to guide the Court and the potential requesting state. And it covers the Court's most representative jurisprudence. However, it also brings some difficulties as it is not conclusive. As pointed out by Judge Sir Gerald *Fitzmaurice*, *Lauterpacht*'s requirement that there should be a standing antecedent instrument (or instrument, as in the case of mutual "optional clause" declarations) can scarcely apply if the Court's jurisdiction could be established on a basis of *forum prorogatum* (delayed jurisdiction, not jurisdiction invoked, but jurisdiction completed subsequently).[145] The examples of recognizing the jurisdiction on *forum prorogatum* can be found in the Court's jurisprudence. In the *Legality of the Use of Force* (YUGOSLAVIA v. USA) and (YUGOSLAVIA v. SPAIN), YUGOSLAVIA claimed Article 38, paragraph 5 of the Rules of the Court as the second alternative basis for jurisdiction of the Court "when the applicant State proposes to found the jurisdiction of the Court upon a consent thereto yet to be

143 Separate Opinion of Judge Sir Hersch *Lauterpacht* appending to the Order of 24 October 1957, *Interhandel*, (Interim Measures), ICJ Reports 1957, p. 118.

144 *Ibid.*, p. 111.

145 *Fitzmaurice*, *supra* note 115.

given or manifested by the State against which such application is made, the application shall be transmitted to that State. It shall not however be entered in the General List, nor any action be taken in the proceedings, unless and until the State against which such application is made consents to the Court's jurisdiction for the purposes of the case". The UNITED STATES observed that it "has not consented to jurisdiction under Article 38, paragraph 5 and will not do so". Therefore, the Court concluded that it manifestly lacked jurisdiction to entertain the application and in turn could not indicate any provisional measures. Facing the complexity of the jurisdictional issue, the relevant facts always differ from one case to another. It is difficult to draw any conclusive test on the Court's practice on the examination of the jurisdiction over the merits. Nevertheless, Judge *Lauterpacht*'s test has made great contributions to the study on the Court's practice on provisional measures. He emphasized the Court's very conservative attitude on the examination of the jurisdiction over the merits. The Court prefers to rely on some definite instruments, rather than to make any inference from any remote grounds.

(4) Jurisprudence

The Court's jurisprudence shows that it has recognized four sources of jurisdiction. This was stated by Judge *Hackworth* in the *Anglo-Iranian Oil Co.* case. He stated: "It necessarily follows that, unless a State has by special agreement, by treaty or convention, or by a declaration made under the Optional Clause of Article 36, paragraph 2, of the Statute, accepted jurisdiction, the Court is without jurisdiction."[146] More support is revealed by the authoritative literature on this point.[147] At the stage of provisional measures, cases could be divided into four categories. For the first category of cases, it is claimed that the parties have reached a special agreement that confers jurisdiction on the Court. A good example is the 1961 Agreement in the *Fisheries Jurisdiction* case. This category of cases provides the most definite basis of the jurisdiction of the Court. In the second category of cases, the Applicant claims to base the jurisdiction of the Court under Article 36, paragraph 2 of the Statute, namely both parties have made declarations accepting the compulsory jurisdiction of the Court concerning specific matters and the rights which the request for provisional measures aims to protect fall within the scope of the declaration. As for the third category of cases, the Applicant maintains that *prima facie* jurisdiction of the Court could be based on the conventions or treaties under Article 36, paragraph 2 of the Statute and there exists a dispute falling within

146 *Anglo-Iranian Oil Co.*, (UK v. IRAN), Order of 5 July 1951, ICJ Reports 1952, p. 139.

147 *Rosenne* lists the jurisdiction of the Court as being of four main kinds: consensual, conventional, prorogated and compulsory. *Rosenne*, The INTERNATIONAL COURT OF JUSTICE: an essay in political and legal theory, (1957), p.284.
Sir Gerald *Fitzmaurice* summarized the sources of the Court's jurisdiction as *ante hoc*, *ad hoc* and *post hoc*. *Fitzmaurice*, *supra* note 115, p. 496.

the provisions of the conventions or the treaties. Apart from these three categories of cases based on jurisdiction *ante hoc*, there is a category of cases that are based on jurisdiction *post hoc*. In these cases, the Applicant State proposes to found the jurisdiction of the Court upon "a consent thereto yet to be given or manifested by the State against which such application is made" under Article 38, paragraph 5 of the Rule of the Court.

This classification of the cases is based on the jurisdictional basis that has been recognized by the Court's present practice. As the international law develops, the consents of the parties to the jurisdiction of the Court in new forms might be recognized. This classification is purely academic and not conclusive. However, the Court has shown a conservative attitude to recognize any inferred consent of the parties as the basis for jurisdiction in practice. This can lead to a natural conclusion that any attempt to establish the jurisdiction based on inferred consent would not be considered at the stage of provisional measures. The Court shows a clearly unwilling attitude to accept any other form of jurisdictional basis. In the *Bosnian Genocide* case (BOSNIA and HERZEGOVINA v. YUGOSLAVIA (SERBIA and MONTENEGRO)), the Applicant firstly raised the letter of 8 June 1992 as a *prima facie* basis of jurisdiction of the Court. The Court found that

> "at the present stage of the proceedings, and on the basis of the information before the Court, it is by no means clear to the Court whether the letter was intended as an 'immediate commitment' by the two Presidents, binding on Yugoslavia, to accept unconditionally the unilateral submissions to the Court of a wide range of legal disputes (cf. *Aegean Sea Continental Shelf*, I.C.J. Reports 1978, p.44, para.108); or whether it was intended as a commitment solely to submission to the Court of the three questions raised by the Chairman of the Committee; or as no more than the enunciation of a general policy of favoring judicial settlement, which did not embody an offer or commitment;"[148]

Therefore, it could not constitute a *prima facie* basis for the jurisdiction of the Court.

As for the jurisdiction *post hoc*, it is the recognized practice that the forthcoming consent could be shown both by express response and also by conduct. However, due to the cursory nature of the consideration of jurisdictional issue at the present stage, the Respondent's simple assertion to negate the intention to consent is sufficient for the Court to conclude that it manifestly lacks jurisdiction. It is an inappropriate and unrealistic attempt to take into account the elements that could manifest the consent. Article 38, paragraph 5 has been raised in the *Legality of Use of Force* cases (YUGOSLAVIA v. USA) and (SERBIA and MONTENEGRO v. ITALY). The UNITED STATES and ITALY respectively observed that it "has not consented to

148 *Bosnian Genocide* (BOSNIA and HERZEGOVINA v. YUGOSLAVIA (SERBIA and MONTENEGRO)), Order of 8 April 1993, ICJ Reports 1993, p.19, para.31.

jurisdiction under Article 38, paragraph 5 and will not do so". Therefore, the Court concluded that it manifestly lacked jurisdiction to entertain the application and in turn could not indicate any provisional measures.[149]

Among the four categories of cases, deciding whether the jurisdiction on a special agreement or on a consent yet to be reached or manifested is usually easier, while this happens in rare cases. The 1961 Agreement in the *Fisheries Jurisdiction* cases (FEDERAL REPUBLIC OF GERMANY v. ICELAND), (the UNITED KINGDOM v. ICELAND) is generally regarded as an example of jurisdiction on a special agreement. It contains the clearest sort of jurisdictional clause possible: "The parties agreed that in the event of any dispute in relation to such extension, the matter would, at the request of either party, be referred to the International Court of Justice".[150]

Most of the cases belong to the second and the third category and are much more complicated. As for the cases in which the Applicant relies on the compulsory jurisdiction declarations, the proposed Respondent might firstly challenge the validity of the declarations. In the case concerning *Military and Paramilitary Activities in and against NICARAGUA,* NICARAGUA had never deposited an instrument of ratification of its declaration. Although doubt remained as for the validity of the ratification of NICARAGUA's declaration, this did not itself constitute a bar to the Court's favored conclusion on its jurisdiction over the merits in the proceeding. The Court concluded that, although it had not so far been established to its satisfaction that NICARAGUA had ever deposited an instrument of ratification of that Protocol, it did not believe that the absence of such effective ratification excluded the operation of Article 36, paragraph 5 of the Statute.[151] It can be asserted that a definite instrument itself, which declares the compulsory jurisdiction without reservation, constitutes the *prima facie* basis for jurisdiction. Any challenge

---

149 *Legality of the Use of Force*, (YUGOSLAVIA v. USA), Order of 2 June 1999, ICJ Reports 1999, p. 925; (SERBIA and MONTENEGRO v. ITALY), Order of 2 June 1999, ICJ Reports 1999, p. 491.

150 UK application (1975), ICJ Pleadings, Vol. I, p. 5.

151 The Court stated: "... it has not so far been established to the Court's satisfaction that NICARAGUA ever deposited an instrument of ratification of that Protocol; whereas however the Court is not convinced, by the arguments so far addressed to it, that the absence of such effective ratification excluded the operation of Article 36, paragraph 5, of the Statute of the present Court, and prevented the transfer to the present Court of the declaration as a result of the consent thereto given by NICARAGUA which, having been represented at the San Francisco Conference, signed and ratified the Charter and thereby accepted the Statute in which Article 36, paragraph 5, appears (see *Aerial Incident of 27 July 1955 (Israel v. Bulgaria), I.C.J. Reports 1959,* p.142; *Temple of Preah Vihear, Preliminary Objections, I.C.J. Reports 1961*, p.17);", Case concerning *Military and Paramilitary Activities in and against NICARAGUA* (NICARAGUA v. USA), (Provisional Measures), Order of 10 May 1984, ICJ Reports 1984, p.179-180, para.25.

to the validity of the declaration seems to be disregarded or regarded as not sufficient to overwhelm the certainty that is provided by the declarations.[152]

The second possible assertion the Respondent might maintain is that the reservations exclude its jurisdiction. The obvious reservation such as temporal limitation could manifestly exclude the jurisdiction. For example, the Respondent claimed that the acceptance of the Court's compulsory jurisdiction was deposited or ratified less than 12 months prior to the filing of the application, in the case *Legality of the Use of Force* (SERBIA and MONTENEGRO v. UK).

As for the more ambiguous reservations, the Court tended not to take account of the reservations and simply draw a direct conclusion that the declarations constituted a *prima facie* basis for jurisdiction. In the case concerning *Military and Paramilitary Activities in and against NICARAGUA* (NICARAGUA v. USA), although it remained unclear whether the UNITED STATES Declaration of 6 April 1984 constituted a valid reservation of its declaration of 26 August 1946, the Court concluded that the declarations constituted a *prima facie* basis for the jurisdiction. In the case concerning the *Land and Maritime Boundary between CAMEROON and NIGERIA* (CAMEROON v. NIGERIA), both parties had made a declaration recognizing the compulsory jurisdiction of the Court in accordance with Article 36, paragraph 2 of the Statute. Both declarations were deposited with the SECRETARY-GENERAL of the UNITED NATIONS and neither of them included any reservation. However, NIGERIA had made it clear in its declaration that it was made on the sole condition of reciprocity. NIGERIA raised preliminary objections to the jurisdiction of the Court and claimed that there was no substantive reciprocity in the recognition of the jurisdiction of the Court by the Parties. The Court was of the view that the preliminary objections raised by NIGERIA were not such as to exclude the jurisdiction of the Court. The Court considered that the declarations made by the Parties constituted a *prima facie* basis on which its jurisdiction in the present case might be founded.

From my point of view, a *prima facie* jurisdictional basis can be established if there are definite instruments on the declaration of accepting the compulsory jurisdiction. The Respondent takes the burden of proof of the reservations and preconditions to the declarations. Unless they are as obvious and definite as the temporal limitation, they cannot be taken into account at this preliminary stage. It can be concluded that, in the earlier cases, the Court exerted a liberal standard on the examination of the jurisdiction over the merits.

It is noteworthy that the Court's recent practice reveals its more cautious attitude. In the case concerning the *Arrest Warrant of 11 April 2000* (DEMOCRATIC REPUBLIC OF THE CONGO v. BELGIUM), both parties made declarations recognizing the compulsory jurisdiction of the Court in accordance with Article 36, paragraph 2

152 Case concerning the *Land and Maritime Boundary between CAMEROON and NIGERIA* (CAMEROON v. NIGERIA), (Provisional Measures), Order of 15 March 1996, ICJ Reports 1996, p. 20-21.

of the Statute of the Court. BELGIUM pointed out that its declaration excluded the Court's jurisdiction in respect of a dispute "to which the parties have agreed or may agree to have recourse to another method of pacific settlement". BELGIUM asserted that the issue of the arrest warrant was actively being discussed at the very highest levels between the two states. However, BELGIUM had not provided the Court with any further details of the negotiations. The Court accordingly held that it was not in a position to determine whether the Parties had agreed temporarily to exclude any recourse to the Court on account of the negotiations. Moreover, BELGIUM had not explained to the Court "the precise consequences which it considered the holding of those negotiations, or the holding of negotiations generally, would have in regard to the Court's jurisdiction". Therefore, the Court concluded that BELGIUM's declaration could not be excluded solely by reason of the negotiations referred to by BELGIUM and the declarations constituted the *prima facie* basis on which its jurisdiction could be founded.[153]

It is found from the Court's practice that its attitude is developing. In the case concerning *Military and Paramilitary Activities in and against NICARAGUA*, the Court kept silent on the challenge to the validity of the declarations.[154] In the case concerning the *Land and Maritime Boundary between CAMEROON and NIGERIA* (CAMEROON v. NIGERIA),[155] the Court stated as: "the Court, which has taken note of the opinion expressed by the Agent of NIGERIA with respect to its *prima facie* jurisdiction, is of the view that the preliminary objections raised by that State are not such as to exclude the jurisdiction of the Court". Although the Court incorporated no specific weighing of the evidences as to the reservations to the declarations, it showed greater concern about the preliminary objections raised by the Respondent. In the case concerning the *Arrest Warrant of 11 April 2000* (DEMOCRATIC REPUBLIC OF THE CONGO *v.* BELGIUM),[156] the Court processed a general examination of the reservations to the declaration. The Court's jurisprudence saw its more and more cautious and conservative attitude on examining the States' consent to its jurisdiction. It might be explained by the fact that the disappointing compliance with the provisional measures cautioned the Court to endeavor to reach an Order that the states are more willing to accept.

---

153 Case concerning *the Arrest Warrant of 11 April 2000* (DEMOCRATIC REPUBLIC OF THE CONGO v. BELGIUM), (Provisional Measures), Order of 8 December 2000, ICJ Reports 2000, p. 182-203.

154 Case concerning *Military and Paramilitary Activities in and against NICARAGUA* (NICARAGUA v. USA), (Provisional Measures), Order of 10 May 1984, ICJ Reports 1984, p. 174-180.

155 Case concerning the *Land and Maritime Boundary between CAMEROON and NIGERIA* (CAMEROON v. NIGERIA), (Provisional Measures), Order of 15 March 1996, ICJ Reports 1996, p. 21.

156 Case concerning the *Arrest Warrant of 11 April 2000* (DEMOCRATIC REPUBLIC OF THE CONGO v. BELGIUM), (Provisional Measures), Order of 1 July 2000, ICJ Reports 2000, p. 123.

As for the third category - the Applicant claims to found the jurisdiction of the Court on a treaty or convention, which is acceded by both parties and contains a provision accepting the Court's jurisdiction. Here the Court's jurisprudence is even more complicated because the claimed treaty or convention involves more arguable points, especially on the validity of the treaty or convention. The Respondent could challenge the jurisdiction on the following grounds:
(1) The proposed treaty or convention does not take effect as to the present party or parties;
(2) The rights that the provisional measures aim to protect do not fall within the scope of the treaty or convention;
(3) The reservations exclude the present dispute from the scope of the provision of the treaty or convention;
(4) The conditions of the provision are not satisfied.

Direct challenge to the effect of the treaty or convention to the party was raised by the Respondent in the *Nuclear Test* case. NEW ZEALAND and AUSTRALIA claimed that Article 17 of the General Act of 1928 provided for the jurisdiction of PCIJ. FRANCE, NEW ZEALAND and AUSTRALIA all acceded to the General Act in 1931. Article 36, paragraph 1 and Article 37 of the Statute provided for continuity of jurisdiction between the present Court and the PCIJ. Therefore, NEW ZEALAND and AUSTRALIA claimed to rely on the General Act of 1928 as one basis to establish *prima facie* jurisdiction of the Court. NEW ZEALAND and AUSTRALIA also raised Article 36, paragraph 2 of the Statute as an alternative basis. Citing the oral observations of NEW ZEALAND and AUSTRALIA that "the genuine debate existed between the parties on the reservations to the declarations and the validity of the General Act of 1928", the Court rejected the French contention that the absence of jurisdiction was manifest.[157]

In the *Aegean Sea Continental Shelf* case, GREECE maintained that the Brussels Joint Communiqué of 31 May 1975 was the basis for the jurisdiction of the Court, basing on Article 36, paragraph 1 of the Statute. The other claimed basis for jurisdiction was Article 17 of the General Act to which both GREECE and TURKEY were parties. TURKEY claimed that the Joint Communiqué was insufficient to ground jurisdiction under Article 36, paragraph 1 due to the lack of ratification by TURKEY. Besides, the General Act was no longer in force and even if it was in force, the jurisdiction was excluded by a Greek reservation to Article 17. GREECE asked the Court to consider the Act as being presumptively in force between the two parties and maintained that the subject matter of the present application did not fall within the terms of the Greek reservation. Citing these arguments between the parties but not providing any more analysis, the Court stated that it was not called

157 *Nuclear Tests* (NEW ZEALAND v. ICELAND), (AUSTRALIA v. ICELAND), (Provisional Measures), Order of 22 June 1973, ICJ Reports 1973, p. 138, p. 102.

upon to decide any question of its jurisdiction to entertain the merits of the case and rejected the request on the lack of irreparable risk of prejudice.[158]

In the *Bosnian Genocide* case, the notification of succession by the Government of BOSNIA and HERZEGOVINA to the Genocide Convention was alleged to be invalid because "no rule of general international law gives BOSNIA-HERZEGOVINA the right to proclaim unilaterally that it is now a party to the Genocide Convention merely because the former Socialist Federal Republic of Yugoslavia was a party to the Convention and the Convention was thus applicable to what is now the territory of Bosnia-Herzegovina". YUGOSLAVIA asserted that BOSNIA-HERZEGOVINA's notice could only be regarded as an instrument of accession and could only become effective subsequent to the expiration of 90 days in accordance with Article XIII of the Convention. The Court observed that the SECRETARY-GENERAL had treated BOSNIA-HERZEGOVINA, not as acceding, but as succeeding to the Genocide Convention, and if so the question of the 90 days expiration requirement for accession would not arise. However, the Court noted that even if BOSNIA-HERZEGOVINA were to be treated as having acceded to the Convention, the 90-days period had elapsed between the filing of the Application and the oral proceedings on the request. Therefore the Court observed that "even if its jurisdiction suffers from the temporal limitation asserted by Yugoslavia - which does not now have to decide - this is not necessarily a bar to the exercise to its powers under Article 41 of the Statute". Article IX of the Genocide Convention thus appeared to the Court to afford a basis on which the jurisdiction of the Court might be founded.[159]

Another challenge from the Respondent is that the right sought to be protected does not fall within the scope of the parties' acceptance of compulsory jurisdiction. Facing this sort of argument, the Court usually needs to interpret the scope of the compromissory clause of the treaty or convention and make a rough examination of the facts. The case concerning the *Vienna Convention on Consular Relations* (PARAGUAY v. USA) and the *LAGRAND* case encompassed very similar facts and both involved the compromisory clause of the Vienna Convention on Consular Relations. PARAGUAY based the jurisdiction of the Court on Article 36, paragraph 1 of the Statute of the Court and on Article I of the OPTIONAL PROTOCOL concerning the Compulsory Settlement of Disputes, which accompanied the Vienna Convention on Consular Relations. Article I of the OPTIONAL PROTOCOL was worded as: "disputes arising out of the interpretation or application of the Convention shall lie within the compulsory jurisdiction of the INTERNATIONAL COURT OF JUSTICE and may accordingly be brought before the Court by an application by any party to the dispute being a party to the present Protocol". The UNITED STATES argued that the

158 *Aegean Sea Continental Shelf* (GREECE v. TURKEY), (Provisional Measures), Order of 11 September 1976, ICJ Reports 1976, p. 1-15.

159 *Bosnian Genocide,* (BOSNIA and HERZEGOVINA v. YUGOSLAVIA (SERBIA and MONTENEGRO)), (Provisional Measures), Order of 8 April 1993, ICJ Reports 1993, p. 1-26.

objections raised by PARAGUAY to the proceedings brought against its nationals did not constitute a dispute concerning the interpretation or application of the Vienna Convention. However, PARAGUAY still requested that the *status quo ante* should be restored. The Court held that there existed a dispute as to whether the relief sought by PARAGUAY is a remedy available under the Vienna Convention, and this was a dispute arising out of the application of the Convention within the meaning of Article I of the Optional Protocol. Therefore, the Court found that, *prima facie*, it had jurisdiction under Article I of the Protocol to decide the dispute between the parties.[160] A similar situation arose again before the Court in the case *Legality of the Use of Force* (SERBIA and MONTENEGRO v. UNITED KINGDOM), and its group cases *Legality of Use of Force* (SERBIA and MONTENEGRO v. PORTUGAL), (SERBIA and MONTENEGRO v. NETHERLANDS), (SERBIA and MONTENEGRO v. CANADA), (SERBIA and MONTENEGRO v. BELGIUM), (SERBIA and MONTENEGRO v. ITALY), (SERBIA and MONTENEGRO v. GERMANY), (SERBIA and MONTENEGRO v. FRANCE). YUGOSLAVIA claimed, in the second place, to found the jurisdiction of the Court on Article IX of the GENOCIDE CONVENTION. The Court observed that the dispute as presented by the Parties was not capable of falling within the provisions of the GENOCIDE CONVENTION because the threat or use of force against a State could not itself constitute an act of genocide within the meaning of Article II of the GENOCIDE CONVENTION. Therefore, the Court found that Article IX of the Convention could not constitute a basis on which the jurisdiction of the Court could *prima facie* be founded.[161]

In the case concerning the *Armed Activities on the Territory of the CONGO* (New Application: 2002) (DEMOCRATIC REPUBLIC OF THE CONGO v. RWANDA), several grounds to challenge the jurisdiction were raised by the Respondent. CONGO observed that the Court's jurisdiction over the merits of the case "on the basis of the international conventions and treaties to which the Applicant and the Respondent area parties" under Article 36, paragraph 1 of the Statute of the Court. The Court firstly found that RWANDA was not a party to the Convention against Torture and this convention could not constitute a basis for the jurisdiction. The CONGO then sought to found the Court's jurisdiction on Article 22 of the CONVENTION ON

160 Case concerning *the Vienna Convention on Consular Relations* (PARAGUAY v. USA), (Provisional Measures), Order of 9 April 1998, ICJ Reports 1998, p. 248-258.

161 *Legality of the Use of Force* (SERBIA and MONTENEGRO v. UK), (Provisional Measures), Order of 2 June 1999, ICJ Reports 1999, p. 836-838; (SERBIA and MONTENEGRO v. PORTUGAL), Order of 2 June 1999, ICJ Reports 1999, p. 668-670; (SERBIA and MONTENEGRO v. NETHERLANDS), Order of 2 June 1999, ICJ Reports 1999, p. 554-556; (SERBIA and MONTENEGRO v. CANADA), Order of 2 June 1999, ICJ Reports 1999, p. 270-272; (SERBIA and MONTENEGRO v. BELGIUM), Order of 2 June 1999, ICJ Reports 1999, p. 136-138; (SERBIA and MONTENEGRO v. ITALY), Order of 2 June 1999, ICJ Reports 1999, p.489-491; (SERBIA and MONTENEGRO v. GERMANY), Order of 2 June 1999, ICJ Reports 1999, p. 429-431; (SERBIA and MONTENEGRO v. FRANCE), Order of 2 June 1999, ICJ Reports 1999, p. 370-372.

RACIAL DISCRIMINATION. RWANDA claimed that it had made reservation to Article 22. The CONGO asserted that the reservation "prevent the attainment of the very purposes and object of the treaty" and thus was invalid. Citing that the Convention on Racial Discrimination prohibited reservations incompatible with its object and purpose, under Article 20, paragraph 2 of the Convention, and "a reservation shall be considered incompatible ... if at least two-thirds of the States Parties to this Convention object to it", the Court observed that such had not been the case in respect of RWANDA's reservation. Therefore, RWANDA's reservation to the Article 22 was *prima facie* applicable and this Convention could not constitute a basis for the Court's jurisdiction. The CONGO sought to found the jurisdiction on Article IX of the Genocide Convention. The Court found that RWANDA had made a reservation to it. CONGO challenged the validity of the reservation on the basis of the universal nature of the norms on Genocide. The Court distinguished the norms on genocide and the consent to jurisdiction in genocide disputes. RWANDA's reservation did not bear on the substance of the law, but only on the Court's jurisdiction. Therefore it did not appear contrary to the object and purpose of the Convention. The Genocide Convention constituted a basis for the Court's jurisdiction. The CONGO further sought to found the jurisdiction on Article 66, paragraph (a) of the 1969 Vienna Convention on the Law of Treaties, maintaining that this convention gave the Court jurisdiction to settle disputes arising from the violation of peremptory norms (*jus cogens*) in the area of human rights. The Court found that Article 66 should be read in conjunction with Article 65. It further stated: "...the object of Article 66 was not to allow for the substitution of juridical settlement, arbitration and conciliation procedures under the Vienna Convention on the Law of Treaties for the settlement machinery for disputes relating to the interpretation or application of specific treaties, notably when a violation of those treaties had been alleged." CONGO did not maintain that there was a dispute that could not be resolved under the procedure prescribed in Article 65 concerning a conflict between a treaty and a peremptory norm of international law. The Court accordingly found that Article 66, paragraph (a) could not constitute a basis for the jurisdiction of the Court to entertain the merits in this case. The CONGO further claimed to found the jurisdiction of the Court on Article 29 of the Convention on Discrimination against Women. The Court observed that CONGO had not shown its attempts to enter into negotiations or undertake arbitration proceedings with RWANDA concerning the application of Article 29 of the Convention. Nor had CONGO specified which rights protected by that Convention had allegedly been violated by RWANDA and should be the object of provisional measures. Therefore, the Court concluded that the preconditions on the seisin of the Court set by Article 29 of the Convention did not appear *prima facie* to have been satisfied. The CONGO sought to found the jurisdiction of the Court on Article 75 of the WHO Constitution. The Court found that there also existed preconditions on the seisin of the Court - any question or dispute concerning the interpretation or application of this Convention that is not settled by negotiation or by the Health Assembly. The Court found that CONGO had not shown that the preconditions had been satisfied. The CONGO further claimed to found the jurisdiction of the Court on Article XIV, paragraph 2, of the UNESCO Constitution. This article provided that "any dispute concerning the interpretation of this Constitution shall be referred for determination to the Court or to an arbitral tribunal ..." The Court observed that the object of the Application did not concern the interpretation of the Constitution. Therefore, the Application did not appear to fall within the scope of that article. The UNESCO Constitution thus could not constitute a basis for the Court's jurisdiction. The CONGO lastly sought to found the Court's jurisdiction on Article 14, paragraph 1, of the Montreal Convention. The Court found that the CONGO had not asked the Court to indicate any provisional measures relating to the preservation of rights that it believed it held under the Montreal Convention. Accordingly the Court was not required to rule on its jurisdiction under that Convention nor on the conditions precedent to the Court's jurisdiction contained therein. The Court finally concluded that it did not have the *prima facie* jurisdiction necessary to indicate provisional measures.[162]

In the *Pulp Mills* case (ARGENTINA v. URUGUAY), the two parties were in agreement that the Court had jurisdiction with regard to the rights to which Article 60 of the 1975 Statute applied. However, URUGUAY claimed that such jurisdiction existed *prima facie* only with regard to those aspects of ARGENTINA's request that were directly related to the rights of ARGENTINA which it was entitled to claim under the 1975 Statute. Accordingly URUGUAY insisted that the 1975 Statute did not cover rights claimed by ARGENTINA relating to any alleged consequential economic and social impact of the mills. The Court observed that it did not need at this stage of the proceeding to address this further issue raised by URUGUAY. The Court therefore concluded that it had *prima facie* jurisdiction under Article 60 of the 1975 Statute to deal with the merits and thus may address the present request for provisional measures.[163] Conclusive observation was not required here. In order to establish the jurisdiction over the merits at the stage of provisional measures, the Applicant needs not to prove to the extent that the present dispute fully corresponds with the scope of the provision of the convention. It is sufficient to establish the *prima facie* basis for the jurisdiction of the Court when *some aspects* of the dispute fall within the provisions of the Convention.

In the case concerning the *Application of the International Convention on the Elimination of All Forms of Racial Discrimination* (GEORGIA v. RUSSIAN FEDERATION), the RUSSIAN FEDERATION asserted that the present dispute did not fall within the scope of CERD that GEORGIA relied on to establish the jurisdiction.

---

162 Case concerning the *Armed Activities on the Territory of the Congo* (New Application: 2000), (DEMOCRATIC OF THE CONGO v. RWANDA), (Provisional Measures), Order of 10 July 2002, ICJ Reports 2002, p. 219-251.

163 *Pulp Mills* (ARGENTINA v. URUGUAY), (Provisional Measures), Order of 13 July 2006, ICJ Reports 2006, p. 15.

Even if such a dispute existed, there existed not the slightest attempt to reach a settlement between the Parties. Therefore the lack of jurisdiction would also be manifest since the precondition for the seisin of the Court had not been met. Citing the observations between the parties, the Court stated that "the Parties disagree with regard to the applicability of Article 2 and 5 of CERD in the context of the events in South Ossetia and Abkhazia...consequently, there appears to exist a dispute between the Parties as to the interpretation and application of CERD...this is sufficient at this stage to establish the existence of a dispute between the Parties capable of falling within the provisions of CERD, which is a necessary condition for the Court to have *prima facie* jurisdiction under Article 22 of CERD". Moreover, the Court still needed to ascertain whether the procedural conditions set out in Article 22 of the Convention had been met. The Court observed that the phrase "any dispute...which is not settled by negotiation or by the procedure expressly provided for in this convention" did not, on its plain meaning, suggest that formal negotiations thereof constitute preconditions to be fulfilled before the seisin of the Court. The Court found that some attempts of negotiation existed and Article 22 of the Convention could be applied.[164]

In the case concerning *Questions Relating to the Obligation to Prosecute or Extradite* (BELGIUM V. SENEGAL), BELGIUM was seeking to found the jurisdiction of the Court on Article 30 of the Convention against Torture, and alternatively on the basis of the declarations made by the two States pursuant to Article 36, paragraph 2 of the Statute. BELGIUM contended that a dispute existed between the Parties on the interpretation and application of the said Convention, as Article 30 of the said Convention provided. BELGIUM further contended that by failing to prosecute Mr. Habré, in default of extraditing him to BELGIUM, SENEGAL had violated the Convention against Torture. SENEGAL claimed that there was no dispute over the interpretation or application of the Convention since it followed from the terms of BELGIUM's Application. SENEGAL emphasized that it had already taken appropriate steps to comply with that obligation. The Court concluded that it appeared prima facie that a dispute as to the interpretation and application of the Convention existed between the Parties on the date the Application was filed. The Court went on to consider whether such a dispute continued, prima facie, to exist in the light of the way in which the Parties explained their positions at the hearings. It cited the fact that the Parties seemed to continue to differ on the questions such as the time frame within which the obligations must be fulfilled or that of the circumstances which might be relevant in considering whether or not a failure to fulfill those obligations had occurred. It concluded that it appeared that prima facie a dispute of the kind continued to exist between the Parties, although the scope of that dispute might have changed since the Application was filed. The Court then

164 *Case Concerning Application of the International Convention on the Elimination of All Forms of Discrimination* (GEORGIA V. RUSSIAN FEDERATION), (Provisional Measures), Order of 15 October 2008, ICJ Reports 2008, p. 1-43.

examined whether the procedural conditions laid down by Article 30 of the said Convention had been fulfilled. The Court considered that the diplomatic correspondence showed BELGIUM's attempt to resolve the dispute by negotiation and it could not be concluded that the negotiations had the effect of resolving the dispute. The Court thus concluded that the requirement that the dispute was one that "cannot be settled through negotiation" must be regarded as having been satisfied *prima facie*. As for the arbitration, the Court concluded that the Note Verbale of 2006 contained an explicit offer from BELGIUM to have recourse to arbitration. It further stated that it was sufficient for the Court to note that, even supposing that the Note Verbale of 2006 never reached its addressee, the Note Verbale of 2007 explicitly referred to it, and it had been confirmed that the second Note was communicated to SENEGAL and received by it more than six months before the date of referral to the Court. On this basis, the COURT concluded that, in the light of the foregoing, it had *prima facie* jurisdiction under Article 30 of the Convention against Torture to entertain the case.[165]

It is worth noting that only 11 requests were rejected due to the lack of *prima facie* jurisdiction of the Court over the merits among the 42 requests for provisional measures before the Court from 1947 to 2009.[166] Among them, 2 cases, namely *Legality of Use of Force* (YUGOSLAVIA v. USA) and *Legality of Use of Force* (YUGOSLAVIA v. SPAIN) were removed from the General List due to the manifest lack of jurisdiction.[167] It can be found from the earlier jurisprudence that the Court was inclined to directly make an affirmative conclusion of the jurisdiction when the evidences showed that there existed *prima facie* the instrument such as the special agreement of consents to the Court's jurisdiction, the declarations accepting the

165 Case concerning *Questions Relating to the Obligation to Prosecute or Extradite* (BELGIUM v. SENEGAL), (Provisional Measures), Order of 28 May 2009, ICJ Reports 2009, p.1-18.

166 Please refer to the case concerning the *Armed Activities on the Territory of the Congo* (New Application: 2002) (DEMOCRATIC REPUBLIC OF THE CONGO v. RWANDA) and the cases *Legality of Use of Force* (YUGOSLAVIA v. BELGIUM), *Legality of Use of Force* (YUGOSLAVIA v. CANADA), *Legality of Use of Force* (YUGOSLAVIA v. FRANCE), *Legality of Use of Force* (YUGOSLAVIA v. GERMANY), *Legality of Use of Force* (YUGOSLAVIA v. ITALY), *Legality of Use of Force* (YUGOSLAVIA v. NETHERLANDS), *Legality of Use of Force* (YUGOSLAVIA v. PORTUGAL), *Legality of Use of Force* (YUGOSLAVIA v. the UNITED KINGDOM), *Legality of Use of Force* (YUGOSLAVIA v. USA), *Legality of Use of Force* (YUGOSLAVIA v. SPAIN).

167 In the case *Legality of Use of Force* (YUGOSLAVIA v. USA), the Court recognized that USA's reservation which requires "specific consent of the United States in each case" under Article IX of the Genocide Convention was valid; As for the second alternative jurisdictional basis-Article 38, paragraph 5 of the Rule, the United States observed that it had not consented to jurisdiction under Article 38, paragraph 5 of the Rule and would not do so. Therefore the Court found that it manifestly lacks jurisdiction to entertain this Application. Considering that "to maintain on the General List a case upon which it appears certain that the Court will not be able to adjudicate on the merits would most assuredly not contribute to the sound administration of justice", rejected the request for provisional measures and removed the case from the General List.

compulsory jurisdiction and the treaties, conventions incorporating a compromissory clause. The Court even refrained from any consideration of the challenging bases raised by the Respondent, except in cases of very definite objections such as the temporal limitation. Judge *Schwebel*, in the case concerning the *Military and Paramilitary Activities in and against* NICARAGUA (NICARAGUA v. USA), observed that "the nub of the matter" appeared to be that "the Court gives the defendant the benefit of the doubt".[168] It is therefore not strange that *Thirlway* concluded that the general trends seemed to be towards a very low standard of proof.[169] However, there was also a call to recognize a higher criterion in the separate and dissenting opinions appending to the earlier Orders. In the *Aegean Sea Continental Shelf* case, Judge *Singh* proposed a criterion "higher than only *prima facie*" which he found necessary only in case of the non-appearance of the Respondent. In view of the provisional character of the requested Order and bearing in mind that it in no way prejudges the decision to be taken in the forthcoming proceedings, Judge *Mosler* stated in his separate opinion that, "it is in my view sufficient that the Court, when it actually indicates interim measures, should have reached the provisional conviction, based on a summary examination of the material before it and subject to any objections which may be raised in subsequent proceedings, that it has jurisdiction on the merits of the case. This amounts to an attempted definition of the criteria of a positive *prima facie* test." Facing the precedents that jurisdiction turned out to be lacking in the later stage (such as in the *Anglo-Iranian Oil Co.* case) and the more frequently raised challenges to the jurisdiction by the Respondent in the recent cases, the Court is tending to spend some tentative and summary examination of the challenges raised by the Respondent. Good examples are provided by the case concerning the *Armed Activities on the Territory of the* CONGO (New Application: 2002) (DEMOCRATIC REPUBLIC OF THE CONGO v. RWANDA) and the group cases *Legality of the Use of Force*. It is against the purpose of provisional measures and also unrealistic to examine all the relevant facts and reach a "reasonable probable" extent on the certainty of jurisdiction, however, taking account of the facts present before the Court and making a summary examination of the objecting grounds is possible and appropriate. Bearing in mind of the significance of the consents principle in international court proceedings and the disappointing situation of the compliance of the provisional measures Orders, it could be a wise choice for the Court to hold a criterion "higher than only *prima facie*" on jurisdiction. Too fast and simple conclusion without any consideration to the objecting grounds on jurisdiction would probably lead to great threat of derogation of the Court's dignity due to the possible forthcoming different conclusion at a later stage. Jurisdiction is an issue of great

168 Dissenting Opinion of Judge *Schwebel* appending to the Order of 10 May 1984, case concerning the *Military and Paramilitary Activities in and against NICARAGUA*, (Provisional Measures), ICJ Reports 1984, p. 207.

169 *Thirlway*, *supra* note 44, p. 22.

significance in the international dispute settlement, the Court's disregarding of the objecting grounds on jurisdiction might make the disappointing incompliance with the Provisional Measures Orders even worse. With respect to the question how far the competence of the SECURITY COUNCIL may or can usefully be invoked in face of the refusal of a State to comply with the obligations under a Provisional Measures Order, or where the jurisdiction of the Court is contested, *Rosenne* observed that "if a permanent member of the Security Council was an 'unwilling respondent' in the Court proceedings, the mere existence of its right of veto in the Security Council could prevent any persuasive action by that body to give effect to any indication of provisional measures against it made by the Court". Even in the cases where a permanent member of the SECURITY COUNCIL is not a party, the political fragmentation repeatedly demonstrated in the proceedings of the SECURITY COUNCIL is likewise likely to make it difficult to obtain the required majority of nine members of the SECURITY COUNCIL in favor of any effective majority. Noting the ineffective role of the SECURITY COUNCIL in promoting the compliance of the provisional measures orders, *Rosenne* concluded as follows:

> "the effectiveness of any provisional measures indicated by the Court would depend upon the extent of the real consent by the parties that the Court should settle the dispute, or at least contribute to its settlement. Having regard to the exceptional power which this jurisdiction involves, it may be arguable that it ought to be more closely integrated with the principal jurisdiction to deal with the case on the merits than it sometimes appears to be."[170]

Judging from the Court's most recent jurisprudence, it is apparently adopting a more stringent test on the jurisdiction over the merits, comparing with the earlier cases. To some extent, the "*prima facie* jurisdiction" test that the Court is adopting could be described as more like a "possible jurisdiction" test.

### 2. A *prima facie* case

Controversy also exists on a question. Is the establishment of "a *prima facie* case" as to the right as claimed another condition to the indication of provisional measures, besides the establishment of *prima facie* jurisdiction over the merits?

This question was raised in the *Passage through the Great Belt* case. DENMARK contended that "for provisional measures to be granted it is essential that FINLAND be able to substantiate the right it claims to a point where a reasonable prospect of success in the main case exists". It argued that "not even a *prima facie* case exists in favor of the Finnish contention" since there was not "such a right of passage for

170 *Rosenne*, *supra* note 5, p. 184-185.

structures up to 170 meters high".[171] Citing that the purpose of provisional measures is to preserve "rights which are the subject of dispute in judicial proceedings", the Court answered DENMARK's argument as follows: "the Court notes that the existence of a right of FINLAND of passage through the Great Belt is not challenged, the dispute between the Parties being over the nature and extent of that right, including its applicability to certain drill ships and oil rigs; … such a disputed right may be protected by the indication of provisional measures under Article 41 of the Statute if the Court considers that circumstances require".

The Court's ruling did not expressly point out whether "a reasonable prospect of success in the main case exists" should be required to indicate provisional measures. However, the Court apparently followed DENMARK's assertion and tried to draw a conclusion on whether such a right of passage existed for the structures as specifically involved in the present proceedings. To go even further, the Court seemed to suggest that - it should summarily evaluate the evidences presented before it and find out whether "a *prima facie* case" has been established before it takes into account the "circumstances" which might require the indication of provisional measures under Article 41 of the Statute.

In his separate opinion, Judge *Shahabuddeen* explained his reasoning with respect to the point of law whether a State requesting interim measures must establish a *prima facie* case as to the existence of the right or not.[172] From his point of view, to indicate interim measures without requiring the requesting State to demonstrate some arguable basis for the existence of the right which is sought to be protected would seem to present a problem of reconciliation with the exceptional character of provisional measures. Refuting the assertion that the requirement of showing a *prima facie* case would lead to prejudgment, he argued that a genuine distinction existed between the thorough investigation and the existence of a possibility. To satisfy the test of "existence of a *prima facie* case", the requesting State is not required to meet every challenge on the merits. Therefore a finding that such a possibility exists clearly falls short of constituting an interim judgment. In order to illustrate how the test should be applied, he observed that it would be sufficient if enough material was presented to disclose the possibility of the existence of the right claimed. Listing the evidences that "DENMARK accepts that FINLAND has a right of passage through the Great Belt; DENMARK has been aware of the fact that since 1972 to the present FINLAND has from time to time passed through the Great Belt several drill ships and oil rigs in excess of a clearance height of 65 meters; in full knowledge of this, DENMARK has never objected to their passage and still does not, as indeed it affirmed at the hearing", he concluded that FINLAND had satisfied the test of showing "the existence of a *prima facie* case".

---

171 *Passage through Great Belt* (FINLAND v. DENMARK), (Provisional Measures), Order of 29 July 1991, ICJ Reports 1991, p. 17, para. 21.

172 Separate Opinion of Judge *Shahabudden* appending to the Order of 29 July 1991, *Passage through the Great Belt*, (Provisional Measures), ICJ Reports 1991, p.28-36.

It is worth noting that the Court showed an ambiguous attitude in the early jurisprudence. However, it seemed to apply an implicit test in two cases, namely *Passage through the Great Belt* and *Nuclear Tests*. Academic opinions are also divided on this issue.

Professor *Sztucki* objected the position of requiring in the proceedings before the Court at the stage of provisional measures to show "a *prima facie* case". As he proposed, this is mainly due to the non-anticipatory character of provisional measures. Formally speaking, it is immaterial to show "a *prima facie* case" for possible indication of conservatory measures.[173] He further developed his view from two other perspectives. On the one hand, the law of the Court does not require such a "*prima facie* case" test and as a rule they do not argue this point. On the other hand, due to the complexity of inter-State disputes, the attempts to determine the existence of a "*prima facie* case" in *limine litis* would be of doubtful value. Notwithstanding his opinion not to regard the showing of a *prima facie* case as one of the conditions of indication of provisional measures, he admitted that "the preliminary view on the legal foundation of the principal claim can marginally play a role in the assessment of circumstances of a case in their entirety".[174]

Professor *Merrils*, in referring to "the respective rights of either party", believed that Article 41 should be interpreted as referring to "the rights which the parties claim", rather than "those which they actually have, which cannot be decided at this stage".[175] Based on his opinion, it could be inferred that any showing of existence of the rights is therefore unnecessary.

The supportive view on this point partly rests upon the analogy with the municipal law. If it seems to the judge very likely that the applicant will fail in the main proceedings, he will refuse to grant the relief asked for since it is inconsistent with the exceptional nature of the procedure for provisional protection. This point was raised by Professor *Mendelson*[176] and also expressed by Judge *Winiarski* and Badaw*i Pasha* in their joint dissenting opinion in the *Anglo-Iranian Oil Co.* case[177] and Judge *Gros* in his separate opinion in the *Nuclear Tests* cases.[178] It is also argued that Article 41 impliedly required the rights in question to be at any rate possible. As stated by Professor *Mani*, the object of interim measures is to preserve certain rights, if the rights claimed are not shown to exist or at least a *prima facie* case is not made out as to their existence, the interim measures will have nothing to

173 *Sztucki, supra* note 3, p. 97.

174 *Ibid.*, p. 123-124.

175 *Merrils*, Interim Measures of Protection and the Substantive Jurisdiction of the International Court, Cambridge Law Journal, (1977), Vol. 36, p. 102.

176 *Mendelson*, Interim Measures of Protection in Cases of Contested Jurisdiction, The British Year Book of International Law, (1972-1973), Vol. 46, p. 316.

177 Joint Opinion of Judge *Winiarski* and Badawi *Pasha*, *Anglo-Iranian Oil Co.*, ICJ Reports 1951, p.96-102.

178 Dissenting Opinion of Judge *Gros*, *Nuclear Tests* (NEW ZEALAND V. FRANCE), ICJ Reports 1973, p. 150-158.

preserve.[179] *Essoff* provided a more thorough and all-around comment on this issue. Citing the fact that the *Passage through the Great Belt* decision illustrates the Court’s implicit reliance on the establishment of “a *prima facie* case”, he called for the Court to explicitly recognize such a requirement. He further supported his point that the explicit requirement would support the goal of provisional measures and strengthen the Court’s analysis of provisional measures. Lastly, he invoked the European Court of Justice’s practice (the “ECJ” or “Court of Justice”) of establishing explicit standards for interim relief which included the requirement that the Applicant established a *prima facie* case on the merits in support of the interim measures requested (Article 83(2)) of the Rules of Procedure). He believed that the practice of the ECJ might represent an appropriate source of international law for the ICJ to consider in developing its criterion for provisional measures.[180]

Bearing in mind that it calls for caution in adopting an analogy with the municipal law on the international plane, the counterpart mechanism in municipal law can nevertheless be analyzed for a better understanding of the provisional measures before the ICJ. The prevailing view holds that all municipal systems have to find a solution to the question of the relevance of the merits of the underlying claim to the indication of interim measures. As maintained by *Jacobs*, the requirement of a *prima face* case on the merits is found in some legal systems as a pre-condition for the grant of interim measures. This is the practice of German law and also in English law prior to the decision of the House of Lords in *American Cyanamid Co. v. Ethicon* [1975] AC 396.[181] Professor *Collins* described the situation as “the solution ranges from the English test that there merely be a serious question to be tried on the merits to the more stringent test in civil law countries that there must be a probable, or *prima facie*, prospect of success on the merits”.[182]

It is believed that the general practice of the International Court is to treat the merits as, in theory, wholly irrelevant on the application for provisional measures.[183] However, even for the relatively lower required English test, examining whether a serious question exists could inevitably touch on the merits.

---

179 *Mani*, Notes and Comments on Interim Measures of Protection: ICJ Practice, Indian Journal of International Law, (1973), Vol. 13, p. 265; also.*Mendelson, supra* note 176, p. 317; *Dumbauld, supra* note 51, p. 160-161.

180 *Essoff*, FINLAND v. DENMARK: A Call to Clarify the INTERNATIONAL COURT OF JUSTICE’s Standards for Provisional Measures, Fordham International Law Journal, (1991/1992), Vol.15, p. 839- 901.

181 *Jacobs*, Interim Measures in the Law and Practice of the Court of Justice of the European Communities, In: *Bernhardt* (ed.), Interim Measures Indicated by International Courts, (1994), p. 50.

182 *Collins*, Provisional and Protective Measures, Recueil Des Cours 1992-III, (1993), p. 224. See also *Adede*, The Rules of Interlocutory Injunctions under Domestic Law and the Interim Measures of Protection in International Law, Syracuse Journal of International Law & Commentary (1977), Vol.4, p. 277.

183 *Collins*, *ibid*, p. 225.

In the view of the present writer, it would indeed be against the spirit of the mechanism of provisional measures to protect a manifestly baseless right. This problem would be especially serious in international law comparing to municipal law because provisional measures in international law are exceptional in character to an even greater extent than they are in municipal law. The inappropriately granted provisional measures may be considered as a serious interference with the sovereignty of the Respondent State. Furthermore, it might encourage the state to abuse this procedure if the Court is permitted to indicate provisional measures to protect a manifestly baseless right. Therefore, it is to some extent necessary to pay some attention to the prospect of the case even at the provisional measures stage.

Nevertheless, the showing of "a *prima facie* case" should be restricted to a very limited extent. To be more specific, the examination of the existence of the case should only be implemented summarily, just at the first sight. The Applicant need not satisfy every challenge from the Respondent. Only when the right as claimed is manifestly baseless could the request for provisional measures be rejected. The Court's practice also reveals its attitude. Although Judge *Shahabudeen* listed a series of cases to support his view that the shape of the arguments was objectively designed to prove, or to disprove, the possibility of the existence of the right claimed,[184] in a few cases did the Court tended to answer this question, namely the *Nuclear Tests* and the *Passage through the Great Belt* and the case concerning *Questions Relating to the Obligation to Prosecute or Extradite*. In these cases, the Court did not expressly state that it was requiring the Applicant to establish a *prima facie* case as a condition to the indication of provisional measures. The Court adopted a very low threshold as to the extent to which "a *prima facie* case" should be established. In *Nuclear Tests*, the very existence of a right to redress for damage caused by fall-out from nuclear tests was disputed. The French government contended that the reports of the Australian National Radiation Advisory Committee from 1967 to 1972 had concluded that fall-out from the French tests did not constitute a danger to the health of the population. Accordingly it argued that the Applicant's case was fully groundless. The Court did not expressly indicate whether any rights of NEW ZEALAND or AUSTRALIA were in threat, it instead stated that the information before the Court did not "exclude the possibility that damage to AUSTRALIA (NEW ZEALAND) might be shown to be caused by the deposit" of the fall-out. It further concluded that it could not be assumed *a priori* that the Government of NEW ZEALAND or AUSTRALIA "may not be able to establish a legal interest in respect of these claims entitling the Court to admit the Application."[185] Trying to avoid the danger of touching on the merits, the Court neither expressed any opinion on whether there existed a right in international law to redress the

---

184 The Separate Opinion of Judge *Shahabudeen* appending to the Order of 29 July 1991, *Passage through the Great Belt* (Provisional Measures), ICJ Reports 1991, p. 31-33.

185 *Nuclear Tests* (AUSTRALIA v. FRENCH), (NEW ZEALAND v. FRENCH), (Provisional Measures), Order of 22 June 1973, ICJ Reports 1973, p. 104-105, 140-141.

damages caused by the nuclear fall-out from the perspective of law, nor decided from the factual perspective whether the rights of AUSTRALIA (NEW ZEALAND) were damaged or not. The Court apparently rejected the French contention that the right which the Applicant requested the Court to protect was groundless simply on the ground that it could not be assumed *a priori* that the Applicant might not be able to establish a legal interest in these claims.

The Court followed this low threshold in *Passage through the Great Belt.* Answering DENMARK's argument that there was not even a *prima facie* case existing in favor of the Finnish contention, the Court stated that "the existence of a right of FINLAND of passage through the Great Belt was not challenged" and "the dispute being over the nature and extent of that right". Here the Court summarily reviewed the evidence and found *prima facie* the existence of FINLAND's right of passage through the Great Belt. It did not get itself into the factual information deeper to investigate whether the right of FINLAND of passage through the Great Belt covered the factual situation in the present proceedings.

The case *Passage through the Great Belt* caused strong calls to clarify such a condition both within and outside the Court.[186] After this case, there are two occasions which the Court faced an assertion from the Respondent to disprove "a *prima facie* case" before the Court. In the case concerning *the Arrest Warrant of 11 April 2000*, BELGIUM asserted that "the 'right' claimed to be in need of preservation by the indication of provisional measures was the 'right' of the DEMOCRATIC REPUBLIC OF THE CONGO's Foreign Minister to travel abroad on governmental business" and foreign travel was a function of diplomatic discourse but not a right. Accordingly, BELGIUM maintained that CONGO had not made out "a *prima facie* case" that was required by the indication of provisional measures and the Application should be dismissed. The Court found that the Cabinet reshuffle of 20 November 2000 caused the circumstances to change. It had accordingly not been established that irreparable prejudice might be caused in the immediate future or that the degree of urgency was such that those rights needed to be protected by the indication of provisional measures. The Court therefore did not directly take into account the argument raised by BELGIUM on the failure to establish "a *prima facie* case".[187]

In the *Lockerbie* case (LIBYA v. UK), the UK also argued that LIBYA had failed to establish the possible existence of the rights claimed.[188] Keeping silent on the

---

186 See the above discussion, *Essoff*, *supra* note 180.
Also the Separate Opinion of Judge *Shahabudeen* appending to the Order of 29 July 1991, *Passage through the Great Belt* (Provisional Measures), ICJ Reports 1991, p. 31-33.

187 Case concerning *the Arrest Warrant of 11 April 2000* (DEMOCRATIC REPUBLIC OF THE CONGO v. BELGIUM), (Provisional Measures), Order of 8 December 2000, ICJ Reports 2000, p. 182-203.

188 *Lockerbie* (LIBYA v. UK), (Provisional Measures), Order of 14 April 1992, ICJ Reports 1992, p. 11.

question whether the rights as claimed existed or not, the Court shifted to another point and concluded that the SECURITY COUNCIL RESOLUTION 748 made the rights claimed by LIBYA under the Montreal Convention inappropriate for the protection of provisional measures.

In the case concerning *Questions Relating to the Obligation to Prosecute or Extradite*, BELGIUM pointed out that its request was intended to protect its right to see SENEGAL prosecute Mr. Habré or obtain his extradition. SENEGAL argued that the Convention against Torture created only the right to demand extradition, which could not prevail over the SENEGAL's right to hold a trial. The Court stated that the power to indicate provisional measures should be exercised only if the Court is satisfied that the rights were at least plausible. However, it kept silent on the arguments raised by both parties. It simply concluded as: "at this stage of the proceeding the Court does not need to establish definitively the existence of the rights claimed by Belgium or to consider Belgium's capacity to assert such rights before the Court; ... the rights asserted by Belgium, being grounded in a possible interpretation of the Convention against Torture, therefore appear to be plausible."[189]

The discussion on whether to require the Applicant establish "a *prima facie* case" at the stage of provisional measures in the proceedings before the Court might be inspired by the common practice of the municipal courts. However, it is worth noting that the international courts have only occasionally adopted it.[190] The Court's rather prudential attitude to regard the showing of "a *prima facie* case" as a condition of the indication of provisional measures could be mainly explained by its concern on the danger of prejudgment at this stage of proceedings. Some differences do exist between international law and municipal law in the field of provisional measures. As pointed by Judge *Shahabudeen*, "possibly the most influential factor contributing to a discernible and perhaps understandable general impression that the Court should not consider whether there is a *prima facie* case as to the existence of the right claimed is the need to avoid any appearance of prejudgment", the initial concern of the advocates of the "a *prima facie* case" requirement might be the potential risk of a prejudgment. The prejudgment without providing the parties appropriate opportunities to present the merits before the international courts might lead to more serious effects comparing with that before the municipal courts, because the cases before the international courts usually involve the state parties' sovereignty. The judicial injustice caused by prejudgments in the international courts might sensitively lead to another international crisis that

---

189 Case concerning *Questions Relating to the Obligation to Prosecute or Extradite* (BELGIUM v. SENEGAL), (Provisional Measures), Order of 28 May 2009, ICJ Reports 2009, p.13, para.58-60.

190 The ECJ explicitly provides the showing of the existence of a *prima facie* case as a condition for granting interim relief.

would be totally against the objects of this important procedural instrument in the international dispute settlement.

From the practical perspective, it is an unreasonably difficult task for the Court to decide at this stage whether "a *prima facie* case" has been established as to the existence of right claimed in the usually complicated inter-state disputes. This is partly due to the developing nature of international law. Article 38(1) of the Statute of the Court provides the rules that the Court could apply.[191] It is generally accepted as the basis for the main sources of international law. Unlike the municipal courts, where the well-developed code laws or case laws are applied, it is quite usual to meet new and uncovered issues in an international forum where there are no well-established rules to be applied to. At least, it is rather difficult to find out these rules within such short period of time due to the urgent requirement of provisional measures. As for these complicated and controversial issues, it is difficult to know whether it constitutes a right that has been recognized by contemporary international law or not, not to mention the even more complicated factual background in the specific dispute. For example, in the *Fisheries Jurisdiction* case, the Applicant asked the Court to declare that ICELAND's claim to extend its exclusive fishery jurisdiction to a zone of 50 nautical miles around ICELAND was without foundation in international law.[192] Judge *Nervo* stated in his dissenting opinion that "in a system of progressive development of international law the question of fishery limits has to be reconsidered in terms of the protection and utilization of coastal resources regardless of other considerations which apply to the extent of the territorial sea".[193] In the *Nuclear Tests* case, it was also a controversial issue in contemporary international law whether the parties possessed a right resulting from radio-active fall-out and to what extent the damage should be remedied.[194]

---

191 Article 38 (1) of the Statute of the INTERNATIONAL COURT OF JUSTICE states: The Court, whose function is to decide in accordance with international law such disputes as are submitted to it, shall apply:
a. international conventions, whether general or particular, establishing rules expressly recognized by the contesting states;
b. international custom, as evidence of a general practice accepted as law;
c. the general principles of law recognized by civilized nations;
d. subject to the provisions of Article 59, judicial decisions and the teachings of the most highly qualified publicists of the various nations, as subsidiary means for the determination of rules of law.

192 *Fisheries Jurisdiction* (UK and NORTHERN IRELAND v. ICELAND), (Provisional Measures), Order of 17 August 1972, ICJ Reports 1972, p. 13, (FEDERAL REPUBLIC OF GERMANY v. ICELAND), (Provisional Measures), Order of 17 August 1972, ICJ Reports 1972, p.30.

193 Dissenting Opinion of Judge Padilla *Nervo* appending to the Order of 17 August 1972, *Fisheries Jurisdiction* (UK and NORTHERN IRELAND v. ICELAND), (Provisional Measures), ICJ Reports 1972, p.23; *Fisheries Jurisdiction* (FEDERAL REPUBLIC OF GERMANY v. ICELAND), (Provisional Measures), ICJ Reports 1972, p. 40.

194 *Nuclear Tests*, (NEW ZEALAND v. FRANCE), (Provisional Measures), Order of 22 June 1973,

Therefore, the endeavor to assess whether a "*prima facie* case" as to the existence of the right as claimed has been established or not, at the provisional measures stage, would be in theory appealing while in practice disappointing. These points, I believe, could to some extent explain the Court's hesitance to adopt the popular test in municipal courts that requires the Applicant to establish "a *prima facie* case".

One may probably take the practice of European Court of Justice (ECJ) to argue that it is also the practice of international courts, as proposed by *Essoff*. However, ECJ encompasses some special nature. As pointed out by *Jacobs*, one of the principle functions of ECJ is to review the measures adopted by the other Community institutions, namely the Council, the Commission and the European Parliament. In these cases, "the issue of interim measures calls for comparison with national administrative law, in particular the administrative law of the Member States of the European Communities. ECJ can more appropriately be compared with a national court in these cases".[195] *Jacobs* stressed in the same paragraph that "in some respects its functions can be compared with those of an international court, especially where the issue of interim measures arises in the course of proceedings brought against Member States, particularly those brought by the Commission of the European Communities against Member States for failure to fulfill their Treaty obligations".[196] But this could neither be regarded as a sound ground for the ICJ to plant ECJ's practice of expressly providing the establishment of "a *prima facie* case" as a prerequisite of the indication of provisional measures. On the one hand, the number of these cases is rather limited comparing to the cases reviewing the measures adopted by other Community institutions. On the other hand, even for the cases brought against Member States, the subjects of the proceedings are usually the treaty obligations of the Member States. Accordingly the work of assessing the establishment of "a *prima facie* case" would be more appropriate and realistic in the ECJ than in the ICJ. Last but not least, it is observed that "the Court has used varying formulations in its interpretation of the requirement imposed by Article 83(2) of the Rules of Procedure relating to the pleas of fact and law establishing a *prima facie* case for interim measures."[197] This might also demonstrate the difficulty brought by the explicit provision to require the establishment of "a *prima facie* case" (by the Applicant) as the condition of provisional measures. Therefore, it is not surprising that the INTERNATIONAL COURT OF JUSTICE did not tend to expressly require the establishment of "a *prima facie* case" as to the existence of the right as claimed as the condition of the indication of provisional measures. Nevertheless, it is still necessary for the Court to exclude those requests that are designed to abuse provisional measures, as discussed above. The Court recognized

---

ICJ Reports 1973, p.135-147; (AUSTRALIA v. FRANCE), (Provisional Measures), Order of 22 June 1973, ICJ Reports 1973, p.99-110.

195 *Jacobs*, *supra* note 181, p. 37.

196 *Ibid.*

197 *Jacobs*, *supra* note 181, p. 48-50.

in *Nuclear Tests* and *Passage through the Great Belt* that it would not indicate provisional measures when there was manifestly no case. And it also recognized in the case concerning *Questions Relating to the Obligation to Prosecute or Extradite* that its power to indicate provisional measures should be exercised only if the Court was satisfied that the rights asserted by a party were at least plausible.

To conclude this part, I find it difficult to encourage *Essoff*'s advocacy to regard the establishment of "a *prima facie* case" as an additional condition to the indication of provisional measures. Nevertheless, the Court will not keep silent when it finds that the right as claimed by the Applicant is manifestly baseless after a very summary view of the evidences. In other words, the Court will reject to indicate provisional measures on the ground of the failure to establish "a *prima facie* case" only for the sake of preventing the abuse of provisional measures. This assertion is also in accordance with the Court's present practice of examining the evidences in a very preliminary and summary manner to avoid the obviously groundless claims.

### 3. The admissibility of the main claim

As generally accepted, a dispute must be admissible before the Court will exercise jurisdiction.[198] The Court expressed its position in the *Border and Transborder Armed Actions* case. It stated that before it would act, it must establish "first, that the dispute before it is a legal dispute, in the sense of a dispute capable of being settled by the application of principles and rules of international law, and secondly, that the Court has jurisdiction to deal with it, and that that jurisdiction is not fettered by any circumstance rendering the application inadmissible".[199] The Court stated that it might make a declaratory judgment but only if this was consistent with the judicial nature of its function.[200] Therefore, it can be observed that the non-existence of a judiciable dispute is an objection based on admissibility.

Apart from this, an objection based on admissibility can also be the alleged procedural defects in a state's application to the Court. As showed by the Court's practice, the failure to exhaust local remedies, undue interference with the domestic affairs of states, lack of legal subject matter and undue delay have been alleged as grounds of the objection on admissibility. Should the Court examine the admissibility of the main claim when it considers the requests for provisional measures? It has been discussed for several times within the Court.

In the *Anglo-Iranian Oil Co.* case, the Iranian government claimed that the Application was inadmissible principally on the ground of the UNITED KINGDOM Government's lack of competence to refer to the Court a dispute that had arisen

198 *Dixon*, Textbook on International Law, (2007), p.286.

199 *Border and Transborder Armed Actions* (NICARAGUA V. HONDURAS), (Jurisdiction and Admissibility), ICJ Reports 1988, p.69.

200 *Dixon*, *supra* note 198.

between the Iranian Government and the Anglo-Iranian Oil Company.[201] To be more specific, it was regarded as a dispute between a state and a private legal person, which is not competent party before the Court. The Court summarily stated that "it appears from the Application by which the Government of the UNITED KINGDOM instituted proceedings, that that Government has adopted the cause of a British company and is proceeding in virtue of the right of a diplomatic protection". The Court did not expressly rule on the issue whether the admissibility of the main action was the precondition of the indication of provisional measures. Instead, it apparently recognized that the present evidences did not lead to a conclusion that the action was inadmissible.

Judge *Gros*, in his dissenting opinion in *Nuclear Tests*, proposed to regard the objections to the jurisdiction of the Court and the admissibility of the claim as both having "a character of absolute priority". He argued that the language of Article 41 made the admissibility also a precondition of the indication of provisional measures. He believed that if there were no rights, there was nothing to protect. Therefore, if the claim had no subject, the principal application fell to the ground. Then the Court could not exercise the power to indicate provisional measures. He stated:

> "Article 41 obliges the Court to see whether the circumstances require it to use the power of indicating measures, and, even if circumstances so require, it can only exercise that power if its decision will be able to preserve the respective rights of either party. But if the State cited as respondent invokes the Court's total absence of power, and if the subject of the claim is really non-existent, what rights would there be to preserve?"[202]

He took the non-existence of the right as claimed as an objection on the admissibility of the claim.

NIGERIA raised objection on the admissibility of the claim in the case concerning *the Land and Maritime Boundary between* CAMEROON *and* NIGERIA (CAMEROON V. NIGERIA). It claimed that CAMEROON's Application described the dispute between the Parties as concerning the whole of the frontier, that no such dispute existed, and that consequently the Application was not even *prima facie* admissible.[203] Considering NIGERIA's preliminary objection to the admissibility of the Application, the Court observed as follows:

---

201 *Anglo-Iranian Oil Co.* (UK V. IRAN), (Provisional Measures), Order of 5 July 1951, ICJ Reports 1951, p.92.

202 Dissenting Opinion of Judge *Gros* appending to the Order of 22 June 1973, *Nuclear Tests* (Provisional Measures), ICJ Reports 1973, p.157.

203 Case concerning *the Land and Maritime Boundary between CAMEROON and NIGERIA* (CAMEROON V. NIGERIA), (Provisional Measures), Order of 15 March 1996, ICJ Reports 1996, p. 21, para. 32.

"whereas without ruling on the question whether, faced with a request for the indication of provisional measures, the Court must, before deciding whether or not to indicate such measures, ensure that the Application of which it is seised is admissible *prima facie*, it considers that, in this case, the consolidated Application of Cameroon does not appear *prima facie* to be inadmissible in the light of the preliminary objections raised by Nigeria."[204]

It remained ambiguous whether the Court regarded the *prima facie* admissibility of the Application as a condition to the indication of provisional measures. The Court was apparently not tending to rule on this question at that moment. Nevertheless, the Court applied a negative determination that the Application did "not appear *prima facie* to be inadmissible in the light of the preliminary objections" and finally indicated provisional measures. *Thilway*, basing on this case, seemed to believe that the question of admissibility should also be considered when the Court considered a request for provisional measures.[205] Judge *Ranjeva,* in his separate opinion, also observed that the Order explained the Court's position on "a possible additional condition for the indication of provisional measures, that is, the *prima facie* admissibility of the principal Application".[206]

The assertion to challenge the Application's admissibility was again taken by the Respondent in the case concerning *Armed Activities on the Territory of the* CONGO. UGANDA argued that CONGO's request for the indication of provisional measures concerned essentially the same issues as the SECURITY COUNCIL RESOLUTION 1304(2000). UGANDA fully accepted this resolution and was complying with it. Therefore CONGO's Application was inadmissible and moot. The Court did not accept this argument. It stated:

"the Security Council Resolution 1304(2000), and the measures taken in its implementation, do not preclude the Court from acting in accordance with its Statute and with the Rules of the Court … in the present case the Security Council has taken no decision which would *prima facie* preclude the rights claimed by the Congo from 'being regarded as appropriate for protection by the indication of provisional measures'".[207]

---

204 *Land and Maritime Boundary* (CAMEROON v. NIGERIA), (Provisional Measures), Order of 15 March 1996, ICJ Reports 1996, p.21, para.33.

205 *Thirlway, supra* note 81, p. 86.

206 Declaration of Judge *Ranjeva* appending to the Order of 15 March 1996, case concerning *the Land and Maritime Boundary between CAMEROON and NIGERIA* (Provisional Measures), ICJ Reports 1996, p. 29.

207 Case concerning *Armed Activities on the Territory of the Congo*, (DEMOCRATIC REPUBLIC OF THE CONGO v. UGANDA), (Provisional Measures), Order of 1 July 2000, ICJ Reports 2000, p. 126-127, para. 36, para. 38.

The Court's concern was whether the SECURITY COUNCIL RESOLUTION had the effect to turn the Application inadmissible, rather than whether admissibility should be a condition to indicate provisional measures. Judge *Oda*, in his declaration, held that the Court was not in a position to grant measures because the case "is, - and has from the outset been, inadmissible". Here objection on admissibility was based on the non-judiciable nature of the dispute because of the action of the SECURITY COUNCIL. (This issue will be elaborated in Chapter E.)

*Merrils*, however, expressed his concern about the unreasonableness of the Court's embarking on a detailed investigation of the complex admissibility questions such as *locus standi*, the exhaustion of local remedies or the existence of a case in international law. He believed that the investigation would "certainly prolong proceedings at the interim measures stage" and might be quite "impractical".[208]

From the above outline, it is revealed that although the Respondent repeatedly adopted this argument to challenge the indication of provisional measures, some judges and authors also expressed their favorable attitude towards this view, the Court kept silent on this point. However, judging from the Court's practice, it is observed that the Court has not recognized the admissibility of the main claim as an additional condition of the indication of provisional measures. Nevertheless, the Court is not taking the admissibility of the main claim as absolutely irrelevant to the indication of provisional measures. It can be inferred from the Court's orders in the above-mentioned cases that the Court would not grant provisional measures if the right claimed is manifestly not existent.

It is not the function of provisional measures to reach issues that are as complex and closely relevant to the merits as admissibility. It is sufficient for the Court to take a summary view over the evidences at this stage, just for the sake of eliminating the requests for provisional measures that are a manifest abuse of this remedy.

### 4. The admissibility of the request

Besides the above-mentioned conditions, there is another condition to the indication of provisional measures, namely the admissibility of the request. As being discussed in Part C of this dissertation, the purpose of provisional measures is to "preserve the respective rights of the Parties pending the decision of the Court". This leads to an assertion that there is an implied condition - any provisional measures indicated must be designed to preserve the rights that are the subject of the main claim submitted before the Court. Additionally, the request for provisional measures needs to satisfy the procedural requirement provided by the Rules of the Court.

208 *Merrils*, *supra* note 175, p. 101.

### a) Correspondence between the provisional measures and the main claim

Both the Permanent Court and the present Court stated this point as: “provisional measures should have the effect of protecting the rights forming the subject of the dispute submitted to the Court”.[209] The Court explicitly stated its position in the Order of 16 July 2008, in the case concerning the *Request for Interpretation of the Judgment of 31 March 2004 in the Case Concerning Avena and other Mexican Nationals*:

> “whereas the Court, when considering a request for the indication of provisional measures, ‘must be concerned to preserve … the rights which may subsequently be adjudged by the Court to belong either to the Applicant or to the Respondent’ (*Land and Maritime Boundary between Cameroon and Nigeria* (Cameroon v. Nigeria), Provisional Measures, Order of 15 March 1996, I.C.J. Reports 1996(I), p. 22, para. 35); whereas a link must therefore be established between the alleged rights the protection of which is the subject of the provisional measures being sought, and the subject of the principle request submitted to the Court;”[210]

The Court was trying to define the link between a request for provisional measures and the main claim through its case-law. It dismissed the request for provisional measures on the ground that the rights that the provisional measures aimed to preserve were not the subject matter of the present main proceedings. In the case concerning *the Arbitral Award of 31 July 1989* (GUINEA-BISSAU v. SENEGAL), the Republic of GUINEA-BISSAU instituted proceedings against the Republic of SENEGAL in respect of a dispute concerning the existence and validity of the arbitral award that was delivered on 31 July 1989 by the Arbitration Tribunal for the Determination of the Maritime Boundary between the two States. Claiming that the Senegalese Navy took actions in a maritime area that was regarded by GUINEA-BISSAU as a disputed area between the Parties, GUINEA-BISSAU requested the Court to indicate provisional measures refraining SENEGAL from any action during the whole duration of the proceedings. SENEGAL confirmed that these incidents occurred while claiming that these incidents were within its maritime sovereignty, relying on a presumption of the validity of the 1989 Award.

---

209 *Polish Agrarian Reform*, (GERMANY v. POLAND), (Interim Measures), PCIJ, Series A/B, No. 58, p. 177, *Aegean Sea Continental Shelf*, (GREECE v. TURKEY), (Interim Measures), ICJ Reports 1976, p. 11, para. 34.

210 *Request for Interpretation of the Judgment of 31 March 2004 in the Case Concerning Avena and other Mexican Nationals* (MEXICO v. UNITED STATES OF AMERICA), (Provisional Measures), Order of 16 July 2008, ICJ Reports 2008, p. 15.

GUINEA-BISSAU recognized in its Application that the dispute of which it had seised the Court was not the dispute over maritime delimitation brought before the Arbitration Tribunal, but a "new dispute...relating to the applicability of the text issued by way of award of 31 July 1989". In other words, the subject matter of present dispute was the validity and application of the 1989 Arbitral Award. What GUINEA-BISSAU sought to protect by provisional measures should have been the delimitation status, basing on the presumption of the validity of the 1989 Award, rather than the respective rights of the Parties, without the effect of the 1989 Award. Accordingly, GUINEA-BISSAU's request for provisional measures did not satisfy its link with the subject matter of the main claim. However, GUINEA-BISSAU argued that "provisional measures may be requested, in the context of judicial proceedings on a subsidiary dispute, to protect rights in issue in the underlying dispute ... the only link essential for the admissibility of measures is the link between the measures contemplated and the conflict of interests underlying the question or questions put to the Court ... "[211]

GUINEA-BISSAU's argument aimed to a liberal interpretation of the link that is required between the request for provisional measures and the main claim. The Court disregarded this view. Citing that the Application asked the Court to pass upon the existence and validity of the award but did not ask the Court to pass upon the respective rights of the Parties in the maritime areas in question, the Court observed that the purpose of exercising the power to indicate provisional measures was to protect "rights which are the subject of dispute in judicial proceedings",[212]and accordingly dismissed the request because the alleged rights sought to be protected by provisional measures were not the subject of the proceedings before the Court. To be more specific, the decision on the validity and existence of the Arbitral Award would not determine the actual rights of the Parties in the disputed area.

Judge *Shahabuddeen*'s separate opinion supported the Court's position. Basing on the prerequisite that the purpose of provisional measures is to preserve the respective rights of the parties pending the proceedings before the Court, the function of provisional measures is to help to sustain the situation of a possible decision in favor of the Applicant. In the present case, GUINEA-BISSAU challenged the validity and existence of the Arbitral Award 1989 in the main claim. Accordingly, the provisional measures should have been designed to be consistent with the status, presuming the validity of that Award. If GUINEA-BISSAU succeeded in the main claim, the effect of this final judgment would be that the Arbitral Award was invalid

---

211 Case concerning the *Arbitral Award of 31 July 1989*, (GUINEA BISSAU v. SENEGAL), (Provisional Measures), Order of 2 March 1990, ICJ Reports 1990, p. 64-71.

212 *Aegean Sea Continental Shelf* (GREECE v. TURKEY), (Provisional Measures), Order of 11 September 1976, ICJ Reports 1976, p. 9, para. 25; Case concerning the *Diplomatic and Consular Staff in Tehran*, (USA v. IRAN), (Provisional Measures), Order of 15 December 1979, ICJ Reports 1979, p. 19, para. 36.

and both parties were at liberty to act within the limits allowed by international law. This is inconsistent with the effect of GUINEA-BISSAU's request of provisional measures that were meant to restrict both parties from any act or action pending the proceedings.[213]

A comparison between the case *Request for Interpretation of the Judgment of 31 March 2004 in the Case Concerning Avena and other Mexican Nationals* (MEXICO v. USA) and the case concerning *the Arbitral Award of 31 July 1989* (GUINEA-BISSAU v. SENEGAL) is helpful to address the point. In that case, the UNITED STATES submitted that MEXICO's request for the indication of provisional measures aimed to prohibit the UNITED STATES from carrying out sentences with regard to Mexican nationals prior to the conclusion of the Court's proceedings on MEXICO's Request for interpretation. In the main claim, MEXICO asked the Court to interpret the Avena Judgment to mean that the UNITED STATES must not carry out sentences “unless the individual affected has received review and reconsideration and it is determined that no prejudice resulted from the violation of the Vienna Convention”. Responding to UNITED STATES' argument that provisional measures requested by MEXICO went beyond the subject of the proceedings before the Court on the Request for interpretation, the Court stated:

> “whereas, in proceedings on interpretation, the Court is called upon to clarify the meaning and the scope of what the Court decided with binding force in a judgment … whereas MEXICO seeks clarification of the meaning and the scope of paragraph 153(9) of the operative part of the 2004 Judgment in the *Avena* case, whereby the Court found that the United States is under an obligation to provide, by means of its own choosing, review and reconsideration of the convictions and sentences of the Mexican nationals, taking into account both the violation of the rights set forth in Article 36 of the Vienna Convention and paragraph 138 to 141 of the Judgment; whereas it is the interpretation of the meaning and scope of the obligation, and hence of the rights which MEXICO and its nationals have on the basis of paragraph 153(9) that constitutes the subject of the present proceedings before the Court on the Request for interpretation; whereas MEXICO filed a request for the indication of provisional measures in order to protect these rights pending the Court's final decision.”[214]

The situation in these two cases is quite similar. However, because the Applicants framed the scope of the main claims differently, the Court made opposite decisions

---

213 Separate Opinion of Judge *Shahabudden* appending to the Order of 1 November 1989, case concerning *the Arbitral Award of 31 July 1989*, (Provisional Measures), ICJ Reports 1989, p.77-78.

214 *Request for Interpretation of the Judgment of 31 March 2004 in the Case Concerning Avena and other Mexican Nationals* (MEXICO v. USA), (Provisional Measures), Order of 16 July 2008, ICJ Reports 2008, p.15-16, para.63.

on the question whether the link between the provisional measures and the subject of the main dispute was satisfied. As for the request to restrict both parties from any act or actions pending the proceedings before the Court, if GUINEA-BISSAU had framed the subject of its main Application as the delimitation of maritime territory or the rights of the parties in the disputed area, the request would not have been rejected because of the inconsistence between the right sought to be protected by provisional measures and the subject of the main claim.

From the above discussion, it has become apparent that the Court will reject the request of provisional measures if the rights that the provisional measures aim to protect do not fall within the scope of the subject of the main claim. However, the case concerning the *Arbitral Award of 31 July 1989* does not mean that the Court was adopting a stringent standard on the link between the subject of the main claim and that of the request for provisional measures. It is apparent from the Court's case-law that a direct link of cause and effect would be sufficient.

In the *Fisheries Jurisdiction* case (UNITED KINGDOM v. ICELAND), it was the British fisheries rights that the requested provisional measures sought to preserve. And the main claim was about whether the declarations relating to the question whether ICELAND's claim to an exclusive fisheries zone of 50 miles was valid in international law.[215] The Court's reasoning reads as follows:

> "whereas in the Application by which the Government of the United Kingdom instituted proceedings, that Government, by asking the Court to adjudge that the extension of fisheries jurisdiction by ICELAND is invalid, is in fact requesting the Court to declare that the contemplated measures of exclusion of foreign fishing vessels cannot be opposed by ICELAND to fishing vessels registered in the United Kingdom. Whereas the contention of the Applicant that its fishing vessels are entitled to continue fishing within the above-mentioned zone of 50 nautical miles is part of the subject-matter of the dispute submitted to the Court, and the request for provisional measures designed to protect such rights is therefore directly connected with the Application filed on 14 April 1972."[216]

The Court's reasoning inferred that the judgment on whether ICELAND's claim to an exclusive fisheries zone of 50 miles was valid in international law would consequently affect the British fisheries rights. The subject matter that the main claim dealt with would directly affect the rights that the Applicant sought to be protected by provisional measures. Therefore, the link between the subject of the main claim and the rights that the provisional measures sought to protect can justify the indication of provisional measures.

---

215 *Fisheries Jurisdiction* (UK and NORTHERN IRELAND v. ICELAND), (Provisional Measures), Order of 17 August 1972, ICJ Reports 1972, p. 12.

216 *Fisheries Jurisdiction* (UK and NORTHERN IRELAND v. ICELAND), *ibid.*, p. 15.

The case *Anglo-Iranian Oil Co.* might be even more typical to illustrate the "direct cause and effect" link. Provisional measures were indicated for the protection of the company's property rights, although the UNITED KINGDOM's primary claim was only for a declaration that IRAN was under a duty to submit the dispute to arbitration. The link here between the "company's property rights" and "IRAN's duty to submit the dispute to arbitration" is at the first sight too far to justify the indication of provisional measures. However, a positive judgment on the IRAN's duty to submit the dispute to arbitration would overrule IRAN's allegation that the nationalization of the company was within its national jurisdiction. Accordingly, the Iranian Government would not be free to dispose of the company's property rights. The determination whether IRAN had the duty to submit the dispute to arbitration had the effect of a determination whether IRAN's power of disposal of the company's property was within its national jurisdiction or was restricted by the claimed international agreement. Accordingly, the company's property rights that were sought to be protected by provisional measures were directly affected by the judgment on the main claim, namely "IRAN's duty to submit the dispute to arbitration". The company's property rights also constituted the subject of the main dispute. This observation could justify the assertion that the provisional measures as requested had the effect of protecting the rights that form the subject of the main claim.

In the case concerning *Certain Criminal Proceedings in* FRANCE, CONGO claimed that the irreparable prejudice would be the continuation and exacerbation of the prejudice already caused to the honor and reputation of the highest authorities of the CONGO, and to internal peace in the CONGO, to the international standing of the CONGO and to Franco-Congolese friendship. The Court observed that these rights as claimed by the CONGO which would suffer irreparable prejudice were not the rights which were claimed by the CONGO in the main Application, namely the right to require a state (FRANCE) to abstain from exercising universal jurisdiction in criminal matter in a manner contrary to international law, and the right to respect by FRANCE for the immunities conferred by international law on the Congolese Head of State. The Court's position seemed to be also rather ambiguous. It stated that "...the prejudice might, in the circumstances of the case, be regarded as such as to *affect* irreparably the rights asserted in the Application."[217](emphasis added) It apparently accepted this "irreparable prejudice" as sufficiently relevant to the indication of provisional measures. The prejudice was not directly to the rights claimed in the Application, but would "affect irreparably" these rights. At least it shall be taken into consideration as a circumstance of auxiliary character. The Court seemed to establish that the link had been established between the right sought to be protected by provisional measures and the subject of the main claim.

---

217 Case concerning *Certain Criminal Proceedings in FRANCE* (CONGO v. FRANCE), (Provisional Measures), Order of 17 June 2003, ICJ Reports 2003, p. 102.

The Court's case-law shows that provisional measures are not necessarily required to directly preserve the subject of the dispute submitted to the Court. In fact, there are very few occasions where a direct and exact link to the subject of the main claim could be established in the requests of provisional measures. On the one hand, the purpose of provisional measures determines that the rights that were sought to be protected by provisional measures must fall within the scope of the subject of the main claim. On the other hand, in order to ensure the effectiveness of provisional measures, a direct link of cause and effect between the provisional measures requested and the subject of the main dispute would be sufficient to satisfy the requirement of the link between the two.

b) The requirements of the form of the request

Article 73 of the Rules of the Court provides the requirement of the form of the request. Non-compliance with the requirement will lead to a request being dismissed as inadmissible. It provides that the request for provisional measures shall be in written form. It shall be made during the course of the proceedings in the case in connection with which the request is made. This restricts the time of the making of the request. It also requires the link between the request and the main claim. Accordingly, any requests raised after the conclusion of the proceedings shall be considered as inadmissible. Any requests that bear no connection with the main claims are inadmissible. It further provides that the request shall specify the reasons therefore, the possible consequences if it is not granted, and the measures requested.

## II. The necessity to indicate provisional measures

### 1. Irreparable prejudice

Bearing in mind that the main purpose of provisional measures is to ensure that the irreparable prejudice is not caused to the rights which are the subject of a dispute in judicial proceedings, the Court must examine whether the irreparable prejudice to the rights exists or not. The assessment of "irreparable prejudice" is the most important part of the consideration of the "circumstances" which require the indication of provisional measures.

a) the abandonment of the "absolute irreparability in law" criterion

Then what is the exact meaning of "irreparable"? To what extent could the situation constitutes "irreparable prejudice" justifying provisional measures? It is a very elusive concept.

The interpretation that distinguishes "reparable" from "irreparable" according to whether an appropriate remedy could be provided by monetary damages was once adopted in the Permanent Court's early jurisprudence. President Huber expressly expounded it in the order in the *Sino-Belgian Treaty* case. He stated that interim protection was indicated because possible infractions of certain rights in question "could not be made good simply by the payment of an indemnity or by compensation or restitution in some other material form."[218] According to this criterion, only the rights which pecuniary compensation is inadequate could be protected by provisional measures. *Dumbauld*, commented on this criterion that provisional protection was improper where an appropriate remedy lay in damages for any wrong done.[219] This criterion is believed to be influenced by "the traditional rule as to the availability of injunctions in common law systems: the Court will not grant an injunction to restrain an actionable wrong for which damages are the proper remedy".[220]

President Huber's criterion was believed to be obsolete. *Stzucki* observed that there would have been rare rights that could be protected by provisional measures according to this criterion. He stated as follows:

> "Indeed, there are no violations of rights which could not be made good in law by reparation. This is true not only of financial or other economic injury but also of all other injuries not measurable in pecuniary terms. This was most clearly demonstrated in the *U.S. Staff* Case when the applicant asked the Court to adjudge reparation for breaches of the obligations relating to the inviolability

---

218 *Sino-Belgian Treaty* (BELGIUM V. CHINA), (Interim Measures), Order of 8 January 1927, PCIJ, Series A, No. 8, p.7.

219 *Dumbauld, supra* note 51, p.147-153.

220 *Goldsworthy*, Interim Measures of Protection in the INTERNATIONAL COURT OF JUSTICE, The American Journal of International Law, (1974),Vol. 68, p. 270.
For the rules on injunction in common law system, it is presented that "the plaintiff must also as a rule be able to show that an injunction until the hearings is necessary to protect him against irreparable prejudice; mere inconvenience is not enough. By the term 'irreparable injury' is meant, substantially, injury that could never be adequately remedied or atoned for by damages. An injunction may, however, be granted even where the injury is capable of compensation in damages, if the act in respect of which relief is sought is likely to destroy the subject-matter in question", *Halsbury*, The Laws of England, (1911), p.219.

of the diplomatic and consular personnel and to its privileges and immunities; and when the Court adjudged in accordance with this submission."[221]

He then continued:

"to say that provisional measures should not be indicated when the prejudice in question might be capable of reparation by some appropriate means would amount to the proposition that such measures should not be indicated at all, except when it is shown with substantial credibility that the magnitude of the prejudice in a given case would exceed the respondent's resources available for reparation or would cause a total collapse and disappearance of the actual beneficiary of the prospective reparation ... Such a criterion of granting interim protection would be clearly at variance with the principle of sovereign equality of States and of their equality before the law."[222]

This criterion has not been included in the Court's Orders any more since the *Sino-Belgian Treaty* case. An exception is the Order in the *Aegean Sea Continental Shelf* case. The Court's invoking of this criterion is widely criticized. (It will be analyzed in detail later.) The Court's invoking of this criterion is widely criticized.) It is nowadays widely believed that the Court has abandoned this criterion.[223]

b) the less stringent criterion

In the *South-Eastern Greenland* case, the Norwegian Government asked the Court to give judgment to the effect that the placing of the disputed area - the South-Eastern Greenland under the sovereignty of Norway was legally valid and that accordingly the said territory was subject to the sovereignty of Norway. It also requested provisional measures to abstain the Danish Government from any coercive measures directed against the Norwegian nationals in the said territory. The Court observed that the circumstances require provisional measures when "the damage threatening these rights would be irreparable *in fact* or in law".[224] (emphasis added) However, the Court did not go on to expound the term

221 The pecuniary reparation was granted in paragraph 5 and 6 of the operative part of the final judgment, ICJ Report 1980, p. 45, para. 95. The restoration was adjudged in paragraph 3(c) of the operative part of the final judgment, ICJ Report 1980, p.45, para.95.

222 *Sztucki, supra* note 3, p.109-110.

223 See *eg. Sztucki, supra* note 3, p. 111.

224 *South-Eastern Greenland* (NORWAY v. DENMARK), PCIJ Ser. A/B, No. 48, p. 284. The Court rejected the request for provisional measures on the ground that it had not established the prejudice to any recognized right of Norway. Norway was seeking interim measures solely to prevent "regrettable events and unfortunate incidents".

"irreparable in fact or in law" specifically. It simply rejected the request for provisional measures on the ground that it had not established the prejudice to any recognized right of Norway. Norway was seeking interim measures solely to prevent "regrettable events and unfortunate incidents".

In the *Electricity Company* case, to state the purpose of provisional protection, the Court observed that provisional measures were required to "to prevent ... the performance of acts likely to prejudice ... the respective rights which may result from the impending judgment."[225]

The present court has not adopted in the Orders any term either as "could not be made good simply by the payment of an indemnity or by compensation or restitution in some other material form" or "irreparable in law or in fact". In the *Anglo-Iranian Oil Co.* case, the Court indicated provisional measures requiring the joint control of the contested company with profits to be deposited in escrow account although it is arguable that the rights sought to be protected is susceptible to reparation by award of damages.[226] To examine whether the present state of affairs justified provisional measures, the Court stated that it was "concerned to preserve … the rights which may be subsequently adjudged … belong either to the Applicant or to the Respondent".[227] In *Fisheries Jurisdiction,* the Court ordered ICELAND to refrain from enforcing the extension of its fishery jurisdiction although the right of Applicants is also arguably remediable by damages. The Court stated that "the immediate implementation by ICELAND of its Regulation would, by anticipating the Court's Judgment, prejudice the rights claimed by the United Kingdom and affect the possibility of their full restoration in the event of a judgment in its favor".[228] This statement generally reflects the Court's recent attitude on the assessment of the "irreparability of the prejudice" to the rights asserted in the main proceedings.[229] More recently and more frequently it was stated as "the Court must be concerned to preserve by such measures the performance of acts likely to prejudice ... the respective rights which may be subsequently adjudged ... to belong either to the Applicant or to the Respondent",[230] as in the case concerning the *Application of the International Convention on the Elimination of All Forms of Racial Discrimination*[231] and *Request for Interpretation*

225 PCIJ Series. A/B, No.79, p.199.

226 *Anglo-Iranian Oil Co.* (UK v. IRAN), (Provisional Measures), Order of 5 July 1951, ICJ Reports 1951, p. 89, 94.

227 *Anglo-Iranian Oil Co.*, *ibid.*, p. 93.

228 *Fisheries Jurisdiction*, (UK and NORTHERN IRELAND v. ICELAND), (Provisional Measures), Order of 17 August 1972, ICJ Reports 1972, p. 16, para. 22.

229 *Fisheries Jurisdiction*, (UNITED KINGDOM v. ICELAND), Order of 17 August, ICJ Reports 1972, p. 12, 13.

230 *Anglo-Iranian Oil Co.*, *Anglo-Iranian Oil Co.* (UK v. IRAN), (Provisional Measures), Order of 5 July 1951, ICJ Reports 1951, p. 93.

231 Case concerning the *Application of the International Convention on the Elimination of All Forms of Racial Discrimination* (GEORGIA v. RUSSIAN FEDERATION), (Provisional

*of the Judgment of 31 March 2004 in the Case Concerning Avena and Other Mexican Nationals.*[232] The same statement is also found in the case concerning the *Application of the Convention on the Prevention and Punishment of the Crime of Genocide*[233] and the case concerning *Land and Maritime Boundary between CAMEROON and NIGERIA.*[234]

In the *Fisheries Jurisdiction* cases, the Court mentioned the effects of the possible actions the parties might take during the pending of the judgment. The Government of ICELAND had issued Regulations to the effect of extension of fisheries jurisdiction until the requests for provisional measures. The Court concluded that "whereas the immediate implementation by ICELAND of its Regulations would, by anticipating the Court's judgment, prejudice the rights claimed by the Federal Republic and affect the possibility of their full restoration in the event of a judgment in its favor;"[235] To this extent, "irreparable prejudice" is relevant to the concept of "anticipation of the final judgment". "Anticipating" in this context means "acting in the belief that the judgment were in his favor", as discussed in Chapter C, Part III. If there is any risk that the parties would take any actions to change the present state of rights to the direction in his favor and the effect of these actions would not be erased, this situation constitutes the "irreparable prejudice" that justifies provisional measures. To this extent, the literal meaning of "irreparable" has been modified. Then, the diction of "irreversible prejudice" might be more appropriate to reflect the Court's practice, rather than the diction of "irreparable prejudice".

To interpret the recent criterion of "irreparability" adopted by the Court, *Stzucki* observed that it should be understood in the sense that "it makes the full execution of the impending judgment impossible and thereby the full restoration of the prejudiced position of the prospective judgment creditor impossible and, in principle, regardless of whether he might be compensated for the non-execution of the judgment or not".[236] This statement underlines that the purpose of the examination on the "irreparability of the prejudice" is consistent with the purpose of provisional measures - to ensure the full execution of the final judgment.

---

Measures), ICJ Reports 2008, p. 33, para. 118.

232 *Request for Interpretation of the Judgment of 31 March 2004 in the Case Concerning Avena and Other Mexican Nationals* (MEXICO v. USA), (Provisional Measures), Order of 16 July 2008, ICJ Reports 2008, p.15, para. 58.

233 *Bosnian Genocide* (BOSNIA and HERZEGOVINA v. YUGOSLAVIA (SERBIA and MONTENEGRO)), (Provisional Measures), Order of 13 September 1993, ICJ Reports 1993, p. 19, para. 34.

234 Case concerning the *Land and Maritime Boundary between CAMEROON and NIGERIA* (CAMEROON v. NIGERIA), (Provisional Measures), Order of 15 March 1996, ICJ Reports 1996(I), p.22, para. 35.

235 *Fisheries Jurisdiction* (REPUBLIC OF GERMANY v. ICELAND), (Provisional Measures), Order of 17 August 1972, ICJ Reports 1972, p.34, para.23.

236 *Sztucki, supra* note 3, p. 110.

A closer examination of the Court's practice in the specific practice might do more help to our study than the abstract and ambiguous statement as quoted above. With the presumption that the character and the gravity of the prejudices in different cases might be importantly relevant to the assessment of "whether the final judgment could be fully executed", this dissertation attempts to categorize the cases before the present Court into several groups according to the nature of the breaches as claimed by the Applicants. The categorization is only for the purpose of study on this specific issue and it is not exhaustive. It should be borne in mind that it's difficult to simply categorize the cases because some of them involve more than one category of breaches.

(1) Privation, hardship, anguish and danger to life and death

In the *Nuclear Tests* case (NEW ZEALAND v. FRANCE), the Government of NEW ZEALAND alleged that any exposure to radiation may have irreparable effects and the uncertain physical and genetic effects would cause the people of NEW ZEALAND acute apprehension, anxiety and concern, and the erosion of the rights can not be fully restored in the event of a judgment in NEW ZEALAND's favor.[237] In response to NEW ZEALAND's allegation, the French Government alleged that the appropriate precautionary measures had been taken and the Reports did not show any danger to the health of the populations of the two countries. In the Order of 22 June 1973, in the Nuclear Tests case, the Court spent a long writing to establish the "irreparability" of the prejudice: "... that the uncertain physical and genetic effects to which contamination exposes the people of NEW ZEALAND causes them acute apprehension, anxiety and concern; and that there could be no possibility that the rights eroded by the holding of further tests could be fully restored in the event of a judgment in NEW ZEALAND's favor in these proceeding;"[238] The Court went on to react to the French Government's argument that the concern as to the long term effects of testing was based on conjecture. (The French Government argued that it would take every precaution to ensure the safety and harmlessness of the tests and the recent Research Reports showed that the fall-out had never involved any danger to the health of the population.) The Court concluded that the information submitted to the Court "*does not exclude the possibility* that damage to NEW ZEALAND might be shown to be caused by the deposit on NEW ZEALAND territory of radio-active fall-out resulting from such tests and to be irreparable".(emphasis added)[239]

Another case involving the prejudice to human life is the case concerning the *UNITED STATES Diplomatic and Consular Staff in Tehran.* With respect to

237 *Nuclear Tests* (NEW ZEALAND v. FRANCE), (Provisional Measures), Order of 22 June 1973, ICJ Reports 1973, p.140-141, para.28.

238 *Ibid.*

239 *Nuclear Tests* (NEW ZEALAND v. FRANCE), (Provisional Measures), Order of 22 June 1973, ICJ Reports 1973, p.141, para.30.

"irreparable prejudice", the Court observed that "the continuance of the situation in question *exposed* the human beings concerned to privation, hardship, anguish and even danger to life and death and thus *to a serious possibility* of irreparable harm".[240] (emphasis added)

In the case concerning the *Application of the Convention on the Prevention and Punishment of the Crime of Genocide*, the Court again quoted the paragraph that the power to indicate provisional measures "presupposes that irreparable prejudice shall not be caused to rights which are the subject of dispute in judicial proceedings".[241] However, the Court, in the subsequent paragraph, stated that "the Court ... ought not to indicate measures for the protection of any disputed rights other than those which might ultimately form the basis of a judgment in the exercise of that jurisdiction". Accordingly, the Court's purpose to invoke the quoted paragraph is to stress the consistency between the rights sought to be protected by provisional measures and the subject of the main claim, rather than going on to examine the issue of "irreparability".[242] The fact that the Court indicated the provisional measures without any assessment of the "irreparability" in this case reflects its liberal attitude in the cases involving genocide.

In the case concerning the *Application of the International Convention on the Elimination of All Forms of Discrimination*, the Court considered that "violations of the right to security of persons and of the right to protection by the State against violence or bodily harm could involve potential loss of life or bodily injury and could therefore cause irreparable prejudice."[243]The Court further considered that

---

240 Case concerning *United States Diplomatic and Consular Staff in Tehran* (UNITED STATES v. IRAN), (Provisional Measures), Order of 15 December 1979, ICJ Reports 1979, p.20, para. 42.

241 Paragraph 34 of the Order reads: "whereas the power of the Court to indicate provisional measures under Article 41 of the Statute of the Court has as its object to preserve the respective rights of the parties pending the decision of the Court, and presupposes that irreparable prejudice shall not be caused to rights which are the subject of dispute in judicial proceedings; and whereas it follows that the Court must be concerned to preserve by such measures the rights which may subsequently be adjudged by the Court to belong either to the Applicant or to the Respondent;" *Bosnian Genocide* (BOSNIA and HERZEGOVINA v. SERBIA and MONTENEGRO), (Provisional Measures), Order of 8 April 1993, ICJ Reports 1993, p.20, para.34.

242 The Court stated in paragraph 35 of the Order that "whereas the Court, having established the existence of a basis on which its jurisdiction might be founded, ought not to indicate provisional measures for the protection of any disputed rights other than those which might ultimately form the basis of a judgment in the exercise of that jurisdiction; whereas accordingly the Court will confine its examination of the measures requested, and of the grounds asserted for the request for such measures, to those which fall within the scope of the Genocide Convention.", *Bosnian Genocide* (BOSNIA and HERZEGOVINA v. SERBIA and MONTENEGRO), (Provisional Measures), Order of 8 April 1993, ICJ Reports 1993, p.20, para.35.

243 Case concerning the *Application of the International Convention on the Elimination of All*

"violations of the right to freedom of movement and residence within a State's borders could also cause irreparable prejudice in situations where the persons concerned are exposed to privation, hardship, anguish and even danger to life and death."[244]

In these listed cases, the breaches in the specific situation might lead to privation, hardship, anguish and danger to life and death. These breaches would make the execution of the prospective judgment impossible. Then the "irreparability" of the prejudice alleged is well-justified. Therefore, it can be concluded that it is the nature of the prejudice that makes the Court not hesitate to conclude that the "irreparable prejudice" has been established.

It is noteworthy that the Court also takes the preliminary issue, namely the possibility of the occurring of prejudice into consideration. In other words, the impossibility of the occurring of the prejudice is a ground to challenge the justification of provisional measures. As reflected by the jurisprudence, the Court exerts a quite loose test on the possibility of the prejudice in the cases concerning "the privation, hardship, anguish and danger to life and death". As shown by the *Nuclear Tests* cases, provisional measures are believed to be justified by the Court when the evidences do not "exclude the possibility" that the damage might be shown to be caused by the infringement. If the evidences can not exclude the possibility of the occurring of that prejudice, the Court concludes that there exists "irreparable prejudice".

(2) Execution of a national, the meaning and scope of whose rights are in question

There is another group of cases in which the prejudice to the life of one or some individuals, rather than the uncertain large amount of people as in the last group of cases, that justifies provisional measures.

In the case concerning *the Vienna Convention on Consular Relations* (PARAGUAY v. USA), the Court concluded that the execution of a national, the meaning and scope of whose rights are in question, before the Court delivers its judgment on the Request for interpretation "would render it impossible for the Court to order the relief that his national State seeks and thus cause irreparable harm to the rights it claims".[245] A similar example is the LAGRAND case. The Court directly stated that the execution of the German nationals would cause irreparable harm to the right claimed by GERMANY in the main proceedings. The Court's Orders in the case concerning *Avena and other Mexican Nationals* and the case

---

*Forms of Racial Discrimination* (GEORGIA v. RUSSIAN FEDERATION), (Provisional Measures), Order of 15 October 2008, ICJ Reports 2008, p. 39, para. 142.

244 *Ibid.*

245 *Vienna Convention on Consular Relations* (PARAGUAY v. USA), (Provisional Measures), Order of 9 April 1998, ICJ Reports 1998, p. 257, para. 37.

*Request for Interpretation of the Judgment of 31 March 2004 in the Case Concerning Avena and Other Mexican Nationals* also followed the two precedents.

(3) Armed activities on the territory

In the case concerning *Military and Paramilitary Activities in and against NICARAGUA*, the Court directly adopted the diction of "to preserve the respective rights of either party pending the decision of the Court" instead of "irreparable prejudice". It stated that the circumstances required it to indicate provisional measures in order to preserve the rights claimed, namely, the right to be free of use or threat of force, the right of sovereignty, the right of action without interference or intervention by a foreign State, and the right of self-determination of the Nicaraguan people.

In the *Frontier Disputes* case, although the authors are divided on the question whether the provisional measures were based on the Court's power to prevent aggravation or extension of the dispute independently of the existence of irreparable prejudice,[246] the Chamber stated that the facts giving rise to the requests "expose the persons and property in the disputed area, to serious risk of irreparable damage".[247]

In the case concerning the *Armed Activities on the Territory of the* CONGO (CONGO V. UGANDA), the Court observed that "the rights which are the subject of the dispute are essentially its rights to sovereignty and territorial integrity and to the integrity of its assets and natural resources, and its rights to respect for the rules of international humanitarian law and for the instruments relating to the protection of human rights".[248] The Court was of the opinion that the persons, assets and resources present on the territory of the CONGO, particularly in the area of conflict, remained extremely vulnerable, and that there was a serious risk that the rights in issue might suffer irreparable prejudice.[249]

(4) Territorial dispute involving the loss of life

In the case concerning the *Land and Maritime Boundary between* CAMEROON *and* NIGERIA, the dispute arose from the boundary delimitation, but it further brought about military conflicts. The Court concluded that "the events that have given rise to the request, and more especially the killing of persons, have caused irreparable damage to the rights that the Parties may have over the Peninsula; whereas persons

246 Please refer to Chapter C, Part V of this dissertation.

247 *Frontier Disputes*, (BURKINA FASO/MALI), (Provisional Measures), Order of 10 January 1986, ICJ Reports 1986, p.10, para.21.

248 Case concerning the *Armed Activities on the Territory of the Congo* (CONGO V. UGANDA), (Provisional Measures), Order of 1 July 2000, ICJ Reports 2000, p. 127, para. 40.

249 *Ibid.*, p. 128, para. 43.

in the disputed area and, as a consequence, the rights of the Parties within that area are exposed to serious risk of further irreparable damage ... "[250]

(5) Dispute involving financial prejudice

The cases involving financial prejudice are special in nature in the context of provisional measures, comparing with the cases involving human rights breaches. Financial prejudice is apparently difficult to be regarded as justifying provisional measures because it could be appropriately and sufficiently remedied by pecuniary compensation. Contrarily, it is a more acceptable argument that the prejudice is irreparable in the cases with the subject matter of human health, life or the environment because the effects of the prejudice could not be reversed or restored by any prospective judgment. This argument is actually a natural inference of President *Huber*'s "absolute irreparability in law" criterion.

The Court's jurisprudence on this issue is not so consistent. In the *Anglo-Iranian Oil Co.* case, the Iranian Parliament passed the Iranian Oil Nationalization Act that affected the property and position of the Anglo-Iranian Oil Company. This company was claimed to be a UNITED KINGDOM national. The government of the UNITED KINGDOM requested the Court to preserve its rights to assure its nationals to be treated in accordance with the international law and have the full benefits that it is entitled under the Convention concluded. The UNITED KINGDOM filed a request for interim measures to prevent the operation of the company from interference by the Iranian government, ensure that no further steps of any kind are taken capable of prejudicing the right of the UK to have a decision of the Court in its favor on the merits of the case executed, should the Court render such a decision, ensure that no step of any kind is taken by both governments capable of aggravating or extending the dispute.... It might be strongly arguable that the interruption of the operation activities of the *Anglo-Iranian Oil Company* could be made good simply by monetary compensation. However, the Court spent no writing on addressing whether the infringement is remediable by pecuniary reparation or not. After concluding that the claim cannot be accepted *a priori* that the claim falls completely outside its jurisdiction, the Court simply observed that the state of affairs justifies the indication of provisional measures.

In the *Fisheries Jurisdiction* cases, the Court did not examine whether the prejudice could be made up by compensation, either. It directly indicated provisional measures on the ground that the possible "immediate implementation" of the Regulation of the Fisheries Jurisdiction Extension would "anticipate" the final judgment and affect the possibility of the full restoration of the rights of the creditor of the judgment in its favor.

250 Case concerning the *Land and Martime Boundary between CAMEROON and NIGERIA*, (CAMEROON v. NIGERIA), (Provisional Measures), Order of 15 March 1996, ICJ Reports 1996, p. 23, para. 42.

The *Interhandel* case was about the release of assets in the UNITED STATES of a Swiss company named Interhandel. The assets in question were shares in the General Aniline and Film Corporation, incorporated under the UNITED STATES Law. The UNITED STATES believed that the General Aniline and Film Corporation belonged to a German company or was controlled by it through the said Swiss company. This under the Second World War fell under the operation of the Trading with the Enemy Act. SWITZERLAND asserted that Interhandel had severed its ties with the German company and that, consequently, the assets in question were neutral property at the time of the entry into force of the Trading with the Enemy Act. SWITZERLAND proposed to settle the dispute through conciliation or arbitration but the UNITED STATES declined this proposal. SWITZERLAND instituted proceedings against the UNITED STATES before the Court, asking the Court to adjudge and declare that the government of the UNITED STATES is under the obligation to restore the assets to Interhandel. SWITZERLAND also filed a request for interim protection to the effect that, pending the final decision in the case, the government of the UNITED STATES is requested to take no ... step to part with the property which is claimed to be Swiss property ... and in particular, not to sell the shares of the General Aniline and Film Corporation ... in general, the government of the UNITED STATES should so act that no measure whatever is taken which would prejudice the right of SWITZERLAND to execution of the judgment which the Court will deliver ... [251] If the Court does not indicate interim measures of protection of the kind which will be specified hereafter, the Swiss Government has serious grounds for believing that, in the event of its claims as just stated being upheld by the Court, *it may be impossible for the Court's decision to be carried out*, should the Interhandel property vested in the Alien Property Custodian, the restitution of which is claimed, have been meanwhile transferred to third parties. *This impossibility to execute a judgment in favor of* SWITZERLAND *would involve irreparable damage*, the mere possibility of which, according to the jurisprudence of the PERMANENT COURT OF INTERNATIONAL JUSTICE, justifies interim measures of protection. The Court found that there was "no need to indicate interim measures of protection" since the sale of the disputed shares could be affected only upon unfavorable conclusion of the judicial proceedings which were pending before the U.S. courts and in respect of which there was "no indication as to its speedy conclusion"[252]. (emphasis added) Here, the Court again did not mention whether the rights in issue were remediable by pecuniary compensation or not. Instead, the Court examined the possible events the Government of the USA would probably take before the delivery of the final judgment. To be more specific, the Court implicitly found that the speedy conclusion of the judicial proceedings that affected the sale of the

---

251 *Interhandel*, (SWITZERLAND v. USA), (Provisional Measures), Order of 24 October 1957, ICJ Reports 1957, p. 105.

252 *Interhandel*, *ibid.* p. 141.

disputed shares would make the subject-matter of the claim impossible to be executed under the final judgment.

In *Fisheries Jurisdiction,* the Applicant claimed that the immediate implementation by ICELAND of its Regulation to unilaterally extend its fisheries jurisdiction would, by anticipating the Court's judgment, prejudice the rights claimed by the Applicant and affect the possibility of their full restoration in the event of a judgment in its favor. The Court directly granted the requests for provisional measures ordering ICELAND to refrain from enforcing the extension of its fishery jurisdiction although it is arguable that the possible "immediate implementation" by ICELAND of its Fisheries Jurisdiction Regulation pending the proceedings would just cause financial prejudice to the fisheries industries of the Applicants and in turn could be appropriately made good by damages.

The above-quoted cases reflect that the financial nature of the prejudice does not itself exclude the possibility of the indication of provisional measures. Comparing it with the initial stringent test of "could not be made good simply by the payment of an indemnity or by compensation or restitution in some other material form", the Court has recently adopted a rather liberal standard on the concept of "irreparability" justifying the indication of provisional measures, namely "to preserve the rights which may be subsequently adjudged to belong either to the Applicant or to the Respondent".

One might argue that the Court did not follow the liberal standard in the *Aegean Sea Continental Shelf* case. The Court rejected the request for provisional measures on the ground of the non-existence of irreparable prejudice because the alleged breach by TURKEY of the exclusivity of the right claimed by GREECE to acquire information concerning the natural resources of areas of continental shelf is one that might be capable of reparation by *appropriate means.*[253] The Court's observation that the "alleged breach by TURKEY" is one that "might be capable of reparation by appropriate means" was echoing the President *Huber*'s "absolute irreparability in law" criterion. Moreover, the observation of "reparation by appropriate means" is doubtable because the interests alleged to be prejudiced, namely the exclusivity of knowledge, is subjective in nature and is not susceptible of pecuniary ascertainment.[254]

It is interesting to find that little analysis was provided on how the prejudice can be made good by appropriate means. Indeed, if we take the Court's recent position that "irreparable prejudice" in the context of provisional measures means the prejudice which would make the "full execution of the final judgment impossible", regardless of whether the non-execution could be made up by compensations or not, it is difficult to agree with the Court's finding that the alleged breach by TURKEY "might be capable of reparation by appropriate means". Because of the special

253 *Aegean Sea Continental Shelf* (GREECE v. TURKEY), (Provisional Measures), Order of 11 September 1976, ICJ Reports 1976, p. 3.

254 *Elkind, supra* note 4, p.213-218.

character of the right to information, the exclusivity to acquire information concerning the natural resources of the areas of continental shelf are not able to be restored once it is infringed. The alleged prejudice, namely the seismic activities by TURKEY, would definitely make the position of GREECE incapable of full restoration.

The Court did not spend much time to specifically explain by which means the alleged breach by TURKEY can be restored by which measures, although the diction of "reparation by appropriate means" was adopted. Instead, much attention was spent on the actual prejudice the seismic exploration might have on the rights claimed by GREECE to acquire information concerning the natural resources of areas of continental shelf, "...according to information before the Court, the seismic exploration undertake by TURKEY, of which GREECE complains, is carried out by a vessel traversing the surface of the high seas and causing small explosions to occur at intervals under water; ... the purpose of these explosions is to send sound waves through the sea-bed so as to obtain information regarding the geophysical structure of the earth beneath it;" It concluded that "no complaint has been made that this form of seismic exploration involves any risk of physical damage to the sea-bed or subsoil or to their natural resources". Furthermore, the exploration was of "transitory character" and "did not involve any establishment of installations". "No suggestion had been made that TURKEY had embarked upon any operations involving the actual appropriation or other use of the natural resources of the areas of the continental shelf in dispute". The concentrated examination of the evidences on the state of TURKEY's seismic exploration reflects the Court's doubt on the possibility of the actual occurrence of the prejudice. It is the possibility of the prejudice rather than the "reparability" that was influencing the Judges' minds.

In the *Passage through the Great Belt* case, the Court found that the prejudice would not occur during the period between the request for provisional measures and the Court's judgment on the merits because "no physical obstruction of East Channel will occur before the Court's judgment on the merits".[255]

(6) Prejudice to the diplomatic immunity

In the case concerning the *Arrest Warrant of 11 April 2000*, CONGO requested to annul the arrest warrant issued against its Minister for Foreign Affairs by a Belgian investigating judge on the ground that "irreparable prejudice" would occur to CONGO's right to require a State to abstain from exercising universal jurisdiction in criminal matters in a manner contrary to international law and the right to the immunity of Heads of State. After arguing that the CONGO Government failed to establish *prima facie* jurisdiction over the merits and failed to make out a case for the existence of a right required the indication of provisional measures, the Belgian

255 *Passage through the Great Belt* (FINLAND v. DENMARK), (Provisional Measures), Order of 29 July 1991, ICJ Reports 1991, p. 12.

Government turned to the requirement of irreparable prejudice and urgency. It asserted that the fact that Mr. Ndombasi ceased to be the Foreign Minister indicated that there was no irreparable prejudice to those rights. It maintained that "we were presented with virtually no evidence of any prejudice having occurred to the rights of the Democratic Republic of the Congo since 11 April (or 12 July) 2000..."[256] The Court accepted BELGIUM's assertion that the prejudice would not exist any more after the Minister of Foreign Affairs shifted to the position of Minister of Education.[257]

In the case concerning the *Certain Criminal Proceedings in FRANCE*, the court examined the evidences and concluded that "in any event the Court notes that it has not been informed in what practical respect there has been any deterioration internally or in the international standing of the CONGO, or in Franco-Congolese relations, since the institution of the French criminal proceedings, nor has any evidence been placed before the Court of any serious prejudice or threat of prejudice of this nature." The Court continued to examine the question whether the criminal proceedings entailed a risk of irreparable prejudice to the right of the CONGO to respect by FRANCE for the immunities of the Head of State. The French government argued that the French Code of Criminal Procedure provided that the president's evidence could not be taken without the express agreement of the CONGO. "A request for a written deposition from President had been sent by the investigating judge to the French Ministry of Foreign Affairs, it had been retained by the Ministry, and that the current proceedings therefore had not caused and cannot cause any damage to the Congo by way of breach of immunities of the President." The Court accepted French's argument that there was at then no risk of irreparable prejudice to the immunities of the Congolese Head of State.

(7) Prejudice to the environment, economy and society

In the *Pup Mills* case, ARGENTINA requested to suspend URUGUAY's construction of the project basing on the ground that it would cause irreparable damage to the environment and also to its economy and society. In the Order of 13 July 2006, the Court was not convinced that, if it should later be shown that URUGUAY had failed fully to adhere to the provisions of Chapter II of the 1975 Statute as claimed, any such violations would not be capable of being remedied at the merits stage of the proceedings. Moreover, ARGENTINA had not provided any evidence that suggested that any pollution resulting from the construction would be of a character to cause

256 Case concerning the *Arrest Warrant of 11 April 2000* (DEMOCRATIC REPUBLIC OF THE CONGO v. BELGIUM), (Provisional Measures), Order of 8 December 2000, ICJ Reports 2000, p. 192, para. 34.

257 Case concerning the *Arrest Warrant of 11 April 2000* (DEMOCRATIC REPUBLIC OF THE CONGO v. BELGIUM), (Provisional Measures), Order of 8 December 2000, ICJ Reports 2000, p. 201, para. 72.

irreparable damage. The Court discriminately treated the two arguments of ARGENTINA. As for the procedural rights of ARGENTINA under the 1975 Statute, the Court fundamentally negated its "irreparability". The Court stated that the violation might be found to have been committed by URUGUAY would be capable of being remedied at the merits stage of the proceedings. As to the right of substantive nature invoked by ARGENTINA, namely the right to protect its environment, the Court seemed to impliedly affirm its "irreparability". However, it objected ARGENTINA's argument on the factual ground, namely the lack of evidence to prove the environmental prejudice, the lack of imminence of the prejudice if it were established.[258]

Meanwhile, URUGUAY argued that the blocking of international roads and bridges connecting ARGENTINA to URUGUAY encouraged by ARGENTINA would cause extremely serious impact on URUGUAY's economy and tourist industry. If it were obliged to halt the project in order to protect its economy, as a consequence of the pressure exerted upon it, the project would be lost in its entirety and the prejudice suffered would therefore be irreparable. The Court was of the view that, notwithstanding the blockades, the construction of the project progressed significantly. The Court was not convinced that those blockades risked prejudicing irreparably the rights as claimed by URUGUAY. The Court consequently found that the circumstances of the case were not such as to require the indication of the first provisional measures requested by URUGUAY, to "prevent or end the interruption of transit" between the two states and *inter alia* the "blockading of the bridges and roads" linking them. The Court's attention is apparently on the factual aspect, specifically on whether the blockades actually affected the rights that URUGUAY claimed in the present case, without addressing the issue whether the prejudice would constitute the "irreparable" degree if it actually occurs.[259]

(8) Cases within which "irreparable prejudice" is not considered

In the group cases *Legality of Use of Force* and the case concerning the *Armed Activities on the Territory of the* CONGO (CONGO v. RWANDA), the Court did not need to discuss the issue of "irreparable prejudice" because the Applicant failed to establish the *prima facie* jurisdiction over the merits. In the case concerning the *Arbitral Award of 31 July 1989*, the request for provisional measures was dismissed on the ground that the alleged rights sought to be made the subject of provisional measures are not the subjects of the proceedings before the Court on the merits of the case. In the two *Lockerbie* cases, the requests for provisional measures were rejected on the ground that the SECURITY COUNCIL RESOLUTION under Chapter VII

258 *Pulp Mills* (ARGENTINA v. URUGUAY), (Provisional Measures), Order of 13 July 2006, ICJ Reports 2006, p. 1-21.

259 *Pulp Mills* (ARGENTINA v. URUGUAY), (Provisional Measures), Order of 23 January 2007, ICJ Reports 2007, p. 1-14.

of the Charter had made the rights under the Montreal Convention (the rights sought to be protected by provisional measures) inappropriate to be protected. The question of irreparable prejudice was therefore not considered in these cases.

### c) Comprehensive assessment of the circumstances

It is observed from these cases that the Court has recently adopted a quite broad criterion on the assessment of "irreparable prejudice". To invoke the Court's terms, it intends to interpret the "irreparability" as "impossibility of full execution of the final judgment", regardless of whether the infringement could be made good in some material form or not. This criterion actually follows the criterion established by the Permanent Court in the *South-Eastern Greenland* case --- the circumstances require interim protection of the rights in dispute when "the damage threatening these rights would be irreparable *in fact* or in law". That means, even if the infringement could be made good by appropriate means, the Court could grant the provisional measures if otherwise it would prejudice the full execution of the final judgment. To this extent, it might be inappropriate to understand the term "irreparable prejudice" literally in the context of provisional measures.

Nevertheless, it should be borne in mind that the Court's examination of the circumstances in a certain case is discretionary. The assessment of "irreparable prejudice" is based on the comprehensive consideration of all the circumstances.

#### (1) The possibility of the prejudice

As discussed above, a prejudice is deemed to be "irreparable" if it makes the full execution of the prospective judgment impossible, regardless of whether the creditor of the judgment might be compensated for the non-execution of the judgment or not.[260] It is much more liberal than the criterion of "absolute irreparability in law".

Since the abandonment of the "absolute irreparable in law" criterion and the adoption of the new criterion "make the full execution of the final judgment impossible", the Court has shown less effort to distinguish the alleged prejudice between "irreparable" and "reparable" from the theoretical perspective, basing on whether the prejudice could be made up by pecuniary compensation or not. In the field of international law, a majority of the disputes involve human rights, sovereignty to territory, rights to environment and natural resources, etc. Although municipal laws have widely recognized the infringement to human life, health, dignity as remediable by pecuniary compensation and is "reparable in law", it is difficult to draw an analogy in international law as great doubt might be raised to the "reparability in law" of human rights and national sovereignty. Moreover,

260 *Stzucki*, *supra* note 3, p. 110.

because of the special character of the rights, these rights are usually related to the dignity and sovereignty of a nation and the effect of the infringement to these rights are certainly "irreversible".

Even in cases mainly concern financial prejudice, such as the *Anglo-Iranian Oil* Co., *Fisheries Jurisdiction*, the subject-matter of the dispute is not as purely financial as the property rights in municipal law. The Court adopted a criterion much broader than the traditional common law approach. The subject of these cases is usually a state's right to protect its nationals' legal economic activities from intervention or to protect the State's property right from intervention. Comparing to the cases involving financial prejudice in municipal law, the cases involving financial prejudice in international law concerns not only property rights, but also the State's welfare and status in international community, at least in an indirect manner. Therefore, the financial nature of the prejudice itself does not exclude its possibility of justifying provisional measures.

Therefore, the distinction between "irreparable prejudice" and "reparable prejudice", basing on whether it could be made good by pecuniary compensation, which is strongly rooted in municipal law, turns to be not so significant in the practice of the Court. Good examples are provided by the *Aegean Sea Continental Shelf* case and the case concerning the *Certain Criminal Proceedings in FRANCE*. In the former case, the Court put close examination on the actual state and effects of the seismic exploration, instead of assessing the "irreparability". In the latter case, the Court accepted the French Government's argument that "a request for a written deposition from President had been sent by the investigating judge to the French Ministry of Foreign Affairs, it had been retained by the Ministry, and that the current proceedings therefore had not caused and cannot cause any damage to the Congo by way of breach of immunities of the President." The Court's jurisprudence shows that it tends to focus on the possibility of the actual occurrence of the prejudice in order to assess whether "irreparable prejudice" could be established.

(2) The nature of the rights under threat

The Court's assessment of "irreparable prejudice" is the comprehensive consideration of all the involved circumstances. The Court's reasoning in its Order to reject the request for provisional measures in the *South-Eastern Greenland* case well demonstrated the point:

> "having regard to the character of the alleged rights in question, considered in relation to the natural characteristics of the territory in issue, even 'measures calculated to change the legal status of the territory' could not, according to the information now at the Court's disposal, affect the value of such alleged rights, once the Court in its judgment on the merits has recognized them as

appertaining to one or other of the Parties, and as, in any case, the consequences of such measures would not, in point of fact, be irreparable."[261]

The Court takes the concerning elements into consideration, such as the nature of the rights under threat, the nature of the infringement, the possibility of the occurring of the prejudice and its possible impact on the parties or even on the international community.

It is not difficult to find from the Court's jurisprudence that these circumstances influence the decision of "irreparable prejudice" interactively. As for the financial prejudice, the Court may require a higher degree of the possibility of the occurring of the prejudice. As for the non-financial prejudice like prejudice to human rights, environment, territorial sovereignty, a lower degree of possibility of the occurring of the prejudice is required. A comparative study of the *Nuclear Tests* cases and the *Aegean Sea Continental Shelf* case well demonstrates this observation. Because "the uncertain physical and genetic effects to which contamination exposes the people of NEW ZEALAND causes them acute apprehension, anxiety and concern and that there could be no possibility that the rights eroded by the holding of further tests could be fully restored in the event of a judgment in NEW ZEALAND's favor in these proceeding", the Court lied a quite low standard as to the possibility of the prejudice in the *Nuclear Tests* cases. It granted the provisional measures when the evidences "did not exclude the possibility" that damage might be shown to be caused by the infringement. Contrarily, as discussed in the last part of this dissertation, the alleged breach by TURKEY of the exclusivity of the right claimed by GREECE to acquire information concerning the natural resources of areas of continental shelf really can make the position of prospective judgment creditor incapable of full restoration in the *Aegean Sea Continental Shelf* case. The Court nevertheless refused to indicate provisional measures. It is inferred from the Court's rather detailed examination of the actual effects of the seismic exploration and the present state of the exploration that the Court seemed to expect a quite high degree of possibility of the occurring of the prejudice to grant provisional measures in the case mainly involving financial prejudice.

#### d) The irreparable prejudice to human life other than the subject matter of the main claim

It is a question worth noting whether the "irreparable prejudice" to the property and life other than the subject matter of the dispute in the main claim could be considered as one of the circumstances justifying provisional measures. To be more

261 Case concerning the *Legal Status of the South-Eastern Territory of Greenland*, (NORWAY v. DENMARK), (Provisional Measures), PCIJ, Series A/B, No. 48, p.288.

specific, can the prejudice to the life on the disputed territory justify the indication of provisional measures in a case that the sovereignty of the territory is the subject of the dispute in question? Could the "irreparable prejudice" to the related loss of life, property other than the subject matter of the dispute in the main claim also be considered as one of the circumstances requiring provisional measures? If the answer is yes, then to what extent could it be considered?

Judge *Oda* proposed this point in his declaration appending to the Court's Order to indicate provisional measures in the case concerning the *Land and Maritime Boundary between* CAMEROON *and* NIGERIA. He drew attention to the principle that provisional measures should be directed to the rights in issue in the case, and those of the State Parties to the case. He then held that the loss of life in the disputed area itself was without doubt distressing, however, it seemed not to be within the scope of the rights in issue in the present case.[262] This question is also relevant to the issue discussed in Chapter C, Part V of this dissertation, namely whether the Court has the power to indicate provisional measures purely to prevent the aggravation of the dispute. The Court seemed to admit that the right to protect the population in the disputed area was beyond the scope of the rights in issue. It stated that "the rights in issue in these proceedings are sovereign rights which the Parties claim over territory". However, it was quite concerned about the protection of the life in the disputed area. The Court admitted that irreparable prejudice was not existed to the rights in issue in the case while trying to ground the indication of provisional measures on the necessity to prevent aggravation or extension of the dispute.

It is interesting to find that the Court seemed to be trying to alternatively ground the indication of provisional measures on establishing the "irreparable prejudice". It stated that "the rights at issue in these proceedings are sovereign rights which the Parties claim over territory, and whereas these rights also concern persons; and whereas armed actions have regrettably occurred on territory which is the subject of proceedings before the Court".[263] The provisional measures aiming to prevent the aggravation of the dispute, independently of the existence of irreparable prejudice, have been adopted once by the Court. However, it is not appropriate and not so effective, as has been elaborated in Chapter C, Part V. Considering the unbearable gravity of the prejudice to human life, the Court widely interpreted the term "rights at issue in the proceedings" by adopting the dictum of "these rights also concern persons". In other words, the danger to human life was directly caused by the breach of the right at issue in the case, namely the breach of the sovereignty over the territory in dispute in the present case. As has been discussed in Chapter D, Part I, point 4, one of the prerequisites for the indication of provisional measures is that

262 Declaration of Judge *Oda* appending to the Order of 15 March 1996, case concerning the *Land and Maritime Boundary between CAMEROON and NIGERIA*, ICJ Reports 1996, p. 27.

263 Case concerning the *Land and Maritime Boundary between CAMEROON and NIGERIA*, (CAMEROON v. NIGERIA), (Provisional Measures), Order of 15 March 1996, ICJ Reports 1996, p. 22, para. 39.

the right sought to be protected by provisional measures is consistent with the subject of the main claim. The Court, in the case concerning the *Land and Maritime Boundary between* CAMEROON *and* NIGERIA, liberally interpreted this prerequisite. It is arguable that the right to protect its population from any military attacks could be regarded as an important part of the state's sovereignty rights over the territory. The great concern on the human life might be one of the important factors that influence the Court's decision on whether the "irreparable prejudice" justifying provisional measures exists or not.

## 2. Urgency

The term "urgency" is not explicitly provided in Article 41 of the STATUTE OF THE INTERNATIONAL COURT OF JUSTICE as the term "irreparable prejudice". However, taking the statutory purpose of provisional measures into consideration,[264] urgency is regarded as an implied requirement of the Court's power to indicate provisional measures. The judges in practice made the formal introduction of urgency into the law of provisional measures. The judges examined the circumstances to find whether the urgency of the matter could justify the indication of provisional measures.[265] The Court's Orders provided the concept of "urgency" as follows: "whereas provisional measures under Article 41 of the Statute are indicated pending the final decision of the Court on the merits of the case, and are therefore only justified if there is urgency in the sense that action prejudicial to the rights of either party is likely to be taken before such final decision is given."[266] It observed on the same issue in the case concerning *Certain Criminal Proceedings in* FRANCE:

> "whereas this power to indicate provisional measures has as its object to preserve the respective rights of the Parties, pending a decision of the Court, and presupposes that irreparable prejudice shall not be caused to rights which are the subject of dispute in judicial proceedings; whereas it follows that the

264 The Court's Order in the *Fisheries Jurisdiction* cases stated the statutory purpose of the Article 41 of the Statute as, "whereas the right of the Court to indicate provisional measures as provided for in Article 41 of the Statute has its object to preserve the respective rights of the Parties pending the decision of the Court, and presupposes that irreparable prejudice should not be caused to rights which are the subject of dispute in judicial proceedings, and that the Court's judgment should not be anticipated by reason of any initiative regarding the measures which are in issue."

265 *Rosenne*, *supra* note 5, p. 135.

266 *Passage through the Great Belt*, (FINLAND v. DENMARK), (Provisional Measures), Order of 29 July 1991, ICJ Reports 1991, p. 17, para. 23. See also *Pulp Mills* (ARGENTINA v. URUGUAY), Preliminary Objections, Order of 23 January 2007, ICJ Reports 2007, p. 11, para. 32

Court must be concerned to preserve by such measures the rights that may subsequently be adjudged by the Court to belong either to the Applicant or to the Respondent; and whereas such measures are only justified if there is urgency;"[267]

As observed by the authoritative writers, in the law relating to provisional measures in the INTERNATIONAL COURT OF JUSTICE, "urgency appears in two forms and with two meanings". "Urgency is a matter of procedure, relevant to the convening of the Court if not in session when the request is made. Urgency is a matter of substance among the circumstances justifying provisional measures."[268] As for the urgency in the form of procedure, Article 74, paragraph 2 of the Rules of the Court provides that the Court shall be convened immediately for the purpose of proceeding to a decision on the request for provisional measures as a matter of urgency. Article 54, paragraph 2 provides that when fixing the date for the opening of oral proceedings, priority shall be granted to oral proceedings on a request for provisional measures. On the other hand, the term "urgency" has been also used in the Court's Orders to require the expedient progress of procedure. The examination of jurisdiction over the merits is required to be operated in an expedient, *prima facie* manner, compatible with the requirement of urgency.[269] Urgency in the substantive sense, as one of the circumstances justifying provisional measures, is to be discussed in the following paragraphs.

### a) "urgency" and "irreparable prejudice"

"Urgency" is a concept closely related to "irreparable prejudice". Provisional measures are only justified if there is urgency in the sense that action prejudicial to the rights of either party is likely to be taken before such final decision is given. To some extent, the concept of urgency is developed upon the basis of "irreparable prejudice". As observed by *Rosenne*, "only if the Court finds that the potential damage would be irreparable, will urgency come to the forefront".[270]

---

267 Case concerning *Certain Criminal Proceedings in FRANCE* (DEMOCRATIC REPUBLIC OF THE CONGO V. FRANCE), (Provisional Measures), Order of 17 June 2003, ICJ Reports 2003, p. 107, para. 22.

268 *Rosenne, supra note* 5, p. 137. See also *Sztucki, supra* note 3, p. 112-113.

269 As in the case concerning the *Military and Paramilitary Activities in and against NICARAGUA*, the Court began the examination of substantive jurisdiction with the statement: "Having given the matter the fullest consideration compatible with the requirement of urgency imposed by a request for the indication of provisional measures ...", Order of 10 May 1984, ICJ Reports 1984, p.179, para.25.

270 *Rosenne, supra* note 5, p. 135.

*Thirlway* observed: "at the outset of proceedings, the date on which the final decision will be given is fairly unforeseeable."[271] He further observed that the assessment of urgency is "not an absolute, but may be a matter of degree".[272] It is a comprehensive consideration of all the surrounding circumstances, such as the nature of the alleged irreparable prejudice, the nature of the rights sought to be protected and the state of the proceedings when the request is instituted.

The Court's jurisprudence shows that "irreparable prejudice" and "urgency" are regarded as closely interrelated. The assessment of urgency is only necessary when the irreparable prejudice justifying provisional measures has been established. Furthermore, the nature, gravity and certainty of the alleged prejudice are relevant to the assessment of urgency. The Court's jurisprudence well demonstrates that, in cases that human rights are alleged to be under threat of prejudice, the Court seems to be in the opinion that the "irreparable prejudice" itself meanwhile shows the urgency. Whenever the evidences show that the alleged prejudice would probably occur in the near future, it could satisfy the requirement of urgency, taking into account the great irreparability of the alleged prejudice. The cases involving the execution of a national, the meaning and scope of whose rights are in question, the cases involving armed activities and the cases of human rights violation are good examples.[273] Due to the extreme irreparability of the rights at issue, the Court raises a liberal standard on "urgency" in these cases.

In the *Nuclear Tests* cases, the Government of AUSTRALIA (NEW ZEALAND) alleged that a series of nuclear tests had been carried out by the French Government in the Pacific during the period from 1966 to 1972; that there had been a growing body of reports, not denied by the French Government, to the effect that the French Government was planning to carry out a further series of nuclear tests in 1973; that the French Government indicated in a statement that, regardless of the protest made by AUSTRALIA and other countries, it did not envisage any cancellation or modification of the program of nuclear testing as originally planned. The Court held that these evidences could satisfy the "urgency" requirement. It stated as: "Those allegations give substance to the AUSTRALIA Government's contention that there is an *immediate possibility* of a further atmospheric nuclear test carried out by FRANCE in the Pacific."[274] (emphasis added)

---

271 *Thirlway*, *supra* note 44, p. 25.

272 *Ibid.* p. 26.

273 As in the cases concerning *the Trial of Pakistani Prisoners of War*, Order of 13 July 1973, *Application of the Convention on the Prevention and Punishment of Genocide*, *Land and Maritime Boundary between CAMEROON and NIGERIA*, *Vienna Convention on Consular Relations*, *LAGRAND*, *Avena and Other Mexican Nationals*, *Armed Activities on the Territory of the Congo*, *Application of the International Convention on the Elimination of All Forms of Racial Discrimination.*

274 *Nuclear Tests* (AUSTRALIA v. FRANCE), (Provisional Measures), Order of 22 June 1973, ICJ Reports 1973, p.104, para.26; (NEW ZEALAND v. FRANCE), (Provisional Measures), Order of 22 June 1973, ICJ Reports 1973, p.140, para.27.

In the case concerning the *Military and Paramilitary Activities in and against NICARAGUA*, the Court invoked NICARAGUA's claim that "the urgent need for the requested measure is shown by the fact that 'the lives and property of NICARAGUA citizens, the sovereignty of the State and the health and progress of the economy are all immediately at stake', that the UNITED STATES has given no indication that it is willing to 'desist from its unlawful actions', but is seeking the resources to continue and intensify its activities."[275] The Court accepted NICARAGUA's claim and indicated the provisional measures.

A similar situation was again met in the case concerning the *Application of the Convention on the Prevention and Punishment of the Crime of Genocide*, the Court invoked the allegation of BOSNIA-HERZEGOVINA that the facts stated in the Application showed that YUGOSLAVIA was committing acts of genocide and "there was no reason to believe that Yugoslavia would voluntarily desist from this course of conduct while the case was pending before the Court". The Court concluded that there was a grave risk of acts of genocide being committed and both parties were under a clear obligation to prevent the commission of any such acts in the future. It can be inferred that the "risk of acts of genocide being committed" was sufficient to justify provisional measures. No exact anticipation of the prejudice was required. When "irreparable prejudice" has been established, "urgency" is presumed to be existed. The burden of proof is on the Respondent State. If the Respondent State fails to establish that it would desist from the alleged actions before the final judgment, "urgency" is established.

In the case concerning the *Land and Maritime Boundary between CAMEROON and NIGERIA*, the Court reiterated that provisional measures were only justified if there was urgency.[276] However, the issue whether the killing of persons in the disputed area could also justify provisional measures overshadowed the assessment of urgency. Nevertheless, the Court's conclusion that "persons in the disputed area and, as a consequence, the rights of the Parties within that area are exposed to serious risk of further irreparable damage" implies its satisfaction with the urgency in the cases concerning human life.

For the cases in which the execution of a national, the meaning and scope of whose rights are in question, the issue of "urgency" is obvious. In the case

275 Case concerning the *Military and Paramilitary Activities in and against NICARAGUA*, (NICARAGUA v. USA), Order of 10 May 1984, ICJ Reports 1984, p. 182, para. 32.

276 "Whereas this power to indicate provisional measures has as its object to preserve the respective rights of the Parties, pending a decision of the Court, and presupposes that irreparable prejudice shall not be caused to rights which are the subject of dispute in judicial proceedings; whereas it follows that the Court must be concerned to preserve by such measures the rights which may subsequently be adjudged by the Court to belong either to the Applicant or to the Respondent; and whereas such measures are only justified if there is urgency;" Case concerning the *Land and Maritime Boundary between CAMEROON and NIGERIA*, (CAMEROON v. NIGERIA), (Provisional Measures), Order of 15 March 1996, ICJ Reports 1996, p. 22, para. 35.

concerning the *Vienna Convention on Consular Relations*, PARAGUAY asked the Court to consider its request as a matter of the greatest urgency "in view of the extreme gravity and immediacy of the threat that the authorities ... will execute a Paraguayan citizen". The Court reiterated that provisional measures were only justified if there was urgency. Finding that the execution of the Paraguayan citizen was ordered and such an execution would render it impossible for the Court to order the relief that PARAGUAY sought and caused irreparable harm to the rights it claimed. The Court accordingly concluded that "in the light of the aforementioned considerations, the Court finds that the circumstances require it to indicate, as a matter of urgency, provisional measures in accordance with Article 41 of its Statute". Similar assessment of "urgency" was proceeded by the Court in its Order in the case concerning *Avena and other Mexican Nationals* and the case *Request for Interpretation of the Judgment of 31 March 2004 in the Case Concerning Avena and Other Mexican Nationals.*

In the *LAGRAND* case, the extent of "urgency" was even greater. On 3 March 1999, at 9.00 a.m. (The Hague time), the representative of the German Government stated that Walter LAGRAND would be executed the same day at 3.00 p.m. (Phoenix time). He emphasized the extreme urgency of this situation and asked the Court to indicate, without holding any hearing, provisional measures *proprio motu*. The Court observed that it could exercise the power under Article 75, paragraph 1 of the Rules of the Court to "examine *proprio motu* whether the circumstances of the case require the indication of provisional measures…". It accordingly decided to indicate provisional measures, as a matter of greatest urgency and without holding oral hearings. Contrarily, the Court spent more attention to assess the requirement of urgency in the cases that the occurring of the irreparable prejudice is less certain.

b) The element of time

The time of the occurrence of the alleged prejudice is relevant to the assessment of urgency. Besides, the state of the proceedings when the request is made, and the estimated period likely to elapse before the decision of the Court or tribunal on the principal claim, is also an element relevant to the determination of the urgency of the matter.[277] The Court is not ready to indicate provisional measures if the final judgment could be rendered before the occurrence of the alleged prejudice.

However, neither the time when the alleged prejudice occurs, nor the time of when the request for provisional measures is instituted, can itself determine "urgency". What really matters is the situation at the moment of the instituting of the request, to be more specific, whether there is a possibility that the Respondent State will take any action that will cause irreparable prejudice to the rights of the

277 *Rosenne, supra* note 5, p. 135.

creditors of the prospective judgment before the delivery of the final judgment. This position was explicitly expressed by the Court in its Order in the *Passage through the Great Belt* case. It stated: "whereas provisional measures under Article 41 of the Statute are indicated 'pending the final decision' of the Court on the merits of the case, and are therefore only justified if there is urgency in the sense that action prejudicial to the rights of either party is likely to be taken before such final decision is given".[278]

In the case concerning the *Trial of* PAKISTAN *Prisoners of War*, PAKISTAN instituted proceedings against INDIA in respect of a dispute concerning charges of genocide against 195 PAKISTAN nationals, prisoners of war or civilian internees, in INDIA custody. PAKISTAN claimed that, under Article VI of the 1947 Convention on the Prevention and Punishment of the Crime of Genocide, to which PAKISTAN and INDIA were both parties, exclusive jurisdiction in respect of such prisoners was vested in PAKISTAN. PAKISTAN therefore requested the Court to indicate provisional measures to protect the process of repatriation of the prisoners from interruption by virtue of charges of genocide against a certain number of individuals detained in INDIA and to refrain INDIA from transferring these prisoners to Bangladesh for trial till such time as PAKISTAN's claim to exclusive jurisdiction in this respect had been adjudged by the Court. On 11 July 1973, PAKISTAN informed the Court that negotiations would soon take place between PAKISTAN and INDIA on issues that were the subject of the Application and asked the Court to postpone further consideration of its request for interim measures in order to facilitate those negotiations. The Court stated: "it is of the essence of a request for interim measures of protection that it asks for a decision by the Court as a matter of urgency, as it is expressly recognized by the Court in Article 66, paragraph 2, of the Rules of the Court;" The Court concluded: "whereas it is of the essence of a request for interim measures of protection that it asks for a decision by the Court as a matter of urgency; as is expressly recognized by the Court in Article 66, paragraph 2, of its Rules of Court;[279] Whereas the fact that the Government of PAKISTAN now asks the Court to postpone further consideration of its request … signifies that the Court no longer has before it a request for interim measures which is to be treated as a matter of urgency; and whereas the Court is not therefore called upon to pronounce upon the said request."[280]

The Court accordingly did not continue to consider the request for provisional measures and decided that the proceedings shall first be addressed to the question of the jurisdiction of the Court to entertain the dispute.

---

278 *Passage through the Great Belt* (FINLAND v. DENMARK), (Provisional Measures), Order of 29 July 1991, ICJ Reports 1991, p. 17, para. 23.

279 The Rules of the Court 1972.

280 Case concerning the *Trial of Pakistani Prisoners of War* (PAKISTAN v. INDIA), (Provisional Measures), Order of 13 July 1973, ICJ Reports 1973, p. 330, para. 13, 14.

## E. The SECURITY COUNCIL RESOLUTION and the indication of provisional measures

Besides the regular examination of the circumstances as above discussed, the Court's jurisprudence on provisional measures raises one special issue: Does the SECURITY COUNCIL RESOLUTION influence the Court's decision on provisional measures? How does the Court exercise the power to indicate provisional measures when the same dispute is simultaneously presented before the SECURITY COUNCIL? The concurrent jurisdiction of the INTERNATIONAL COURT OF JUSTICE and the SECURITY COUNCIL has gained great academic attention since the inter-state disputes usually involve both legal and political aspects and are frequently presented to the legal and political forums simultaneously. This difficulty also occurs when the Court is considering the request for provisional measures.

### I. The cases

#### 1. The Aegean Sea Continental Shelf case

In the *Aegean Sea Continental Shelf* case, GREECE filed an Application, on 10 August 1976, to institute proceedings against TURKEY in respect of a dispute concerning the delimitation of the continental shelf appertaining to both states in the Aegean Sea, and concerning the respective legal rights of the two States to explore and exploit the continental shelf of the Aegean. On the same day, GREECE requested the indication of provisional measures. Simultaneously with the proceedings before the Court in respect of the request for interim measures of protection, the UNITED NATIONS SECURITY COUNCIL had also been seised of the dispute. On 25 August, the SECURITY COUNCIL adopted a resolution urging both governments "to do everything in their power to reduce the present tensions in the area so that the negotiating process may be facilitated" and calling for the resumption of "direct negotiations over their differences". In the recitals to the resolution, the SECURITY COUNCIL recalled the governments "the principles of the Charter of the United Nations concerning the peaceful settlements of disputes" and the need "to respect each other's international rights and obligations and to avoid any incident which might lead to the aggravation of the situation".

 E. The SECURITY COUNCIL RESOLUTION and the indication of provisional measures

The Court, taking "cognizance of the fact that the United Nations Security Council also has been seized of the dispute", cited the statements of both Foreign Ministers that showed both States' willingness to accept the resolution.[284] Then the Court delivered the following paragraph:

> "whereas both GREECE and TURKEY, as Members of the United Nations, have expressly recognized the responsibility of the Security Council for the maintenance of international peace and security; whereas, in the above-mentioned resolution, the Security Council has recalled to them their obligations under the United Nations Charter with respect to the peaceful settlement of disputes, ... these obligations are clearly imperative in regard to their present dispute ... and it is not to be presumed that either State will fail to heed its obligations under the Charter of the United Nations or fail to heed to the recommendation of the Security Council addressed to them with respect to their present dispute. ... Accordingly, it is not necessary for the Court to decide the question whether Article 41 of the Statute confers upon it the power to indicate interim measures of protection for the sole purpose of preventing the aggravation or extension of the dispute."[285]

The Court then found, by 12 votes to 1, that the circumstances were not such as to require the exercise of its power to indicate interim measures of protection. The Court's response to the Greek Government's request for interim measures could be divided into two parts. In the first place, the Court analyzed from the perspective of the lack of irreparable prejudice. It stated that "in the present instance, the alleged breach by TURKEY of the exclusivity of the right claimed by GREECE to acquire information concerning the natural resources of areas of continental shelf, if it were established, is one that might be capable of reparation by appropriate means;"[286] Accordingly the Court was unable to find such a risk of irreparable prejudice which requires provisional measures. In the second place, the Court went on to deal with GREECE's request to indicate interim measures of protection in order to prevent the aggravation or extension of the dispute, independently of its request regarding the

284 "Whereas the Foreign Minister of GREECE stated in the SECURITY COUNCIL following the adoption of resolution 395(1976) that he trusted that the resolution would 'clear away the obstacles to a resumption of the dialogue with TURKEY and lead to the solution of the problem of the continental shelf by peaceful means'; and whereas the Foreign Minister of TURKEY stated, following the adoption of the resolution, that the paragraph of the resolution calling for a resumption of direct negotiations was 'fully in accord with the policy that has been consistently pursued by TURKEY", *Aegean Sea Continental Shelf* (GREECE v. TURKEY), Provisional Measures, Order of 11 September 1976, ICJ Reports 1976, p. 13, para. 40.

285 *Aegean Sea Continental Shelf* (GREECE v. TURKEY), Provisional Measures, Order of 11 September 1976, ICJ Reports 1976, p. 13, para. 41, 42.

286 *Ibid.*, p.11, para.33.

preservation of its rights. The Court noted that it would need to determine whether, under Article 41 of the Statute, the Court has such an independent power to indicate interim measures to prevent the aggravation of the dispute. The Court cited the SECURITY COUNCIL RESOLUTION and the statements of both the FOREIGN MINISTERS in the SECURITY COUNCIL. The statements implied that both States would obey the obligations under the CHARTER OF THE UNITED NATIONS and the SECURITY COUNCIL RESOLUTION, therefore there would be no threat of aggravation or extension of the dispute. Accordingly the Court did not consider it necessary to answer the question "whether Article 41 of the Statute confers upon it the power to indicate interim measures of protection for the sole purpose of preventing the aggravation or extension of a dispute" in this case.

Although the Court expressed no explicit opinion on the issue of the concurrent jurisdiction between the SECURITY COUNCIL and the Court, either on the issue of the possible influence that the SECURITY COUNCIL RESOLUTION might have on the Court's indication of provisional measures, it is observed from the reasoning of the Court's Order quoted above, that the Court was regarding the SECURITY COUNCIL RESOLUTION merely as one of the *circumstances* that shall be taken into consideration. Considering the recalling of the parties' obligations under the UNITED NATIONS CHARTER with respect to the peaceful settlement of disputes and the plausible expectation of both parties to respect the SECURITY COUNCIL RESOLUTION with good will, the Court was of the opinion that there would rarely be any possibility of aggravation of a dispute, regardless whether the Court was statutorily conferred any power to indicate provisional measures for the sole purpose of preventing the aggravation of a dispute. There was no implication, as to the question whether the Court was refraining from exercising its jurisdiction, due to the fact that the case was also seised by the SECURITY COUNCIL. To be more specific, the Court's Order in this case did not reflect any opinion that the exercise of its power under Article 41 of the Statute could be precluded or interfered by the SECURITY COUNCIL's simultaneous exercising of jurisdiction.

The separate and dissenting opinions of the judges appending to the Court's Order demonstrated the above assertion. Judge Jiménez de *Aréchaga*, in his separate opinion, noted that the question of the jurisdiction of the Court could only be regarded as one among the circumstances and the essential justification for provisional measures was the threat of irreparable prejudice. He argued that "the Court's specific power under Article 41 of the Statute is directed to the preservation of rights 'sub-judice' and does not consist in a police power over the maintenance of international peace nor in a general competence to make recommendations relating to peaceful settlement of disputes."[287]

Judge *Lachs*, in his separate opinion, called for the Court's "own constructive, albeit indirect, contribution, helping to pave the way to the friendly resolution of a

---

287 Separate Opinion of Judge Jiménez de *Aréchaga* appending to the Order of 11 September 1976, *Aegean Sea Continental Shelf*, Provisional Measures, ICJ Reports 1976, p. 16.

dangerous dispute". He noted that there was no statutory bar to its (the Court's) spelling out the legal consequences of the SECURITY COUNCIL RESOLUTION and the official statements of the representatives of the two States. The pronouncements of the Council did not dispense the Court, an independent judicial organ, from expressing its own view on the serious situation in the disputed area.[288]

Judge *Tarazí* specifically expressed his opinion on the role of the Court as an organ of the UNITED NATIONS and its place in the process of peaceful settlement of international disputes. He observed that, "at the same time it requested the Court to indicate interim measures, GREECE turned to the Security Council to request it to examine the situation which it had already described in the Application. This was not an example of the simultaneous use of two parallel remedies, inasmuch as the Security Council, unlike the Court, is a political organ. The rule *electa una via* did not have to be applied." He continued that "the Security Council bears an essential responsibility for the maintenance of international peace and security. The Court, if the circumstances so require, ought to collaborate in the accomplishment of this fundamental mission."[289]

Judge *Elias* more elaborately presented this position. He observed that both organs were competent each in its own sphere to deal with the matter submitted to it and come to its own conclusions thereon.[290]

## 2. The case concerning UNITED STATES Diplomatic and Consular Staff in Tehran

The case concerning *UNITED STATES Diplomatic and Consular Staff in Tehran* is another concerned case. The dispute arose from the Iranian demonstrators' seizure and holding as hostages of the members of the US diplomatic and consular staff in Tehran. It was asserted by the US Government that the Iranian Government failed to take any measures to lessen the tension. On 29 November 1979, the UNITED STATES Government instituted proceedings at both the SECURITY COUNCIL and the INTERNATIONAL COURT OF JUSTICE. On the same day, the UNITED STATES requested provisional measures. IRAN did not appear at the Court. It sent a letter to the Court, stating that the question of the hostages "represents only a marginal and secondary aspect of an overall problem" and that "the Court cannot examine the American Application divorced from its proper context, namely the whole political dossier of the relations between IRAN and the United States over the last 25

288 Separate Opinion of Judge *Lachs* appending to the Order of 11 September 1976, *ibid.*, p. 20.

289 Separate Opinion of Judge *Tarazi* appending to the Order of 11 September 1976, *ibid.*, p. 33.

290 Separate Opinion of Judge *Elias* appending to the Order of 11 September 1976, *ibid.*, p. 28.

years."[291] Furthermore, it asserted that the Islamic revolution was a "revolution of a whole oppressed nation" and "any examination of the numerous repercussions thereof" was "a matter essentially and directly within the national sovereignty of IRAN."[292] On 15 December 1979, the Court held that "no provision of the Statute or Rules contemplates that the Court should decline to take cognizance of one aspect of a dispute merely because that dispute has other aspects, however important".[293] The Court went on to state that, since the present dispute involved the interpretation or application of multilateral conventions, it was "one which by its very nature falls within international jurisdiction".[294] It accordingly granted the provisional measures requested by the UNITED STATES.

The SECURITY COUNCIL adopted Resolution 457(1979) on 4 December. The Resolution stated that the level of tension between IRAN and the UNITED STATES could have grave consequences for international peace and security and called for the immediate release of the staff of the embassy. It also requested the SECRETARY-GENERAL to lend his good offices for the immediate implementation of the resolution and to take all appropriate measures to that end.

In the judgment on the merits, the Court elaborated on the concurrent jurisdiction of the INTERNATIONAL COURT OF JUSTICE and the SECURITY COUNCIL:

> "in the preamble to this second resolution the Security Council expressly took into account the Court's Order of 15 December 1979 indicating provisional measures; and it does not seem to have occurred to any member of the Council that there was or could be anything irregular in the *simultaneous* exercise of their *respective* function by the Court and the Security Council. Nor is there in this any cause for surprise. Whereas Article 12 of the Charter expressly forbids the General Assembly to make any recommendation with regard to a dispute or situation while the Security Council is exercising its functions in respect of that dispute or situation, no such restriction is placed on the functioning of the Court by any provision of either the Charter or the Statute of the Court. The reasons are clear. It is for the Court, the principle judicial organ of the United Nations, to resolve any legal questions that may be in issue between parties to a dispute; and the resolution of such legal questions by the Court may be an important, and sometimes decisive, factor in promoting peaceful settlement of the dispute. ... It follows that neither the mandate given by the Security

291 *United States Diplomatic and Consular Staff in Tehran* (UNITED STATES OF AMERICA v. IRAN), (Provisional Measures), Order of 15 December 1979, ICJ Reports 1979, p. 11, para.3.

292 *Ibid.*

293 *United States Diplomatic and Consular Staff in Tehran* (UNITED STATES OF AMERICA v. IRAN), (Provisional Measures), Order of 15 December 1979, ICJ Reports 1979, p. 15.

294 *United States Diplomatic and Consular Staff in Tehran* (UNITED STATES OF AMRICA v. IRAN), (Provisional Measures), Order of 15 December 1979, ICJ Reports 1979, p. 16, para.25.

> Council to the Secretary-General in Resolution 457 and 461 of 1979, nor the setting up of the Commission by the Secretary-General, can be considered as constituting any obstacle to the exercise of the Court's jurisdiction in the present case."[295]

The Court's statement reaffirmed its position in the *Aegean Sea Continental Shelf* case: The prior SECURITY COUNCIL RESOLUTION does not preclude the Court from exercising its judicial jurisdiction. Accordingly the Court's jurisdiction, in particular, its power to indicate provisional measures shall not be interfered by the simultaneous jurisdiction of the SECURITY COUNCIL.

### 3. The case concerning Military and Paramilitary in and against NICARAGUA

In the case concerning *Military and Paramilitary in and against* NICARAGUA, the question of the simultaneous jurisdiction between the Court (the Court's jurisdiction to indicate provisional measures, specifically in this dissertation) and the SECURITY COUNCIL was explicitly taken by the Respondent State as one of the grounds to challenge the admissibility of the request for provisional measures. NICARAGUA instituted proceedings in the SECURITY COUNCIL on 4 April 1984. The proceedings led to the SECURITY COUNCIL RESOLUTION 530 on 19 May, 1983, which recalled the Charter principles governing the peaceful settlement of disputes and reaffirmed "the right of NICARAGUA and of all other countries of the area to live in peace and security, free from outside interference."[296]

NICARAGUA instituted proceedings against the UNITED STATES before the Court, on 9 April 1984. It claimed that the UNITED STATES were using military force against NICARAGUA and intervening in NICARAGUA's internal affairs, in violation of NICARAGUA's sovereignty, territorial integrity and political independence and of the most fundamental and universally-accepted principles of international law. NICARAGUA simultaneously requested the Court to indicate provisional measures to ask the UNITED STATES to cease and desist from any further military and paramilitary activities in and against NICARAGUA.

At the hearings of the proceedings of provisional measures, the UNITED STATES disputed the admissibility of the request for provisional measures on the ground[297]

295 Case Concerning *United States Diplomatic and Consular Staff in Tehran* (USA v.IRAN), (Merits), ICJ Reports 1980, p.21, para. 40, p. 23-24, para. 44.

296 See UN Doc. S/16463.

297 Challenges to the admissibility of the request for provisional measures were also raised on two other grounds: Firstly, NICARAGUA's request for provisional measures is inextricably linked to the rights and interests of the other States of Central America, and that an indication of such measures would interfere with the Contadora negotiations. These other Central American States are indispensable parties in whose absence the Court cannot

that "NICARAGUA's Application appears on its face to request a definitive legal determination regarding an alleged illegal use of armed force in the midst of on-going hostilities. In the circumstances of this case, where the United Nations and the Organization of American States have approved the Contadora process, such questions regarding the use of force during hostilities are more properly committed to resolution by the political organs of the United Nations and of the Organization of American States".[298]

The UNITED STATES observed that "the primary responsibility for the maintenance of international peace and security is assigned by the Charter of the United Nations to the Security Council", that Chapter VIII of the Charter provides for regional arrangements for the maintenance of international peace and security, and that while all situations involving the threat or use of force "necessarily involve Article 2(4) and Article 51 of the United Nations Charter or other issues of law or legally significant fact", nevertheless "that does not mean that this Court can, or should, take cognizance of the legal aspects of those situations in the midst of hostilities, and while the political processes of the United Nations and the OAS (the Organization of American States) are still engaged".[299]

The Court invoked the fact that the Agent of NICARAGUA "referred to previous decisions of the Court as establishing the principle that the Court is not required to decline to take cognizance of one aspect of a dispute merely because that dispute has other aspects, and that the Court should not decline an essentially judicial task merely because the question before the Court is intertwined with political question". The Court accordingly rejected the UNITED STATES' request to terminate the proceedings on the main Application and on the request for the indication of provisional measures by the removal of the case from the list.

During the proceedings on provisional measures, the Court provided no more detailed reasoning to reject the UNITED STATES' contention that the Court's jurisdiction should be precluded by the political processes of the SECURITY COUNCIL. However, the UNITED STATES at the proceedings on the merits again raised this issue. The UNITED STATES disputed the admissibility of the Application. According to the UNITED STATES, the unlawful use of armed force against NICARAGUA as alleged by NICARAGUA, was "a matter which is committed by the Charter and by practice to the competence of other organs, in particular the United

properly proceed. Case concerning *Military and Paramilitary Activities in and against NICARAGUA* (NICARAGUA v. USA), (Provisional Measures), Order of 10 May 1984, ICJ Reports 1984, p. 184, para. 35; Secondly, that "Contadora itself is a properly instituted regional process seeking to resolve complex and interrelated social, political, and economic issues, as well as security matters underlying the current turmoil in Central America. This Court cannot take cognizance of NICARAGUA's Application or indicate the interim measures NICARAGUA requests without detrimentally affecting that process in unpredictable and irremediable ways", p. 184-185, para. 36.

298 *Ibid.*, p. 185, para. 37.

299 *Ibid.*.

Nations Security Council",[300] accordingly the allegations were confined to the political organs for consideration and determination. Moreover, the UNITED STATES asserted that "since NICARAGUA's Application in effect asks the Court for a judgment in all material respects identical to the decision which the Security Council did not take, it amounts to an appeal from an adverse consideration in the Security Council."[301]

The Court rejected these allegations. It observed that "it was asked to pass on judgment on certain legal aspects of a situation which have also been considered by the Security Council, a procedure which is entirely consonant with its position as the principle judicial organ of the United Nations."[302] Even when the questions presented involve issues of political elements, they are, according to the Court, "issues which it has competence, and is equipped, to determine."[303]

With reference to the UNITED STATES' argument that the seeking for a judgment amounted to an appeal from an adverse consideration in the SECURITY COUNCIL, the Court answered that the responsibility conferred upon the SECURITY COUNCIL for the maintenance of international peace and security was "primary", but not "exclusive". It concluded that the Council had functions of a political nature assigned to it and the Court exercised purely judicial functions, both organs could perform their separate but complementary functions with respect to the same event.[304]

This observation reaffirmed the Court's position in the last two precedents. The Court's exercising of jurisdiction (specifically the power to indicate provisional measures in this dissertation) is not precluded either because the dispute involves political elements, or because the SECURITY COUNCIL has simultaneously seised of the same dispute.[305]

The Court further observed that even if the SECURITY COUNCIL was seised of the matter, not under Chapter VI but under Chapter VII of the Charter, both organs were still competent to separately perform their functions. It stated as follows: "until the Security Council makes a determination under Article 39, a dispute remains to be dealt with by the methods of peaceful settlement provided under Article 33, including judicial settlement; and even after a determination under Article 39, there is no necessary inconsistency between Security Council action and adjudication by

300 Case concerning *Military and Paramilitary Activities in and against NICARAGUA* (NICARAGUA v. USA), (Jurisdiction of the Court and Admissibility of the Application), Order of 26 November 1984, ICJ Reports 1984, p. 412-413, para. 47.

301 *Ibid.*, p. 432-433, para. 91.

302 *Ibid.*, p. 436.

303 Case concerning the *Military and Paramilitary Activities in and against NICARAGUA* (NICARAGUA v. USA), (Merits), ICJ Reports1986, p. 28.

304 *Ibid.*, p. 435.

305 The Court's jurisprudence in this respective is concluded by the literature as: the principle in municipal law such as the litispendence principle and the political doctrine could not be analogously applied in international plane.

the Court. From a juridical standpoint, the decisions of the Court and the actions of the Security Council are entirely separate."[306]

**4. The Bosnian Genocide case**

In the *Bosnian Genocide* case, BOSNIA-HERZEGOVINA asked the Court to adjudge and declare that YUGOSLAVIA had committed acts of genocide and was in violation of customary and treaty law regarding the non-use of force.[307] With respect to the same dispute, the SECURITY COUNCIL had adopted the resolution 713(1991) which imposed an arms embargo on YUGOSLAVIA. BOSNIA-HERZEGOVINA asserted in its Application that under the circumstances, it had the sovereign right under UNITED NATIONS CHARTER Article 51 and customary international law to defend itself and request the immediate assistance of any State to come to its defense. Accordingly it asked the Court to adjudge and declare that the SECURITY COUNCIL RESOLUTION 713(1991) "must be construed in a manner that shall not impair the inherent right of individual or collective self-defense of Bosnia and Herzegovina";[308] It also asked the Court to declare that "the Security Council resolution 713(1991) and all subsequent Security Council resolutions referring thereto or reaffirming thereof must not be construed to impose an arms embargo upon Bosnia and Herzegovina, as required by Article 24(1) and 51 of the United Nations Charter and in accordance with the customary doctrine of *ultra vires*".[309]

BOSNIA and HERZEGOVINA requested the Court to indicate provisional measures to the effect that YUGOSLAVIA (SERBIA and MONTENEGRO) immediately cease and desist from all acts of genocide, all military or paramilitary activities against BOSNIA and HERZEGOVINA and cease and desist from any support to such activities. On the other hand, it requested that "under the current circumstances, the Government of Bosnia and Herzegovina has the right to seek and receive support from other States in order to defend itself and its people, including by means of immediately obtaining military weapons, equipment, supplies."[310] The actual effect of the provisional measures as requested would be adverse to the SECURITY COUNCIL RESOLUTION 713(1991). YUGOSLAVIA in response contended that "so long as the Security Council is acting in accordance with Article 25 and under that Charter,[311] it would be premature and inappropriate for the Court to indicate

---

306 *Supra* note 300, p.432.

307 *Bosnian Genocide* (BOSNIA and HERZEGOVINA v. YUGOSLAVIA (SERBIA and MONTENEGRO)), (Provisional Measures), Order of 8 April 1993, ICJ Reports 1993, p. 4-7, para. 1,2.

308 *Ibid.*, p. 6.

309 *Ibid.*.

310 *Ibid.*, p.8, para.3.

311 Article 25 of the UNITED NATIONS Charter provides that "the Members of the UNITED NATIONS agree to accept and carry out the decisions of the SECURITY COUNCIL in

provisional measures, and certainly provisional measures of the type which have been requested."[312] The Court observed that this objection was "primarily addressed to those measures requested by Bosnia-Herzegovina which go beyond matters within the scope of the Genocide Convention, and which for that reason the Court cannot consider". The Court held that it "ought not to indicate measures for the protection of any disputed rights other than those which might ultimately form the basis of a judgment in the exercise of that jurisdiction and accordingly the Court will confine its examination of the measures requested, and of the grounds asserted for the request for such measures, to those which fall within the scope of the Genocide Convention."[313] Subsequently, the Court granted the Bosnian requests with regard to genocide while rejecting the Bosnian requests with regard to its rights to defend itself and request the immediate assistance of any State to come to its defense.

The Bosnian Government asserted that "it would be premature and inappropriate for the Court to indicate provisional measures", in consideration of the SECURITY COUNCIL RESOLUTION. Although it is a quite reasonable assertion that the Bosnian requests to defend itself and request the military assistance from any State would be against the SECURITY COUNCIL RESOLUTION 713(1991), the Court did not need to provide any comment on the Bosnian assertion. It invoked the "lack of jurisdiction" as the ground of not examining the measures requested with regard to BOSNIA's right of self-defense. The Court then adopted its observation made in the case concerning *Maritime and Paramilitary in and against NICARAGUA*: "The Council has functions of a political nature assigned to it, whereas the Court exercises purely judicial functions. Both organs can therefore perform their separate but complementary functions with respect to the same events".[314] This observation showed the Court's inclination to simultaneously entertain the dispute if the Court's jurisdiction had not been restricted to the Genocide Convention. It is worth noting that, the *NICARAGUA* dictum did not actually touch on the question of the conflict between the provisional measures as requested and the SECURITY COUNCIL RESOLUTION. In the *Aegean Sea Continental Shelf* case, case concerning the *UNITED STATES Diplomatic and Consular Staff* and the case concerning *Military and Paramilitary Activities in and against* NICARAGUA, the provisional measures as requested were not inconsistent with the SECURITY COUNCIL RESOLUTION. Different from these three cases, the provisional measures requested by BOSNIA and HERZEGOVINA would have the effect of conflicting with the effect of conflicting with the SECURITY COUNCIL RESOLUTION. A problem that had not occurred before was then presented to the Court. Can the Court indicate provisional measures that

accordance with the present Charter." This article is the legal basis of the binding force of the SECURITY COUNCIL decisions.

312 *Supra* note 288, p.18-19, para.33.

313 *Ibid.*, p.19, para.35.

314 *Ibid.*, p.19, para.33.

are directly conflicting with the SECURITY COUNCIL RESOLUTION? It is widely accepted that both the Court and the SECURITY COUNCIL can perform their separate but complementary functions with respect to the same dispute, as we could infer from the provisions in the UNITED NATIONS CHARTER and also from the Court's jurisprudence. However, the question of how the Court could deal with the requests of provisional measures that are in conflict with the SECURITY COUNCIL RESOLUTION remained to be unsettled. Although the Court was in the position not to follow YUGOSLAVIA's contention that the Court ought to defer to the Council, the "restriction of jurisdiction with regard to Genocide" in effect relieved the Court of any examination of the requests for provisional measures with regard to BOSNIA HERZEGOVINA's right of self-defense. This in turn had the consequence of not directly conflicting with the SECURITY COUNCIL RESOLUTION 713(1991). The Court, rejected the Respondent's argument that the involvement of the SECURITY COUNCIL, even in disputes falling under UN Chapter VII, is an obstacle to the consideration of a case under Article 41. Nevertheless, the Court's position seemed to be equivocal. The Court did not touch on an important question - had the Court had the jurisdiction over the issue of BOSNIA HERZEGOVINA's right to self-defense, would it have exercised the power to indicate provisional measures that would probably conflict with the SECURITY COUNCIL RESOLUTION 713(1991)?

## 5. The case concerning Armed Activities on the Territory of the CONGO

In the case concerning *Armed Activities on the Territory of the CONGO*, UGANDA argued that the request for provisional measures was inadmissible as well as moot because the CONGO's request for provisional measures concerned essentially the same issues as the SECURITY COUNCIL RESOLUTION 1304(2000), which UGANDA fully accepted and was complying with. The Court did not accept this argument. With regard to this argument, the Court observed that the "Security Council resolution 1304(2000) and the measures taken in its implementation, do not preclude the Court from acting in accordance with its Statute and with the Rules of Court."[315] The Court again quoted the observation that "both organs can therefore perform their separate but complementary functions with respect to the same events".[316] The Court then turned to the *Lockerbie* cases and stated that, in the

315 Case concerning *Armed Activities on the Territory of the CONGO* (CONGO v. UGANDA), (Provisional Measures), Order of 1 July 2000, ICJ Reports 2000, p.126, para.36.

316 Case concerning the *Military and Paramilitary Activities in and against NICARAGUA* (NICARAGUA v. USA), (Jurisdiction and Admissibility), Judgment of 26 November 1984, ICJ Report 1984, p.434-435, para.95.
*Bosnian Genocide* (BOSNIA and HERZEGOVINA v. YUGOSLAVIA (SERBIA and MONTENEGRO)), (Provisional measures), Order of 8 April 1993, ICJ Reports 1993, p.19, para.33.

present case the SECURITY COUNCIL had taken no decision which would *prima facie* preclude the rights claimed by the CONGO from 'being regarded as appropriate for protection by the indication of provisional measures'.[317]

### 6. *Lockerbie* cases

The *Lockerbie* cases arose from the aerial crash of Pan Am Flight 103 that occurred over LOCKERBIE, SCOTLAND, on 21 December, 1988. According to the US and UK investigations, two Libyan nationals were responsible for the bombing of the Flight. The SECURITY COUNCIL accordingly adopted resolution 731(1992) which called for the extradition of the suspects. LIBYA refused to extradite the two nationals and filed in the REGISTRY OF THE INTERNATIONAL COURT OF JUSTICE on 3 March 1992, instituting proceedings against the UNITED STATES and the UNITED KINGDOM respectively.[318] In the Applications LIBYA stated that "in November 1991, the Lord Advocate of Scotland charged two Libyan nationals (the 'accused') alleging, *inter alia*, that they had caused a bomb to be placed aboard [that flight] ... which bomb had exploded causing the airplane to crash". LIBYA referred to Article 1 of the Montreal Convention, contending that the acts alleged by the indictment constituted an offence within the meaning of that provision. LIBYA claimed that the Montreal Convention was the only appropriate convention in force between the Parties dealing with such offences, and that the UNITED STATES and the UNITED KINGDOM were bound by their legal obligations under the Montreal Convention, which required them to act in accordance with the Convention, with respect to the matter involving Pan Am flight 103 and the accused. LIBYA submitted that, while it had taken all necessary steps to try the suspects and had itself fully complied with all of its own obligations under the Montreal Convention,[319] the UNITED STATES and the

---

317 Case concerning *Armed Activities on the Territory of the Congo* (DEMOCRATIC REPUBLIC OF THE CONGO v. BELGIUM), (Provisional Measures), Order of 1 July 2000, ICJ Reports 2000, p. 126-127, para. 36, para. 38.

318 *Lockerbie*, (LIBYA v. US), (Provisional Measures), Order of 14 April 1992, ICJ Reports 1992, p.115; (LIBYA v. UK), (Provisional Measures), Order of 14 April 1992, ICJ Reports 1992, p.4.

319 Libya asserted that it had itself fully complied with its own obligations under the Montreal Convention as provided for by Article 5 and 8. Article 5(2) provides that: "Each Contracting State shall take such measures as may be necessary to establish its jurisdiction over the offences mentioned in [the Convention], in the case where the alleged offender is present in its territory and it does not extradite him pursuant to Article 8"; Article 5(3) provides that: "This Convention does not exclude any criminal jurisdiction exercised in accordance with national law." Article 8(2) provides that: "If a Contracting State which makes extradition conditional on the existence of a treaty receives a request for extradition from another Contracting State with which it has no extradition treaty, it may at its option consider this Convention as the basis for extradition in respect of the offences. Extradition

UNITED KINGDOM had breached and were continuing to breach their obligations to LIBYA. LIBYA asked the Court to adjudge and declare:

(a) that LIBYA has fully complied with all of its obligations under the Montreal Convention;

(b) that the UNITED STATES (UNITED KINGDOM) has breached, and is continuing to breach, its legal obligations to LIBYA under Article 5(2), 5(3), 7, 8(2), and 11 of the Montreal Convention; and

(c) that the UNITED STATES (UNITED KINGDOM) is under a legal obligation immediately to cease and desist from such breaches and from the use of any and all force or threats against LIBYA, including the threat of force against LIBYA, and from all violations of the sovereignty, territorial integrity, and the political independence of LIBYA.[320]

Later on 3 March 1992, the day on which the Application was filed, the Libyan Government also filed an "urgent request that the Court indicate provisional measures which ought to be taken promptly to preserve the right of Libya".[321] In its request, LIBYA, referring to the statement of facts in its Application, alleged that "the United States (United Kingdom) was actively seeking to bypass the provisions of the Montreal Convention by threatening various actions against Libya in order to compel Libya, in violation of the Convention, to surrender its two accused nationals". LIBYA affirmed that "the United States (United Kingdom) had indicated that it might seek or impose economic, air and other sanctions against Libya if Libya did not comply with the demands of the United States (United Kingdom), and that the latter had refused to rule out the use of armed force against Libya." LIBYA further asserted that "only by granting provisional measures enjoining the United States (United Kingdom) from taking such actions against Libya was it possible to prevent Libya's rights from being irreparably prejudiced".[322] According to LIBYA's assertion, the coercive actions against LIBYA would force LIBYA to surrender the two accused nationals. This would irreparably prejudice LIBYA's right under the Montreal Convention to freely choose to extradite the accused or prosecute them at its national courts. Once the accused nationals had been extradited, the option of prosecuting them by the national courts would in effect disappear.

LIBYA requested the Court to indicate provisional measures to "enjoin the United States from taking any action capable of having a prejudicial effect on the Court's decision in the case and to refrain from taking any step that might aggravate or extend the dispute, as would surely happen if sanctions were imposed against Libya

---

shall be subject to the other conditions provided by the law of the requested State."

320 *Ibid.*, (LIBYA v. US), Order of 14 April 1992, ICJ Reports 1992, p.117-118, para.7; (LIBYA v. UK), Order of 14 April 1992, ICJ Reports 1992, p.6-7, para.7.

321 *Ibid.*, (LIBYA v. US), Order of 14 April 1992, ICJ Reports 1992, p.118, para.8; (LIBYA v. UK), Order of 14 April 1992, ICJ Reports 1992, p.7, para.8.

322 *Ibid.*, (LIBYA v. US), Order of 14 April 1992, ICJ Reports 1992, p.118, para.9; (LIBYA v. UK), Order of 14 April 1992, ICJ Reports 1992, p.7, para.9.

or force were employed."[323] In the course of the oral proceedings, reference was made by both sides to the possibility of sanctions being imminently imposed by the SECURITY COUNCIL on LIBYA in order to require it to surrender the accused to the UNITED STATES or the UNITED KINGDOM. LIBYA accordingly stressed that "provisional measures were urgently required to cause the United States (United Kingdom) to abstain from any action capable of having a prejudicial effect on the Court's decision, and more specifically to refrain from *taking any initiative within the Security Council* for the purpose of impairing that right to exercise jurisdiction, which Libya asks the Court to recognize".[324](emphasis added)

However, on 31 March 1992 (three days after the close of the hearings), the SECURITY COUNCIL adopted RESOLUTION 748 (1992) under Chapter VII of the Charter, in which it demanded that LIBYA extradite the accused nationals.

In the course of the oral proceedings, the UNITED STATES (UNITED KINGDOM) contested the admissibility of the Libyan claim, contending that "the Security Council was actively seised of the situation which was the subject of the Application and ... therefore the Court should not indicate provisional measures." This assertion could easily be rejected by the Court's dictum in the case concerning *Maritime and Paramilitary in and against NICARAGUA* and the *Bosnian Genocide* case.[325]

The Agent of the UNITED STATES stated that the resolution 748(1992) was an "additional reason" to maintain that the Libyan request for provisional measures should be denied. He stated in a letter addressed to the Court on 7 April 1992 that "in order to avoid any conflict with the Security Council the Court should decline the request to indicate provisional measures in this case."[326]

LIBYA, in response to the US assertion, stated that the risk of contradiction between the resolution and the provisional measures requested did not render the

---

323 *Ibid.*, (LIBYA v. US), Order of 14 April 1992, ICJ Reports 1992, p.118, para.10; (LIBYA v. UK), Order of 14 April 1992, ICJ Reports 1992, p.7, para.10.

324 *Ibid.*, (LIBYA v. US), Order of 14 April 1992, ICJ Reports 1992, p.124, para.32,33; (LIBYA v. UK), Order of 14 April 1992, ICJ Reports 1992, p.13, para.32, 33.

325 The Court observed that "while there is in the Charter a provision of a clear demarcation of functions between the GENERAL ASSEMBLY and the SECURITY COUNCIL, in respect of any dispute or situation, that the former should not make any recommendation with regard to that dispute or situation unless the SECURITY COUNCIL so requires, there is no similar provision anywhere in the Charter with respect to the SECURITY COUNCIL and the Court. The Council has functions of a political nature assigned to it, whereas the Court exercises purely judicial functions. Both organs can therefore perform their separate but complementary functions with respect to the same events"., case concerning *Military and Paramilitary Activities in and against NICARAGUA* (NICARAGUA v. USA), (Jurisdiction and Admissibility), Judgment of 26 November 1984, ICJ Reports1984, p.434-435, para.95; *Bosnian Genocide* (Provisional Measures), Order of 8 April 1993, ICJ Reports 1993, p.19, para.33.

326 It was quoted in the Dissenting Opinion of *Bedjaoui* appending to the Order of 14 April 1992, *Lockerbie*, (Provisional Measures), ICJ Reports 1992, p.154.

Libyan request inadmissible, since there was in law no competition or hierarchy between the Court and the SECURITY COUNCIL, each exercising its own competence.[327]

This again raised the question which once appeared but was not substantively touched by the Court in the *Bosnian Genocide* case - When the Court is confronted with a request for provisional measures which are in effect conflicting with the SECURITY COUNCIL RESOLUTION, how should the Court deal with the situation? The observation that both the Court and the Council can perform their separate but complementary functions with respect to the same events naturally leads to the assertion that the SECURITY COUNCIL has simultaneously seised of the same dispute does not make the present dispute before the Court inadmissible. In the same vein, the Court can entertain the requests for provisional measures with the aim to protect the rights, although the rights sought to be protected are under a wider political background and the dispute is simultaneously before the SECURITY COUNCIL. However, this observation seems to be not sufficient to answer the present question. In other words, when the provisional measures as requested do not conflict with the SECURITY COUNCIL RESOLUTION, both the Court and the SECURITY COUNCIL perform its own function in a parallel and complementary manner. Contrarily, when the requested provisional measures are in effect conflicting with the SECURITY COUNCIL RESOLUTION, the problem arises. On this point, Judge *Bedjaoui* observed as follows:

> "if the concomitant exercise of concurrent but not exclusive powers has thus far not given rise to serious problems, the present case, by contrast, presents the Court not only with the grave question of the possible influence of the decisions of a principle organ on the consideration of the same question by another principal organ, but also, more fundamentally, with the question of the possible inconsistency between the decisions of the two organs and how to deal with so delicate a situation."[328]

The Court's attitude on this point in the *Lockerbie* cases seemed to be as equivocal as that in the *Bosnian Genocide* case. It observed as follows:

> "both Libya and the United States, as Members of the United Nations, are obliged to accept and carry out the decisions of the Security Council in accordance with Article 25 of the Charter; ... the Court, which is at the stage of proceedings on provisional measures, considers that prima facie this obligation

327 *Lockerbie* (LIBYA v. US), (Provisional Measures), Order of 14 April 1992, ICJ Reports 1992, p.126, para.39; (LIBYA v. UK), (Provisional Measures), Order of 14 April 1992, ICJ Reports 1992, p.16, para.36.

328 Dissenting Opinion of Judge *Bedjaoui* appending to the Order of 14 April 1992, *Lockerbie* cases, ICJ Reports 1992, p.143, para.2.

extends to the decision contained in resolution 748 (1992); and ... in accordance with Article 103 of the Charter, the obligations of the Parties in that respect prevail over their obligations under any other international agreement, including the Montreal Convention ... the Court, while thus not at this stage called upon to determine definitely the legal effect of Security Council resolution 748 (1992), considers that, whatever the situation previous to the adoption of that resolution, the rights claimed by Libya under the Montreal Convention cannot now be regarded as appropriate for protection by the indication of provisional measures ... furthermore, an indication of the measures requested by Libya would be likely to impair the rights that appear prima facie to be enjoyed by the United Nations by virtue of Security Council resolution 748 (1992)."[329]

The Court accordingly found that "the circumstances of the case are not such as to exercise its power under Article 41 of the Statute to indicate provisional measures." The motivation for the Court's rejection of the request for provisional measures is not clear. Is it because of the Court's intention to avoid a decision directly conflicting with the SECURITY COUNCIL RESOLUTION? Is it because of the Court's awareness on the fact that the provisional measures as requested would be enjoined by the SECURITY COUNCIL RESOLUTION, through the function of Article 103 of the Charter, even if the provisional measures were granted?[330]

The fact that the Court did entertain the request for provisional measures at least demonstrated that the Court did not regard the SECURITY COUNCIL RESOLUTION as an obstacle to the admissibility of the request for provisional measures. Nevertheless, the Court presumed the *prima facie* validity of the SECURITY COUNCIL RESOLUTION and showed its reluctance to adopt any decisions conflicting with the SECURITY COUNCIL RESOLUTION. It stated in the Order that "an indication of the measures requested by Libya would be likely to impair the rights which appear *prima facie* to be enjoyed by the United Kingdom by virtue of Security Council resolution 748 (1992)".[331]

---

329 *Lockerbie* (LIBYA v. US), (Provisional Measures), Order of 14 April 1992, ICJ Reports 1992, p.126-127, para.42-44; (LIBYA v. UK), (Provisional Measures), Order of 14 April 1992, ICJ Reports1992, p.15, para.39-41.

330 On this point, Macdonald observed that the rationale of the decision could have been either that an indication of the provisional measures requested would have had no effect or that the Court felt that it should avoid making a determination that would conflict with a binding resolution of the SECURITY COUNCIL. *Macdonald*, Changing Relations Between the INTERNATIONAL COURT OF JUSTICE and the SECURITY COUNCIL of the UNITED NATIONS, Canadian Yearbook of International Law (1993), Vol. 31, p.21.

331 *Lockerbie* (LIBYA v. US), (Provisional Measures), Order of 14 April 1992, ICJ Reports 1992, p.124, para.33; (LIBYA v. UK), (Provisional Measures), Order of 14 April 1992, ICJ Reports 1992, p.15, para.41.

## II. Concurrent Jurisdiction

The concurrent jurisdiction between the INTERNATIONAL COURT OF JUSTICE and the SECURITY COUNCIL is grounded on the rules in the UNITED NATIONS CHARTER and the Statute of the Court. Article 36, paragraph 1 of the Statute of the Court provides that the Court has jurisdiction in all cases referred to it by the parties in dispute, and in all matters specially provided for in the Charter or in other treaties and conventions in force. Article 36, paragraph 2 provides that the state parties may declare they recognize the jurisdiction of the Court in all legal disputes concerning: (a) the interpretation of a treaty; (b) any question of international law; (c) the existence of any fact which, if established, would constitute a breach of an international obligation; (d) the nature or extent of the reparation to be made for the breach of an international obligation.

Meanwhile, Article 35, paragraph 1 of the UNITED NATIONS CHARTER provides that any Member of the UNITED NATIONS may bring to the attention of the SECURITY COUNCIL or of the GENERAL ASSEMBLY any dispute or any situation which might lead to international friction or give rise to a dispute the continuance of which would be likely to endanger the maintenance of international peace and security.[332]

### 1. The principle of *litispendence* on the international plane?

As discussed above, both the rules in the UNITED NATIONS CHARTER and the Statute of the Court and the practice of the Court and the SECURITY COUNCIL have recognized the concurrent jurisdiction of these two organs. The two organs might render different decisions with regard to the same dispute. It is recognized in municipal law by the principle of *litispendence* that the conflict jurisdiction should be avoided and the unity of proceedings be ensured.[333] One might raise a further

332 Article 35, paragraph 2 of the Charter provides that a State which is not a Member of the UNITED NATIONS may bring to the attention of the SECURITY COUNCIL or of the GENERAL ASSEMBLY any dispute to which it is a party if it accepts in advance, for the purposes of the dispute, the obligations of pacific settlement stipulated in the Charter.

333 It is observed that the doctrine of litispendence has a twofold function: firstly the circumvention of conflicting judgments, and secondly, the avoidance of a proliferation of pending cases on the same issue. See *Elsen*, Litispendence between the INTERNATIONAL COURT OF JUSTICE and the SECURITY COUNCIL, (1986), p.1; *Reichert*, Problems with Parallel and Duplicate Proceedings: The Litispendence Principle and International Arbitrations, Arbitration International (1992), Vol.8, p.237-255, p.239.

question: Could the principle of *litispendence*[334] be applied in the field of international law? To be more specific, could the principle be applied to the question of the concurrent jurisdiction between the Court and the SECURITY COUNCIL?

In municipal law, *litispendence* means that a question pending before one tribunal may not be brought before another tribunal or at least that one of the tribunal shall declare it inadmissible because of its pendency before another tribunal.[335] There are three essential elements which constitute *litispendence*: (a) an identical question; (b) pending between the same parties; (c) before organs which possess jurisdiction of identical or similar character.

The authors are divided on the issue of *litispendence* on the international plane. The prevailing view holds that, the situation of *litispendence* should also be avoided on the international law.[336] An even stronger opinion, which has gained little support, holds that this principle has also been accepted by international law.[337] Dan *Ciobanu* then proposed a middle-way path that admitting the necessity of avoiding *litispendece* on the international plane while at the same time recognizing that in practice the principle of *litispendence* in international law assumed characteristics that sharply distinguish it from the same doctrine in municipal law.[338] Some writers pointed out that the avoidance of *litispendence* is at most a moral obligation rather than a legal one on the international plane.[339] In sum, the

334 In the first place, in international relations, disputes are almost with the nature of both legal and political. Accordingly the "identity of the question" is difficult to define. As for the second condition, in international plane, the State is responsible to protect its nationals' rights, accordingly the dispute could be presented as not only between one State and one national but also between two states. The third condition of litispendence requires that the question must be presented before organs possessing jurisdiction of the same character. This condition is also difficult to satisfy since the inter-state disputes are usually presented before the international organs that are established under some special treaties for any particular purposes.

335 *Frahm*, Multiplication of International Courts and Tribunals and Conflicting Jurisdiction – Problems and Possible Solutions, In: Max Planck Yearbook of UNITED NATIONS Law, *Frowein*, *Philipp*, *Wolfrum* (eds.), (2001), Vol.5, p.77.

336 *Rosenne* considered that *litispendence* should also be avoided on the international plane. *Elsen* commented: "In the opinion of *Rosenne*, it would be salutary that, in principle, political organs refrain from placing on their agenda disputes for which they have recommended judicial settlement. Equally, those States that have themselves instituted proceedings in the Court should not, subsequently, introduce the same dispute in a political organ while the judicial proceedings are pending."

337 *Connell*, International Law, (1965), Vol.I, p.13.

338 *Ciobanu*, Litispendence between the INTERNATIONAL COURT OF JUSTICE and the Political Organs of the UNITED NATIONS, In: The Future of the INTERNATIONAL COURT OF JUSTICE, *Gross* (ed.), (1976), p.216-219. See also, *Elsen*, *supra* note 315, p.12-14;

339 *Ciobanu* quoted a student's writing that "La règle dictée par des considerations de correction et de courtoisie internationales consiste dans l'obligation pour tout organisme internationale de ne pas connaître d'une affaire portée devant une autre institution

prevailing view on this point is that the principle of *litispendece* has not been recognized as a principle in general public international law. As discussed in the last part, neither the Court nor the SECURITY COUNCIL has accepted this doctrine as the law of the UNITED NATIONS.

As observed by *Frahm*, this is due to the character of international jurisdiction, namely organs of a different character created by the states for particular needs not standing in any hierarchical relationship, the prerequisites constituting *litispendence* will be present only in very exceptional cases.[340] Furthermore, even if the principle of *litispendence* were be accepted, it would remain to be questionable whether this principle is applicable to the conflict jurisdiction between the Court and the SECURITY COUNCIL, because of their different character – one is judicial and the other is political.

### 2. Judicial constraint on the international plane?

One might still try to solve the difficulty of the concurrent jurisdiction between the Court and the SECURITY COUNCIL, arguing that a delimitation of jurisdiction between the two organs could be made, because the "judicial constraint" is required in the disputes involving highly political issues.[341] It is argued that the Court's jurisdiction could be excluded in the highly political disputes.

Traditional opinion holds that there exists a distinction between the legal and the political disputes, the justiciable and the non-justiciable disputes, and disputes as to rights and disputes arising out of conflicts of interests.[342] The distinction accordingly leads to a classification between the disputes that by their nature are

---

internationale, à moins qu'il ne soit solicité d'intervenir par l'autorité déjà saisie." And paraphrased the text as follows: "if there was an obligation to discontinue the proceedings in case of litispendence, this was an obligation of comity, or, to put it otherwise, it would be something more than a moral obligation but less than a legal one.", *Ciobanu, ibid., footnote*.95.

340 *Frahm, supra* note 311, p.77.

341 This was argued by America in the *NICARAGUA* case to claim the exclusive power of the SECURITY COUNCIL on the question of the legitimacy of the armed force allegedly taken in self-defence. It was also observed by Takane *Sugihara* that there is a certain limitation on the judicial function of the Court with respect to the cases that involve highly political issues, *Sugihara*, The Judicial Function of the INTERNATIONAL COURT OF JUSTICE with Respect to Disputes Involving Highly Political Issues, In: The INTERNATIONAL COURT OF JUSTICE, Muller *et al.* (*eds.*), p.117-138.

342 See, *e.g., Higgins*, Policy Considerations and the International Judicial Process, In: 17 The International and Comparative Law Quarterly, (1968), Vol.17, p.63; *Mosler*, Political and Justiciable Legal Disputes: Revival of an Old Controversy, In: *Schwarzenberger, Cheng, Brown* (eds.), Contemporary Problems of International Law: Essays in Honour of Georg Schwarzenberger on his Eightieth Birthday, (1988), p.219; and *McWhinney*, Judicial Settlement of International Disputes (1991), p.42.

appropriate for judicial settlement and those that are not. This doctrine has been widely regarded as unsatisfactory nowadays. As *Jennings* noted:

> "It is perhaps a little unfortunate that, in the effort to establish international tribunals, so much effort was devoted to the distinction between legal and political - or justiciable and non-justiciable - questions and disputes, rather at the expense of proper attention to the much more crucial distinction between legal and political determination of a legal dispute. A dispute that is not a legal dispute, that is to say one that is not reduced, or perhaps cannot be reduced, to specific issues of fact or law between the parties (of the sort that can be defined in 'submissions'), admits only of some sort of political or at any rate of a non-legal, determination; but a legal dispute admits of both a legal nature and a political answer."[343]

Professor *Higgins* observed that there was little reality in any definition of a political, or legal, question; what was relevant was the distinction between a political *method* and a legal *method* of solving dispute.[344]

He also pointed out that "a dispute is a 'legal' dispute if it is to be resolved by authoritative legal decision, no matter what the component elements of that dispute".[345]

Further support is found from Judge Sir Robert Jennings' observation: "the rubric of 'legal dispute' should be understood as indicating not only something about the objective character of a dispute submitted to a court, but much more the highly technical procedure whereby the Court and the parties together reduced their dispute into a form which renders it manageable in an adversarial procedure in a court of law; in a word, made 'justiciable' [...]"[346]

This availability of one dispute in both legal and political forms was indeed demonstrated by the *Lockerbie* cases. As observed by Judge *Bedjaoui*, the dispute was political as a problem of international terrorism and Libyan responsibility for the Lockerbie bombing. Meanwhile, it was a legal question brought before the Court as to whether LIBYA was under an international treaty obligation to extradite the accused nationals.

Therefore, it would be unrealistic to delimit the scope of jurisdiction between the Court and the SECURITY COUNCIL by the judicial and political categorization

---

343 *Jennings*, Reflections on the Term 'Dispute', In: *Macdonald* (ed.), Essays in Honour of Wang Tieya on His Eightieth Birthday, (1994), p.403.

344 *Higgins*, *supra* note 318, p.74.

345 *Higgins,ibid.*, p.74; See also *Anand*, Compulsory Jurisdiction of the INTERNATIONAL COURT OF JUSTICE (1961), p.85; and *Gordon*, Legal Disputes under Article 36(2) of the Statute, In: *Damrosch* (ed.), The INTERNATIONAL COURT OF JUSTICE at a Crossroads, (1987), p.200.

346 *Jennings*, *supra* note 319.

according to their inherent nature. Moreover, it is noteworthy that, after the Cold War, more and more essentially political disputes in the traditional sense have been presented to the judicial forums in the attempt to seek judicial legislation.[347] This tendency would demonstrate the necessity and feasibility of settling the inter-state disputes by the cooperative action of both political and judicial organs. Furthermore, the UNITED NATIONS law has not recognized the principle of "separation of powers". The Court stated in the *NICARAGUA* case that the argument of the UNITED STATES excluding the jurisdiction of the Court on the question of the legitimacy of armed actions allegedly taken in self-defense was an attempt to transfer municipal-law concepts of separation of powers to the international plane and these concepts were not applicable to the relations among international institutions for the settlement of disputes.[348]

The Court's practice as in the *Aegean Sea Continental Shelf* case, the case concerning the *US Diplomatic and Consular Staff*, the *Bosnian Genocide* case and the case concerning *Military and Paramilitary Activities in and against NICARAGUA* demonstrates that the Court does not refrain from exercising jurisdiction with regard to the disputes involving political elements. The Court observed that "Article 24 of the Charter confers on the Security Council the primary, not the exclusive, responsibility for the maintenance of international peace and security ... the Council has functions of a political nature assigned to it, whereas the Court exercises purely judicial functions. Both organs can therefore perform their separate but complementary functions with respect to the same events."[349] The "judicial constraint" concept in municipal law could not be applied to the international plane. Therefore, it could be concluded that even in the disputes involving highly political elements, the Court does not have any obligation to be constrained from exercising its jurisdiction.

### 3. The conflicting decisions

As discussed above, both the Court and the SECURITY COUNCIL could concurrently perform their own functions with regard to the same dispute. The Court is not

347 Judge *Gros*, in his Separate Opinion in the Nuclear Tests case, pointed out that "there is a certain tendency to submit essentially political conflicts to adjudication in the attempt to open a little door to judicial legislation". However, he supposed that this tendency would result in the situation, on the international plane, of government by judges. He believed that this notion is opposed to the realities of the present international community and it would undermine the very foundation of jurisdiction; Separate Opinion of Judge *Gros* appending to the Order of 22 June 1973, *Nuclear Tests*, ICJ Reports 1973, p.296-297.

348 Case concerning *Military and Paramilitary Activities in and against NICARAGUA* (NICARAGUA v. USA), (Jurisdiction and Admissibility), ICJ Reports 1984, p.433, para.92.

349 Case concerning *Military and Paramilitary Activities in and against NICARAGUA* (NICARAGUA v. USA), (Jurisdiction and Admissibility), ICJ Reports 1984, p.434-435.

refrained from exercising its power either because the Court has simultaneously seised of the same matter, or because the dispute is highly political. The Court is not excluded from entertaining the requests for provisional measures in the *Lockerbie* cases. This was what the Court actually did. Therefore, the real problem in the *Lockerbie* cases seemed to be the conflicting decisions, rather than the admissibility of the case before the Court. On this point, *Macdonald* observed that "in essence, it is misconceived to treat the decisions of the Court and the Council as conflicting determinations. There is simply no common standard by which a comparison can be made. The *apparent* conflict is with respect to the *effects* of the determinations if they are enforced. (emphasis original)

In other words, both the Court and the SECURITY COUNCIL could perform their "separate but complementary functions with respect to the same events" in the maintenance of the international peace and security. The legal political dichotomy does not stem from the inherent nature of the dispute, but from a political and a legal method of solving the dispute. The Court exercises its judicial function, using juridical concepts, adopting the standards of legality, using the method of legal proof,[350] while the SECURITY COUNCIL examines questions in their political aspects, making decisions upon political considerations. Both organs function in parallel, accordingly, there is no basis for comparison between a political and a legal decision.

Basing on this ground, *Macdonald* observed that the Court "adopted an unnecessarily conservative stance" to mind the apparent conflict between the two determinations. He regarded the Court's failure to determine the rights claimed by LIBYA under the Montreal Convention and to determine whether in the circumstances those rights warranted the protection of provisional measures as they "shied away from the full discharge of its judicial responsibilities". He accordingly asserted that the Court could make a determination on LIBYA's legal rights pursuant to the Montreal Convention of 1971 and go on to entertain the request of provisional measures. He believed that the decisions of the Court and the Council could have been considered *valid within their respective domains*. As for the potential conflict on the effects of the decisions, he proposed that it would have been resolved at a later stage. He stated that, the potential conflict in the results of the decisions of the SECURITY COUNCIL and the Court was easily resolvable, because the status of Resolution 748 was such that it was negated the effects of the determination of the Court.[351]

---

350 Judge *Weeramantry*, in his dissenting opinion in the *Lockerbie* cases, observed that "the concept it (the Court) uses are juridical concepts, its criteria are standards of legality, its method is that of legal proof. Its tests of validity and the bases of its decisions are naturally not the same as they would be before a political or executive organ of the UNITED NATIONS.", ICJ Reports 1992, p.56, p.166.

351 *Mcdonald*, Changing Relations between the INTERNATIONAL COURT OF JUSTICE and the SECURITY COUNCIL of the UNITED NATIONS, Canadian Yearbook of International Law,

His observation tended to advise the Court to take a more active role in the maintenance of international peace and security, to deliver a decision on whether LIBYA was under any obligation to extradite the accused nationals under the Montreal Convention 1971, make a decision on whether the present circumstances justified the provisional measures as requested by LIBYA and leave the possible upcoming conflicting effects of the two decisions to a later stage. In the *Lockerbie* cases, the conflicting effects of the two decisions can be solved because Article 103 of the Charter explicitly provides that in the event of a conflict between Charter obligations and those arising out of any other international agreements, the former are to prevail.

However, the solving of the conflicting effects of the two decisions might not be as effective as *Macdonald* expected in every case because the scope of Article 103 of the UN Charter is limited. In the first place, Article 103 does not apply to the norms of *jus cogens*.[352] In other words, the obligations under the UN Charter are not by Article 103 deemed hierarchically superior to the principles of *jus cogens*. As observed by *Shaw*, the norms of *jus cogens* are not extensive and may not extend beyond the prohibition of the use of force and the violation of certain key human rights such as genocide.[353] It is therefore illogical and wrong for such core rules of international behavior to be breached even by the SECURITY COUNCIL.[354]Judge *Lauterpacht* raised this issue in his Separate Opinion in the *Bosnian Genocide* case, observing that Article 103 of the Charter could not be directly applied to the case because "the prohibition of genocide has generally been accepted as having the status not of an ordinary rule of international law but of *jus cogens*." He declared that "the concept of *jus cogens* operates as a concept superior to both customary international law and treaty. The relief that Article 103 of the Charter may give the SECURITY COUNCIL in case of conflict between one of its decisions and an operative treaty obligation cannot - as a matter of simple hierarchy of norms - extend to a conflict between a SECURITY COUNCIL RESOLUTION and *jus cogens*.[355]

In the second place, it could be argued that Article 103 of the Charter may not apply to customary law rules. As observed by *Shaw*, this is a controversial proposition and much will depend upon the nature of the asserted rule and the nature of the circumstances of the decision in question.[356]

---

(1993), p.3.

352 *Watson*, Constitutionalism, Judicial Review and the World Court, Harvard International Law Journal (1993), Vol.34, p.36-37.

353 *Shaw*, International Law, (1991), p.98-99.

354 *Shaw*, The SECURITY COUNCIL and the INTERNATIONAL COURT OF JUSTICE: Judicial Drift and Judicial Function, In: *Muller et al.* (eds.), The INTERNATIONAL COURT OF JUSTICE - Its Future Role after Fifty Years, (1997), p.230.

355 Separate Opinion of Judge *Lauterpacht* appending to the Order of 8 April 1993, *Bosnian Genocide*, ICJ Reports 1993, p.440.

356 *Shaw*, *supra* note 354, p.231.

This could lead to an observation - although Article 103 apparently solved the conflict between the decisions of Court and the SECURITY COUNCIL, the Court did not substantively solve the problem with regard to the conflict between the decisions of the two organs. When the SECURITY COUNCIL has adopted a resolution exerting obligations to the State parties while the Court is simultaneously requested to adjudge the rights and obligations concerning the same dispute, if these rights and obligations are not under any "other international agreement", then the Court would not be refrained from making a decision that would conflict with the SECURITY COUNCIL RESOLUTION.

Take the present case for example, had LIBYA presented its claim as that "the extradition of the accused nationals would constitute breach of the general public international law rather than the breach of the Montreal Convention",[357] then Article 103 would not have acted as an obstacle to the Court's power to entertain the requests for provisional measures. Then the Court would indicate provisional measures that conflict with the SECURITY COUNCIL RESOLUTION 748, but the problem would still remain unsolved - both decisions would be binding and the conflicts between the two decisions would still exist.

In addition, *Macdonald*'s observation that the concurrent jurisdiction of the Court and the SECURITY COUNCIL would not lead to conflicting decisions since the judicial decisions rendered by the judicial organs through judicial procedures and the political organs rendered by the political organs through political considerations would be totally incomparable is contestable. According to the observation, the decisions of the two organs with respect to the same events are *not in conflict* because there is no standard to compare the two decisions that are made in respective manner and within different domains. Accordingly it is difficult to conclude that they are conflicting or not. The Court, as the judicial organ and the SECURITY COUNCIL, as the political organ of the UNITED NATIONS, are conferred the power to act within their own function in order to obtain the common purpose, namely to maintain the international peace and security. The activities of the two organs are not conflicting. Both organs assume their function independently, complementarily and in parallel. Theoretically speaking, the political decisions don't conflict with the judicial decisions. What could be in conflict are just the actual effects of the decisions. To this extent, *Macdonald*'s observation is quite convincing.

However, it is noteworthy that in practice the two organs might have different conclusions as to the facts and the solutions, even if both organs perform their functions within their jurisdiction, following the procedure, not acting *ultra virus*,

---

357 Judge *Oda* actually took the view that had Libya sought to base its claims on its sovereign rights generally under international law rather than upon the treaty rights in the Montreal Convention, a "totally different litigation" would have ensued and the question of the jurisdiction of the Court would have been "certainly a different matter", Declaration of Judge *Oda*, *Lockerbie*, ICJ Reports 1992, p.19.

with good faith, in a word, with full respect to international law. Due to the inherent nature of the two organs, each organ pays attention to the particular aspects of the facts that it regards as significant. Each organ renders the decision, usually requiring the parties to take some measures that it regards as most appropriate to solve the dispute. However, because of the nature of the rights in dispute and the particular circumstances, it might happen in practice that in some cases the legal rights alleged by the parties would be directly affected by the political measures. Then the decisions of the two organs conflict in effect. In the *Bosnian Genocide* case, the SECURITY COUNCIL had made a decision of arms embargo on BOSNIA. Had the Court seised of the jurisdiction of the right of self-defense, the Court might have decided that BOSNIA could exercise its right of self-defense. The arms embargo is obvious limitation or even deprivation of the Bosnian right of self-defense.[358] It is the appropriate assumption of the responsibility of maintenance of international peace and security and is therefore not beyond the SECURITY COUNCIL's function.

However, it is noteworthy that the above presumption is not always practicable in reality. The organ is not always acting with full respect to international law. Sometimes, it acts beyond its functional scope. This might even add additional risk to the possibility of conflicting decisions between the two organs. In the *Lockerbie* cases, Judge *Bedjaoui* wrote about this point, which I respectfully agree,

> "...the difficulty in the present case lies in the fact that the Security Council not only has decided to take a number of political measures against Libya, but has also demanded from it the extradition of its two nationals. It is this specific demand of the Council that creates an overlap with respect to the substance of the legal dispute with which the Court must deal, in a legal manner, on the basis of the 1971 Montreal Convention and international law in general."[359]

This is actually not a rare occasion in the history of the SECURITY COUNCIL. *Shaw* concluded on the SECURITY COUNCIL's practice as follows:

> "the Security Council has over the last few years been extending its reach by the use of its powers of decision under Chapter VII of the Charter. These activities have moved beyond the determination of threat to or breaches of the peace or acts of aggression to include not only measures to deal with those

---

358 Shaw regarded the Bosnian Genocide case as an example of the SECURITY COUNCIL's resolutions that in effect amount to a legal determination. *Shaw*, *supra* note 354, p.235, p.255.

359 Dissenting Opinion of Judge *Bedjaoui* appending to the Order of 14 April 1992, *Lockerbie*, ICJ Reports 1992, p.145. In the opinion of the present writer, the decisions of arms-embargo could be a purely political determination to take action for the aim of maintaining international peace and security.

immediate threats in a timely and opportune fashion but also the assertion of conclusions of law in particular circumstances."[360]

It could therefore be concluded that the conflicting decisions between the two organs are not illusory. It is found that the concurrent jurisdiction between the Court and the SECURITY COUNCIL is recognized in international law and the municipal principle of *litispendence* and the principle of "judicial restraint" are not recognized by international law. Then it can be observed that the conflicting decisions are the natural consequences of the concurrent jurisdiction. There is not any basis to reject the conflicts of decisions. In other words, because the principle of "*litispendence*" is not recognized on the international plane, so there is room for the existence of conflicting decisions. To get back to the theme of this dissertation, the Court's power to entertain the requests for provisional measures is not excluded by the SECURITY COUNCIL's simultaneous exercise of jurisdiction with regard to the same dispute. The Court does not have any obligation to construct the provisional measures in consistence with the SECURITY COUNCIL RESOLUTION, either.

## 4. The natural consequences of the "concurrent jurisdiction"

The problem of the conflicting decisions between the Court and the SECURITY COUNCIL is inherent to the "concurrent jurisdiction" of the two organs. The two organs are established within the UNITED NATIONS system without any specific mechanism for coordination. There is no provision in international law as to the legal effects of the decisions of two organs which conflict with another with regard to the same dispute. Neither is there any provision, in the UNITED NATIONS Charter, or in the Statute of the Court, which lays out the prevailing character of the decision of one organ to that of the other. Moreover, there exists no mechanism on the international plane that could act as an appellate body to accept the challenges to these conflicting decisions and make a final decision.

As discussed above, normally the conflicting decisions stem solely from the "concurrent jurisdiction". Imagine that both the Court and the SECURITY COUNCIL exercise its own function with regard to the same dispute, with good faith and discretion, not acting *ultra virus*, they might have different conclusions of the facts and provide the solution they regard as appropriate. In this situation, the conflict of the decisions is the natural, normal consequence of the "concurrent jurisdiction". It's difficult to see any basis in international law to avoid the occurrence of this kind of conflict. Within the present scheme of the UNITED NATIONS, making reservations to the jurisdiction might be the only feasible solution to avoid this difficulty. In practice, some states append to their declarations of the acceptance of the

360 *Shaw*, *supra* note 354, p.235, p.255.

compulsory jurisdiction a reservation that the Court's jurisdiction does not apply to disputes with regard to which the parties may have agreed or may agree to have recourse to another mode of pacific settlement. Or even more specifically, some states reserve the rights to suspend the proceedings before the Court in the disputes in respect of which the SECURITY COUNCIL is exercising the jurisdiction.[361]

## III. Jurisdictional Overlap

### 1. Exercise of power beyond its political function

As for the second situation - the overrunning of power beyond the organ's functional scope, one might at the first sight be reminded of the issue of "judicial constraint" which has been discussed above. It is true that the municipal constitutional principle of separation of powers is not recognized on the international plane. The non-recognition of the principle of "judicial constraint" on the international plane means that the Council is not excluded from exercising its jurisdiction because the dispute is highly political. The non-recognition of the principle of "judicial constraint" makes both organs able to deal with one inter-state dispute simultaneously. This might be salutary to the development of international dispute settlement, considering the usually mixed nature of the complicated inter-state disputes.

What is concerned here is another issue. With respect to a specific dispute, the facts can be organized in a form of legal dispute, from the Court's point of view; while as a political dispute, from the Council's point of view. The Court extracts a legal dispute from the facts and deal with the dispute with legal means. The Council abstracts the political elements from the facts and deals with the dispute in a political manner, with political considerations. Each organ acts in a manner consistent with its functional nature. To this extent, it is arguable that a fictitious delimitation within a specific dispute still exists. In other words, the Court can only

361 For example, AUSTRALIA made a reservation in the declaration on 6 February 1954: "And this declaration is subject to the condition that the Government of AUSTRALIA reserves the right to require that proceedings in the Court shall be suspended in any dispute in respect of which the SECURITY COUNCIL of the UNITED NATIONS is exercising the functions assigned to it by the Charter of the UNITED NATIONS, provided that notice to suspend is given within ten days of the notification of the initiation of the proceedings in the Court, and provided also that the suspension shall be limited to a period of 12 months or such longer period as may be agreed by the parties to the dispute or determined by a decision of the SECURITY COUNCIL.

deal with the legal aspects extracted from the dispute while the SECURITY COUNCIL could only deal with the political aspects of the disputes.

In practice, the SECURITY COUNCIL's action beyond the scope of its political function catches more attention from the international community than that of the Court, owing to its quite broad power under Chapter VII of the Charter.[362] This is due to the vagueness of Chapter VII in general and of Art.39 in particular. The SECURITY COUNCIL apparently possesses unlimited discretionary powers to decide whether to act, whether one of the constituent facts of Art.39 is present, and whether to take any measures.

It is noteworthy that Article 39 of the UN Charter does constitute an express, exceptional extension of the SECURITY COUNCIL's political function. Article 39 of the Charter holds that "the Security Council shall determine the existence of any threat to the peace, breach of the peace, or act of aggression and shall make recommendations, or decide what measures shall be taken in accordance with Article 41 and 42, to maintain or restore international peace and security". On this point, Judge *Bedjaoui* stated that "indeed, whether one is in favor of it or not, the Council's freedom of appraisal finds *clear textual warrant* in the Charter. For that reason it could not, as such, very well be the object of legality-control."[363] (emphasis added)

A further question can be raised. What is the scope of the Security Council's power under Article 39? The SECURITY COUNCIL's practice under Article 39 is popularly titled with "the quasi-judicial function of the Security Council".[364] It is even asserted that the determination of the breach of peace under Article 39 is entirely within the discretion of the Council.[365] *Kirgis*, provided an elaboration of this point as follows:

---

362 UN Member States agreed in Article 24 of the Charter to confer on the Council primary responsibility for the maintenance of international peace and security. The specific powers that the Charter gives the Council to achieve this objective are contained in Chapter VII. Chapter VII confers the Council sole authority to determine the existence of "a threat to, or breach of the peace or act of aggression" and the power to make recommendations or take measures in order to restore international peace. See *Simma*, *Mosler* (eds.), The Charter of the UNITED NATIONS: A Commentary, (2002), p.397.

363 However, Judge *Bedjaoui* did not tend to assert that this could lead to the conclusion that the Council could act without any legal limitations. He then went on to state that "on the other hand, as shown by the resolutions discussed above, the same degree of immunity can surely not apply in the domain of the more concrete activities that the Council is led to deploy as a result, in particular, of its qualification of a given situation under Article 39 of the Charter. It is in this area of action undertaken, or of the ways and means decided for having them carried out, that the need may arise and a proper place be found for testing the legality of Security Council resolutions." *Bedjaoui*, The New World Order and the SECURITY COUNCIL: Testing the Legality of its Acts, (1994), p.52-53.

364 *Lauterpacht*, Aspects of the Administration of International Justice, (1991), p.37.

365 Judge *Weeramantry*, *Lockerbie*, (LIBYA V. UK), ICJ Reports 1993, p.66.

> "the Security Council was clearly empowered from the outset to make some other determinations that could be seen as quasi-judicial. Thus, it could expressly, or by necessary implication, brand a state as a potential or actual violator of international law. The obvious example is the Article 39 authority to determine the existence of a threat to the peace, breach of the peace or act of aggression. It was understood all along that this authority entitled the Council to make more than a nonjudgmental, factual determination: it included the authority to determine the aggressor, and to do so with binding effect on member states under Article 25."[366]

The SECURITY COUNCIL, however, seems to be expanding this power in practice too broader than expected. It is not a rare practice that the SECURITY COUNCIL adopts a resolution in a manner more like a legal determination than a directive to determine the situation as a threat or breach to the international peace or act of aggression and calls for measures to restore international peace. *Shaw* listed the typical examples as follows:[367] the resolutions to declare a situation as illegal or invalid, such as the determination in 1970 that the presence of SOURTH AFRICA in NAMIBIA is illegal,[368] the determination that the annexation of KUWAIT by IRAQ was illegal[369] and the determination that "the policy and practice of Israel in establishing settlements in Palestinian and other Arab territories occupied since 1967 have no legal validity"; [370] the resolutions demanding international non-recognition, also regarding the purported annexation of KUWAIT by IRAQ;[371] the resolutions recognizing and dealing with an ousted regime as authoritative rather than the regime in actual control, in the HAITI dispute;[372] the resolutions imposing peace conditions, defining and guaranteeing boundaries, and determining state responsibility issues[373] and even to more remote extent, resolutions to establish judicial or quasi-judicial bodies.[374]

---

366 *Kirgis*, The SECURITY COUNCIL's First Fifty Years, American Journal of International Law (1995), Vol.89, p.527.

367 *Shaw*, *supra* note 354, p.235.

368 S/RES. 276(1970). Jan.30, 1970, para.2, the Council declared that "the continued presence of the South African authorities is illegal and that consequently all acts taken by the Government on behalf of or concerning Namibia after the termination of the Mandate are illegal."

369 UN Doc. S/RES. 662(1990), para.1, in which the Council decided that "the annexation of Kuwait by Iraq under any form and whatever pretext has no legal validity, and is considered null and void."

370 UN Doc. S/RES. 446(1979), Mar.22, 1979, para.1.

371 UN Doc. S/RES. 662(1990).

372 UN Doc. S/RES. 841(1993).

373 UN Doc. S/RES. 687(1991).

374 The SECURITY COUNCIL decided to establish the UNCC and UNIKOM in the Iraqi case, or the ICTY and ICTR in the YUGOSLAVIA and RWANDA cases.

It is asserted that the SECURITY COUNCIL's broadened practice to make quasi-judicial determinations could be justified by the UN Charter.[375] To be more specific, it is asserted to be the implied power of the SECURITY COUNCIL under the UN Charter Art.41[376] since it was a measure necessary for the effective exercise of its powers to maintain or restore international peace and security.[377] It is therefore not strange that some writers observed that the SECURITY COUNCIL's practice to adopt resolutions that in effect amount to legal determinations is "well-established and essentially unchallenged by member states."[378]

## 2. The legal limits to the Council's power

It is widely accepted that "consensus" is the ultimate source of international law. Then it is a plausible inference that the Member States of the UNITED NATIONS expect an organ which serves the common interests of the international community - to maintain the international peace and security, rather than acting as a political organ that actually serves the interests of several great powers. Therefore, the action of the SECURITY COUNCIL shall also be within the limitation of law. Article 24(2) of the UN Charter provides that in discharging its duties with regard to international peace and security "the Security Council shall act in accordance with the Purposes and Principles of the UN". Article 1(1) of the UN Charter declares that one of the aims of the organization is to bring about by peaceful means and in conformity with

---

375 *Hoogh*, Attribution or Delegation of (Legislative) Power by the SECURITY COUNCIL? The Case of the United Transnational Administration in East Timor (UNTAET)", 7 Yearbook of International Peace Operation (2001), p.37.

376 Article 41 of the Charter reads: The SECURITY COUNCIL may decide what measures not involving the use of armed force are to be employed to give effect to its decisions, and it may call upon the Members of the UNITED NATIONS to apply such measures. These may include complete or partial interruption of economic relations and of rail, sea, air, postal, telegraphic, radio, and other means of communication, and the severance of diplomatic relations.

377 It is observed by Armin von *Bogdandy* that the Appeals Chamber of the International Criminal Tribunal of YUGOSLAVIA in the *Tadic* case in effect determined that the SECURITY COUNCIL possessed an implied power to establish the International Criminal Tribunal of YUGOSLAVIA from its express powers in Article 41, since it was a measure necessary for the effective exercise of its powers to maintain or restore international peace and security. *Bogdandy*, Lawmaking by International Organizations, In: Wolfrum, Röben (eds.),Developments of International Law in Treaty Making, p.199. See also, *Sarroshi*, The UNITED NATIONS and the Development of Collective Security, (1999), p.97; *Kirgis*, *supra* note 341, p.522; *Nolte*, The Limits of the SECURITY COUNCIL's Powers and its Functions on the international Legal System: Some Reflections, In: *Byers* (ed), The Role of Law in International Politics, (2000), p.322; Similar opinion see also *Schweigman*, The Authority of the SECURITY COUNCIL under Chapter VII of the UN Charter, (2005), p.155.

378 *Shaw*, *supra* note 354, p.235.

the principles of justice and international law, adjustment or settlement of international disputes or situations that might lead to a breach of the peace.

It can be inferred that it is the implied consensus of the Member States that the SECURITY COUNCIL shall obey the UN Charter and the general international law.

The question whether the SECURITY COUNCIL is also constrained by international law in exercising its functions under the UN Charter Chapter VII is more controversial. One of the views was represented by *Kelsen*, who holds that the SECURITY COUNCIL's actions under Chapter VII to maintain international peace and security is "entirely within the discretion of the Council" and therefore is not subject to any principles of justice or international law.[379] He further observed that "the Council would be empowered to establish justice if it considered the existing law as not satisfactory, and hence to enforce a decision which is considered to be just though not in conformity with existing law. The decision enforced by the Security Council may create new law for the concrete case."[380]

The contrary view is that although it is the political discretion of the SECURITY COUNCIL to determine the existence of threat to international peace, there is still room to assert legal limitations to the SECURITY COUNCIL's actions under Chapter VII of the Charter. It is argued that the SECURITY COUNCIL possesses great discretion to determine such a situation and decide to take measures it regards appropriate, within the legal limits imposed by the purposes and principles of the UN Charter and the general international law. A representative of the writers who hold this view is Judge *Bedjaoui*. He rejected *Kelsen*'s position that the Council can enforce decisions that are not in conformity with law and create new law for the concrete cases. Judge *Bedjaoui* firstly stated that the organs of the UNITED NATIONS are not empowered to create new customs through their concordant, consistent and undisputed practice according to the Charter. Even a plenary and representative organ such as the GENERAL ASSEMBLY can, at most, make "recommendations" to encourage the progressive development of international law.

---

379 *Kelsen* observed that "the purpose of the enforcement action under Article 39 is not: to maintain or restore the law, but to maintain or restore peace, which is not necessarily identical with the law." He therefore doubted whether the SECURITY COUNCIL may take account of the principles of justice and international law when it is under an obligation to decide on collective measures for the maintenance or restoration of peace, within the Chapter VII context. *Kelsen*, The Law of the UNITED NATIONS: A Critical Analysis of its Fundamental Problems, (2000), p.294.
See also *Dulles*, he observed that "The SECURITY COUNCIL is not a body that merely enforces agreed law, it is a law unto itself. If it considers any situation as a threat to the peace, it may decide what measures shall be taken. No principles of law are laid down to guide it; it can decide in accordance with what it thinks is expedient. It could be a tool enabling certain powers to advance their selfish interests at the expense of another power.", *Dulles*, War or Peace, (1950), p.194-195.

380 *Kelsen*, *ibid.*, p.295.

He went on to cite *Dupuy*'s observation on the issue of the rule-making powers of international organizations: "having been created by States, international organizations themselves create legal rules addressed to various entities, all of whose provisions, however, even if they have their due place within the particular legal order of the organization concerned, are subjected to international law."[381]

To reject *Kelsen*'s assertion that the SECURITY COUNCIL may in some cases be able to act not in accordance with international law, Judge *Bedjaoui* observed that it would be impossible for the SECURITY COUNCIL to brush aside, when it resorts to the use of force, fundamental norms of law of war (humanitarian law), or on human rights and self-determination of peoples: norms which express principles rooted in the "universal conscience of mankind".[382]

Judge *Bedjaoui* accordingly concluded his position on this point as follows: "it is found increasingly inadmissible that international political organs should take liberties with the Charter or adopt a relaxed attitude towards international law when it is they, surely, even more than states that have been given the duty of fortifying international law's credibility and reliability."[383]

### 3. The narrow interpretation of the Council's power

Based on the above discussion, it is concluded that the SECURITY COUNCIL's power under Article 39 of the Charter was not without the limitation of international law. Additionally, it is also necessary to probe into the intention of the drafters of the Charter in order to view the scope of the Council's function under Article 39 exactly.

There seems to be quite little attention, both within the Member States and the academic world, on the intention of the drafters of the UN Charter to endow the SECURITY COUNCIL with such a power. Neither has much attention been drawn, from the functional perspective, on the necessity to exert limitations on its power. The drafters' intention to endow the Council with the power to maintain international peace, along with the SECURITY COUNCIL's inherently political character appear to be overwhelmed by the fact that the SECURITY COUNCIL has broadly interpreted its power under Chapter VII and the apparent acquiescence within the international community.[384] However, in the view of the present writer, the function of the Council and the "should-be" scope of the Council's power under Chapter VII of the UN Charter is a point that shall not be ignored.

---

381 *Dupuy*, Droit international public, (1992), p.127, cited in *Bedjaoui*, The New World and the SECURITY COUNCIL, (1994), p.32-33.

382 *Bedjaoui*, The New World and the SECURITY COUNCIL, (1994), p.35.

383 *Bedjaoui*, *ibid.*, p.129-130.

384 *Lauterpacht*, *supra* note 364, p.47.

It would be a plausible interpretation of Chapter VII that the SECURITY COUNCIL is endowed with such a power to maintain the international peace and security, only under extreme circumstances - firstly, the "threat or breach of international peace, or act of aggression" is urgently calling for the action from the international community and a lengthy, strict legal procedure would be impractical for the urgent situation. As observed by *Lauterpacht*, "confronted by an armed attack by one State upon another, it is bound to assess the situation and apply to it the relevant Charter provisions with all appropriate expedition."[385] *Shaw* further elaborated this point as follows: "such enforcement activity could not be accomplished if it were accompanied, for example, by rigorous evidential processes extending over time and involving complicated procedure for the gathering of facts and hearing of witnesses and delayed due to some form of legal appeal mechanism."[386]

Secondly, the facts are very obvious that the SECURITY COUNCIL is able to determine whether it constitutes the "threat or breach of international peace, or act of aggression", without any substantial legal findings. The Council's power under Article 39 of the Charter inevitably involves the finding of facts and also the finding of law, in order to judge whether a state was using force aggressively or defensively.[387] It is concluded that in practice the SECURITY COUNCIL RESOLUTION "rests on a factual finding, as well as on an interpretation of Charter interpretations and a weighing of political considerations, procedures for clarifying the facts have assumed special importance."[388] Nevertheless, this extension of the Council's power is to some extent still plausible because the situation that could constitute a threat to the international peace and security is usually so obvious that the SECURITY COUNCIL would not face complicated problems, such as the interpretation and application of international law.

Accordingly it can be inferred that the UN Charter permits the Council with an exceptional extension of power rather than appointing an additional judicial organ within the UNITED NATIONS system. In other words, there is an implied prerequisite for the SECURITY COUNCIL to exercise its power to maintain the international peace and security - it exercises the power in a manner comparable to its inherent function. As a political organ, the SECURITY COUNCIL's function is intended to be extended, but only to a limited extent. It might not be the intention of the UN Charter drafters to endow an organ with the power to determine whether the situation constitutes "threat to peace", depending on the political decision-making process and

385 *Lauterpacht*, *ibid.*, p.43.

386 *Shaw*, *supra* note 354, p.226.

387 It is pointed out that at Dumbarton Oaks CHINA raised the question who was to judge whether a state was using force aggressively or defensively. The consensus was that it was probably the SECURITY COUNCIL. *Eagleton*, International Government, (1957), p.450. *Russell*, A History of the UNITED NATIONS CHARTER, (1958), p.465-466.

388 *Goodrich*, *Simons*, The UNITED NATIONS and the Maintenance of International Peace and Security, (1995), p.348.

representing the interests of the great powers. A more plausible interpretation could be - Article 39 is provided to permit the Council's exceptional extension of power, with the expectation that the advantages of settling international disputes through the SECURITY COUNCIL, namely the *expeditiousness*[389] and the *enforcement power*,[390] would be the most efficient way to maintain the international peace and security.

This point, I suppose, is the root of a lot of problems of the SECURITY COUNCIL. The SECURITY COUNCIL's practice is criticized, such as its too wide interpretation of the conception "threat of peace";[391] its *ultra vires* action to take measures such as establishing judicial or quasi-judicial bodies;[392] the incompatibility with international law of the consequences of the Council's resolutions[393] and the interference with the Court's competence to indicate provisional measures of

389 *Shaw*, *supra* note 354.

390 The SECURITY COUNCIL shall first decide whether a particular situation calls for action (Article 39). If such a situation has arisen, it may either make recommendations (Article 39), take provisional measures (Article 40), or decide on enforcement measures not involving the use of force (Article 41), in order to remedy the situation. If the Council considers these measures to be ineffective, it may authorize the use of measures involving the use of force, to put an end to a threat or breach of the peace (Article 42). Comparing with this, the enforcement of the Court's decisions depends on the Council (Article 94(2)).

391 *McRae* concluded the situations that could be considered to be threats to international peace as follows: massive violations of human rights in specific situations or serious violations of international law that may provoke armed countermeasures; extreme violence within a state; non-compliance with international obligations; concerns about future conduct of a state (measures with regard to armament); and the massive flow of refugees across international borders. With respect to "the breach of the peace", he concluded the Council's practice as "should include any use of armed force" and "also exists when armed forces are applied by or against an effective independent de facto regime which is not recognized as a state"; With respect to "act of aggression", it was observed that the SECURITY COUNCIL's practice seemed to be influenced by the GENERAL ASSEMBLY's definition of aggression. Moreover, the Council recognized in the *NICARAGUA* case that an "act of aggression" included cases of indirect military intervention of one state in another state. In addition, he observed that the Council used the *erga omnes* justification as the basis for its actions under Chapter VII. He concluded that "although the SECURITY COUNCIL has, in the past few years, extended its definition of a threat to the peace, Article 39 of the Charter, in my view, is not capable of supporting such broad interpretation.", *McRae*, Use of Economic Sanctions under International Law, The Canadian Yearbook of International Law, (2001), Vol.39, p.262-276.

392 For example, the SECURITY COUNCIL adopted resolutions to establish international criminal tribunals in former YUGOSLAVIA and RWANDA.

393 In the *Bosnian Genocide* case, it was argued that the Council's decision to impose a weapons embargo in effect contributed to the ongoing genocide against its populations. Furthermore, it was also argued that the SECURITY COUNCIL's resolution to exert continued sanctions on Iraq is incompatible with the international human rights law. See *eg. Schweigman, supra* note 377, p.301.

protection by adopting resolutions under Chapter VII.[394] All of the problems are related to the Council's over reaching actions that are beyond its political function.

This problem is also addressed by some judges and writers. They observed that it was the SECURITY COUNCIL's discretion to determine the situation of "breach of peace". Some writers meanwhile raised some challenges and called for some limitation to it, at least to some extent. Judge *Bedjaoui*, on the one hand admitted that Article 39 did provide the discretion of appraising the situation of "breach of peace" and could not very well be the object of legality-control, on the other hand raised doubts as to whether "the same degree of immunity" could be applied in the area of enforcement measures which the Council decides to take to restore international peace.[395] It was concluded as "a three-way division" by some literature - firstly, the actual determination of a threat to or breach of the peace or act of aggression; secondly, actions taken consequent upon that determination in order to maintain or restore international peace and security; thirdly, resolutions which in effect amount to a determination or characterization of a legal situation.[396] This opinion was shared by *Lauterpacht*, who observed that a distinction can be drawn between "prescriptions of conduct that are directly and immediately related to the termination of the impugned conduct" and "those findings that, though not unrelated", but have "a general and long-term legal impact that goes beyond the immediate needs of the situation".[397]

As observed by *Franck*, "a problem with Security Council resolutions is that they speak in the covered language of diplomacy, sometimes out of political necessity, sometimes out of the drafters' professional habit. They often fail to address issues of fairness, which leaves Council actions vulnerable to attack as exercises in unprincipled power. This adversely affects the resolution, its capacity to garner voluntary compliance, and perceptions of the process' legitimacy."[398]

The Council does extend its jurisdiction in practice to cover some fields that shall be covered by the judicial organs. Some writers even argue that this practice seems to be accepted with the acquiescence of the Member States.[399] This practice

---

394 See *Lockerbie* cases.

395 *Bedjaoui*, *supra* note 358.

396 *Shaw*, *supra* note 354, p.234-235.; See also *Kelsen*, *supra* note 355.

397 *Lauterpacht* observed that "In many cases, the facts will be so clear that there can be no doubt that the situation amounts to 'a threat to the peace, a breach of the peace or an act of aggression'. The system cannot be criticized for authorizing the SECURITY COUNCIL to identify such a situation. But the question should be asked: is there a line to be drawn between those determinations which it is proper for the SECURITY COUNCIL to make as part of its activity directed to the immediate restoration of peace and those that go beyond that function by making legal determinations that are – in the vocabulary of the common lawyer – quasi-judicial?", *Lauterpacht*, *supra* note 364, p.44.

398 *Franck*, Fairness in International Law and Institutions, (1995), p.230.

399 *White*, The UNITED NATIONS and the Maintenance of International Peace and Security, (1990), p.69.

invokes some thoughts. The fact that the UNITED NATIONS law has not recognized the "judicial constraint" principle does not mean that the SECURITY COUNCIL is free to exercise its power beyond its functional nature. The UN Charter provides that the SECURITY COUNCIL is the main political organ and the Court is the judicial organ. It would be against its political nature and function for the SECURITY COUNCIL to deal with the legal aspects of the dispute and make any legal determinations. In the same vein, it would be against the function of a judicial organ to deal with the political aspects of the dispute. Although up till now a systematic mechanism for the demarcation and coordination of the activities of its subsidiary organs, which is in my view greatly needed, has not been developed in the UNITED NATIONS, there is still an article that indicates the intent of the drafters on this point. Article 36, paragraph 3, stipulates that the SECURITY COUNCIL in making recommendations should take into consideration that legal dispute should as a general rule be referred by the parties to the INTERNATIONAL COURT OF JUSTICE.[400] Bearing in mind that the international disputes usually possess a mixture nature, both legal and political, the categorization of "legal dispute" and "political dispute" is obsolete. Nevertheless, the facts of a dispute can be organized in a form of legal dispute, or as a political one. Accordingly, it is a reasonable inference of Article 36, paragraph 3 of the Charter that the SECURITY COUNCIL, in taking actions, should take into consideration the principle that the "legal aspect of the dispute" should as a general rule be referred to the INTERNATIONAL COURT OF JUSTICE.

Judge *Onyeama*'s Separate Opinion appending to the Court's Namibia Advisory Opinion further demonstrates this position. In the context of considering whether it was the SECURITY COUNCIL's declaration of illegality in Resolution 276(1970) that made the continued presence of SOUTH AFRICA in NAMIBIA illegal, or whether instead the illegality flowed from SOUTH AFRICA's failure to comply with the GENERAL ASSEMBLY's resolution 2145 (XXI), he observed that SECURITY COUNCIL RESOLUTION 276 (1970) was, in effect, a judicial determination, and it was doubtful if any power existed in the Charter for the SECURITY COUNCIL to make such a determination except in *certain well-defined cases* not relevant here.[401]

*Lauterpacht* interpreted the "certain well-defined cases" to refer to the powers of the Council to: (i) make a determination of persistent violation of the Principles of the Charter prior to the making of a recommendation to the General Assembly for the expulsion of a Member State under Art. 6 of the Charter; and (ii) to review a judgment of the International Court prior to making recommendations or deciding upon measures in respect of an unfulfilled judgment of the Court under Art. 94(2) of the Charter.[402]

400 *Kelsen, supra* note 355, p.370.

401 *Legal Consequences for States of the Continued Presences of South Africa in Namibia Notwithstanding SECURITY COUNCIL RESOLUTION* 276 (SOUTH-WEST AFRICA), Advisory Opinion, ICJ Reports1971, p.147.

402 *Lauterpacht, supra* note 364, p.44. *Lauterpacht* also called attention to the Judge Petrén's

Moreover, the representatives from the Member States that act with the mission of gaining for national interests under the voting procedure might not be so legally minded. *Kirgis* expressed his view on this point as follows:

> "the Council has no rules of procedure for fair adjudicative hearings; nor could it reasonably be expected to adopt or follow any such rules. Even if it did adopt procedural rules and try to follow them, it would not likely be regarded as a fair or effective adjudicator. In its fifty years of practice, it has given reason for concern in this regard. It has sometimes - including recently - seemed quite unaware of, or unconcerned about, any limits that ought to apply to its quasi-judicial role."[403]

It was also observed by *White*:

> "although it may be argued that some of the provisions of Chapter VI and the general principles contained in Article 1(1) create a quasi-judicial role for the Council, an examination of most Council debates leading to the adoption of a recommendation towards the pacific settlement of a dispute will illustrate that it is arrived at by political consensus, and that law is often merely a 'tactical

---

Separate Opinion in the Advisory Opinion of the Namibia case: A decision in this respect is to be taken by the GENERAL ASSEMBLY upon the recommendation of the SECURITY COUNCIL. There is nothing to compel either the SECURITY COUNCIL or the GENERAL ASSEMBLY to ask for an opinion of the Court before taking a decision on the question whether the Member State concerned has violated the principles of the Charter. In other words, a political organ is entitled to take a decision upon grounds which are admittedly of a legal nature, but the validity of which cannot be examined by the Court once the political organ has taken its decision within its proper sphere of competence. *Namibia* (S.W. AFRICA), Separate Opinion of Petrén, ICJ Reports 1971, p.132-133. However, Judge Sir Gerald *Fitzmaurice* expressed a different view on this point. He observed that "in the institutional field, the justification for the act of some organ or body may turn upon considerations of a political or technical character, or of professional conduct or discipline, and if so, the political, technical or professional organ or body concerned will, in principle, be competent to make the necessary determinations. But where the matter turns, and turns exclusively, on considerations of a legal character, a political organ, even if it is competent to take any resulting action, is not itself competent to make the necessary legal determinations on which the justification for such action must rest. This can only be done by a legal organ competent to make such determinations." He accordingly believed that "framers of the Charter did confer this particular specific power to expel a member State on the Assembly, in express terms, without indicating whether or not it was one that should only be exercised after a prior determination of the alleged violations by a competent juridical organ. To argue from the power thus specifically conferred by Article 6, that the Assembly must therefore be deemed to possess a general power under the Charter to make legal determinations, is clearly fallacious." *Namibia* (SOUTH WEST AFRICA), Dissenting Opinion of Judge Fitzmaurice, ICJ Reports 1971, p.299-300.

403 *Kirgis*, *supra* note 341, p.532.

device' and a 'weapon in the armoury of rhetoric'".[404]

Furthermore, it might be difficult to assert that the Member States of the UNITED NATIONS intend to confer a power that is not inherent to its political nature to the SECURITY COUNCIL, without adding any explicit provision in the Charter.[405] Although it could be argued that the Council's freedom of appraisal of the situation of "breach of peace" finds *clear textual warrant* in the Charter, it might be more plausible to interpret the discretion as merely the appraisal of "breach of peace". Article 39 does not exclude the possibility for the Council to refer the legal aspects of the dispute to the Court, at least when the Council finds that the situation calls for some legal determinations. The SECURITY COUNCIL's determination under Article 39 shall be consistent with the purpose and principle of the UN Charter. This is correct with the prerequisite that the power is exercised under extreme circumstances - when the situation is urgently calling for action from the international community and a lengthy, strict legal procedure would be impractical. The narrow interpretation of Article 39 would be consistent with the SECURITY COUNCIL's proper role as the guardian of international peace and security and also comparable with the Council's role and function as a political organ.

I respectfully share the opinion of Judge *Bedjaoui* that the SECURITY COUNCIL acted beyond its scope of power to demand LIBYA to extradite its two nationals. The SECURITY COUNCIL "not only has decided to take a number of political measures", but has also touched "the substance of the legal dispute with which the Court must *deal in a legal manner, on the basis of the 1971 Montreal Convention and international law in general.*"[406]

## 4. Rule of Law on the international plane

The SECURITY COUNCIL over-extended its power to the judicial field - this is in my view the primary cause of the Court's difficulty to exercise its power to indicate provisional measures in the *Lockerbie* cases. As have been discussed in Chapter E, Part II, the principles of "*litispendece*" and "judicial constraint" did not constitute the obstacles for the Court to entertain the request for provisional measures. To go one step further, Article 103 of the Charter should have not constituted an obstacle either. The Council should have refrained from touching on the legal aspects of the dispute to adjudge the legal rights and obligations of the parties, namely whether LIBYA possesses the right of freedom to choose to extradite or prosecute the accused

404 *White*, *supra* note 380.

405 See also *Lauterpacht*, *supra* note 364, he observed that "it is doubtful whether the States Members of the UN appreciated when they became Members that they were granting to the SECURITY COUNCIL a quasi-judicial power additional to its political powers."

406 Dissenting Opinion of Judge *Bedjaoui* appending to the Order of 11 April 1992, *Lockerbie*, ICJ Reports 1992, p.34.

nationals under the Montreal Convention. What Article 39 empowers the Council to do is to take measures to restore the immediate breach of the peace directly, rather than the legal adjudging which could be not so urgently needed and might not be so helpful for the restoration of peace actually. It is even difficult to assert that the extradition of the accused would be necessary to restore the peace that was being breached three years ago. Furthermore, it is difficult to see any appropriateness of the Council to reach such a decision more like a legal determination, through political decision-making procedure.

One might propose an approach to solve this problem that the SECURITY COUNCIL waits for the Court to render decisions on the legal issues and then make political decisions itself. This point was actually raised by Judge *Bedjaoui* in his separate opinion. He contested America's request to ask the Court to refrain from exercising its judicial function and bow to the SECURITY COUNCIL "in order to avoid any conflict" with it. He observed:

> "such invitations clearly made to the Court to refrain from exercising its judicial function independently are puzzling. In the past the Security Council awaited the Court's decision. In the *Anglo-Iranian Oil Co.* case, the Council, before which the matter had been brought in 1951 by the United Kingdom, which was asking it to take measures against IRAN, postponed discussion until the Court's decision. In the present case, a number of member States of the Security Council ... have expressed their deep conviction that it is necessary to allow the Court to perform its task and, in fact, they are expecting the Court to lay down international legality."[407]

This approach is without doubt desirable for the ultimate of the international community to introduce "rule of law rather than rule of politics" into the international relations. Moreover, it needs to be borne in mind that the compliance with the SECURITY COUNCIL's decisions depends greatly on the willingness of the States. With the development of the process of "rule of law" in international relations, it is difficult to see the States' willingness to accept a decision with the poorly constructed legal basis. As observed by *Franck*, the actions taken by the council should correspond to the "standards of legitimacy and fairness" in order to gain the support and compliance of the states.[408] Lastly, the public opinion of the whole international community would also push the SECURITY COUNCIL to mind its prestige. This could remind us of the observation by some writers that the SECURITY COUNCIL is trying to construct its resolutions with legal grounding in

407 Separate Opinion of Judge *Bedjaoui* appending to the Order of 11 April 1992, *Lockerbie*, ICJ Reports 1992, p.154, para.23.

408 *Franck*, *supra* note 371, p.219.

international law,[409] although it is still difficult to see the virtual legitimacy of some of its decisions.

Nevertheless, the "rule of law" ultimate might be too ideal to be fulfilled *in the near future*. The history since 1990 witnessed the SECURITY COUNCIL's great enthusiasm to exercise its power. The Resolutions under Chapter VII of the UN Charter, authorizing the use of forces were adopted in the cases of IRAQ,[410] former YUGOSLAVIA,[411] SOMALIA,[412] HAITI[413] and RWANDA.[414] Moreover, it was observed that the SECURITY COUNCIL has "creatively assumed new functions of various kinds under Chapter VII".[415] Some even directly pointed out that the SECURITY COUNCIL "is trying to do too much, too quickly",[416] that the SECURITY COUNCIL's power is being abused due to the control of the great powers, taking advantage of the flaws on its composition and the decision-making mechanisms.[417]

Considering the concurrent jurisdiction between the Court and the Council, some states made reservations to their acceptance of jurisdiction to avoid it, however, this is not obligatory. Moreover, the submission of complicated international disputes that possess a mixed political and legal character would promote the international judicial legislation. This is also in favor of the concept of the "rule of law" being applied on the international plane. Therefore it would be unwise not to encourage it. However, it would be necessary to avoid the over-reaching of power between the two organs, especially the Council's extension of its power to the judicial field. Considering the present world shape of political power, it is difficult to see any

---

409 It is observed that "since the Persian Gulf War, the Council has resumed the practice of citing the chapter and verse that form the basis for its decisions, thereby grounding them in the law." *Bedjaoui*, supra note 375, p.35.

410 *See e.g.*, UNDocs. S/RES/660 (1990), S/RES/662 (1990), S/RES/661 (1990), S/RES/666 (1990), S/RES/670 (1990), S/RES/665 (1990) and S/RES/678 (1990).

411 *See, e.g.*, UNDocs. S/RES/713 (1991), S/RES/757 (1992), S/RES/787 (1992), and S/RES/820 (1993).

412 UNDocs. S/RES/733 (1992).

413 UNDocs. S/RES/841 (1993).

414 UNDocs. S/RES/788 (1992).

415 It was observed that the SECURITY COUNCIL has creatively assumed new functions of various kinds under Chapter VII, *inter alia*, by curtailing the sovereignty of a defeated aggressor state by imposing the conditions of a termination of hostilities (IRAQ), intervening with military force for humanitarian reasons into the anarchy of another state (SOMALIA), limiting the right of self-defense of a UN member state through maintaining an arms embargo (BOSNIA-HERZEGOVINA), imposing sanctions for providing shelter to alleged terrorists (SUDAN and AFGHANISTAN), and ordering Libya to extradite two nationals allegedly responsible for acts of terrorism to the courts of two permanent members of the SECURITY COUNCIL (the *Lockerbie* case), *Schweigman*, *supra* note 377, Introduction part.

416 *Murphy*, The SECURITY COUNCIL, Legitimacy, and the Concept of Collective Security after the Cold War, Columbia Journal of Transnational Law (1994), Vol.32, p.201-288.

417 See, *eg.*, *Caron*, The Legitimacy of the Collective Authority of the SECURITY COUNCIL, American Journal of International Law (1993), Vol.87, p.552-588.

possibility that the Council would be self-restrained to withdraw back to its own boundary of authority. Nevertheless, some writers have raised some approaches to solve the problem, such as establishing a "constitutional Chamber" of the Court with a view to provide ready and speedy opinions to the UN organs as crises develop, or establishing a legal committee under the SECURITY COUNCIL for legal counseling.[418]

## IV. Limited judicial review

Putting an even closer look on the *Lockerbie* cases, it is found that the Court's applying Article 103 of the Charter was made on a prerequisite that the SECURITY COUNCIL RESOLUTION 748(1992) was legal and valid. Then a tentative question could be asked: Could the Court assert a power to review the SECURITY COUNCIL actions?

As discussed above, the prevailing view holds that although the Council possesses the discretion to act under Chapter VII, this power still bears some legal limitations. In the advisory case concerning *Legal Consequences for States of the Continued Presence of South Africa in Namibia*, two of the judges observed that even the manner in which the SECURITY COUNCIL had exercised its discretionary power to determine that a "situation was being dealt with under the head of the maintenance of international peace and security" should have been subjected to judicial review. Judge *Fitzmaurice* observed as follows:

> "Limitations on the powers of the Security Council are necessary because of the all too great ease with which any acutely controversial international situation can be represented as involving a latent threat to peace and security, even where it is really too remote genuinely to constitute one. Without these limitations, the functions of the Security Council could be used for purposes never originally intended … there [was] no threat to peace and security other than as might be artificially created as a pretext for the realization of ulterior purposes."[419]

It is widely accepted that the Court has not been endowed expressly with the power of judicial review and it does not stand as a hierarchically superior organ of judgment upon the other organs of the UNITED NATIONS.[420] The Court affirmed this

418 *Shaw*, *supra* note 354, p.259.

419 Dissenting Opinion of Judge Sir Gerald *Fitzmaurice*, *Namibia* case (SOUTH-WEST AFRICA), Advisory Opinion, ICJ Reports 1971, p.294, para.116.

420 The political framework within which the International Court operates and the institutional status that it has are in no way similar to such domestic courts and the drawing of parallels

point in the *Namibia* case: "undoubtedly, the Court does not possess powers of judicial review or appeal in respect of the decisions taken by the United Nations organs concerned."[421]

Nevertheless, it can be argued that the Court can exert some sort of judicial review over the SECURITY COUNCIL action. Firstly, the judicial review power does exist when the Court is exercising its advisory jurisdiction, although a request for advisory opinion could be rarely raised as to the Council's resolution because of the requirement of veto or majority consensus. Secondly, the Court could still assert the incidental review[422] as to the Council's resolution in the contentious proceedings. On this point, *Skubiszewski* observed that "the Court is not, and it is submitted *de lege ferenda* that it should not become, a tribunal of judicial review with power to declare null and void those acts of the Security Council that it finds contrary to law. But the Court, in view of its function, cannot and in fact did not shy away from pronouncing on the conformity of Security Council acts with law in both contentious and advisory opinions."[423]

*Schweigman* elaborated this point as follows:

> "the Court does have a limited power of review. In contentious cases the Court has to settle disputes brought before it on the basis of international law. Binding decisions of the Council undoubtedly form part of this law. In the exercise of its judicial function, the Court will have to consider for each case whether the particular rule of international law relied upon by one or both of the parties is applicable and valid in the specific circumstances of the case. The Court will have to satisfy itself, for example, as to whether a treaty invoked by a party has entered into force and whether it applies to the relations between the parties. The same holds for the decisions of the Council. If one of the parties relies on or contests the applicability of a Council decision, the Court, in the exercise of its judicial function, should determine whether the decision is indeed *intra vires*, in other words, whether the decision does in fact form part and parcel of international law."[424]

---

are more likely to emphasize such differences than act as a source from which to infer increased institutional powers. See *Reisman*, The Constitutional Crisis in the UNITED NATIONS, American Journal of International Law (1993), Vol.87, p.87; and *Herdegen*, The 'Constitutionalisation' of the UN Security System, Vanderbilt Journal of Transnational Law (1994), Vol.27, p. 145; *Shaw*, *supra* note 354, p.256.

421 *Legal Consequences for States of the Continued Presence of South Africa in Namibia* (SOUTH-WEST AFRICA), ICJ Reports 1971, p.45, para.89.

422 This competence is to be distinguished from a general power of judicial review. See *schweigman*, *supra* note 377, p.271.

423 *Skubiszewski*, The INTERNATIONAL COURT OF JUSTICE and the SECURITY COUNCIL, In: *Lowe*, *Fitzmaurice* (eds.), Fifty Years of the INTERNATIONAL COURT OF JUSTICE (1996), p.606-629.

424 *Schweigman*, *supra* note 377, p.217.

Referring this view to the *Lockerbie* cases, it is arguable that the Court, in finding the applicable law, must take account of the legality and validity of the Council's resolution in so far as it affects the appropriateness of providing provisional protection to the rights sought to be protected by LIBYA.

The incidental review could only be exercised when the Court is also seised of the subject matter that is being entertained by the SECURITY COUNCIL. In other words, the Court can only exercise its power of incidental judicial review to the extent that the jurisdiction conferred by the instrument overlaps with that of the SECURITY COUNCIL decision. It was observed that the instances in which this could happen are very limited.[425] Judge *Bedjaoui* therefore observed that "it seems that the Court was right not to allow itself at any time to be tempted to pronounce on the validity of the way the Security Council had intended to deal with the case of the international responsibility of a state for terrorist activities, which is wider than the dispute here."[426]

Additionally, the Court's incidental judicial review would be operated in a limited manner. It would be based on the presumption that the Council's resolution is legal and valid. *Lauterpacht* mentioned this point in the Genocide case: "it is not to be contemplated that the Security Council would even deliberately adopted a resolution clearly and deliberately flouting a rule of *jus cogens* or requiring a violation of human rights. But the possibility that a Security Council resolution might inadvertently or in an unforeseen manner lead to such a situation cannot be excluded."[427]

He continued: "and that, it appears, is what has happened here ... the Security Council resolutions can be seen as having in effect called on Members of the United Nations, albeit unknowingly and assured unwillingly, to become in some degree supporters of the genocidal activity of the Serbs and in this manner and to that extent to act contrary to *jus cogens*."[428]

The Court in the *Namibia* case again affirmed this view. It stated that "a resolution of a properly constituted organ of the United Nations which is passed in accordance with that organ's rules of procedure, and is declared by its President to have been so passed, must be presumed to have been validly adopted".[429]

It is therefore a plausible inference that the Court would act in a delicate manner and exert a rather strict requirement of proof as to the illegality of the resolution.

---

425 *Schweigman*, *ibid.*, p.285.

426 Dissenting Opinion of Judge *Bedjaoui* appending to the 11 April 1992, *Lockerbie*, ICJ Reports 1992, p.151, para.18.

427 Separate Opinion of Judge *Lauterpacht* appending to the Order of 8 April 1993, *Bosnian Genocide*, ICJ Reports 1993, p.119-120, para.102.

428 *Lauterpacht*, *ibid.*, p.120, para.102.

429 *Legal Consequences for States of the Continued Presence of South Africa in Namibia (SOUTH-WEST AFRICA) notwithstanding SECURITY COUNCIL RESOLUTION 276(1970)*, ICJ Reports 1971, p.22, para.20.

Without any established procedure on judicial review, it would remain to be a very difficult problem the Court needs to deal with. Moreover, with regard to the lack of express authority to judicial review of the SECURITY COUNCIL RESOLUTION, and the necessity to respect the harmonious cooperation between the organs within the UN system, the Court might act with great caution when it finds it necessary to challenge the Council's resolution. It is suggested by *Schweigman* that the Court would couch its determination in careful terms when it pronounces itself on a possible illegality of a Council decision and it would probably refer it back to the Council that would then remedy the defective resolution.[430]

Therefore, it can be concluded that there is little the Court can do to overcome the difficulty in the *Lockerbie* cases. Even if LIBYA had instituted the proceedings on the basis of "violation of general international law" and the jurisdictional condition for the exercise of incidental judicial review had been satisfied, the Court would act very limitedly. Moreover, it is important to note that the Court will not review the validity of the SECURITY COUNCIL RESOLUTION at this phase (provisional measures) because it would be impossible for the Court to touch on the merits and reject the presumption of the resolution's validity at the provisional measures phase.

430 *Schweigman, supra* note 377, p.283.

## Conclusions

Article 41 of the Statute of the Court states that the Court has the power to indicate provisional measures if it considers that circumstances so require. Yet, this article does not provide any further information and it is left to the Court to develop the law. In order to study the Court's practice on provisional measures, Chapter A examines the legal basis for this power - Article 41 of the Statute of the Court is the only source of the power.

Chapter B provides a brief survey of the Court's decisions on provisional measures. The procedure has been much more frequently triggered since 1990. This is on the one hand because more states acceded to the Court's jurisdiction. On the other hand, it is due to the encouraging effects that provisional measures bring to the requesting parties.

With the assumption that studying the purposes for which provisional measures can be claimed is an important step to probe into the Court's practice, Chapter C examines the statutory purpose of provisional measures.

Firstly, provisional measures could be claimed for the purpose of "preserving the respective rights of either party". It requires a standard higher than "to prevent the rights from infringement or breach". The *Case Concerning UNITED STATES Diplomatic and Consular Staff in Tehran* shows that provisional measures are required only when the circumstances show that the rights are going to disappear, or conceivably that the subject-matter of the right is going to be non-existent, or the rights will be without any virtual value to the other party when the final judgment renders if the provisional measures are not granted;

Secondly, for the purpose of "the prevention of irreparable prejudice", provisional measures are designed to prevent a prejudice that would probably occur in the future rather than imposing redress for the wrong already and irreversibly inflicted. In reality, the dividing line between the two is obscure. Most of the time, the rights sought to be protected are being infringed and are in a deteriorating situation;

Thirdly, for the purpose of "protecting certain recognized rights or keeping a certain recognized legal status". The Court's practice shows that the purpose for which provisional measures can be claimed could be extended to cover "the prevention of irreparable prejudice" to the claimed rights, which have not been recognized under the current frame of international law (*Nuclear Tests* cases);

Fourthly, "non-anticipation of Court's decision" is also recognized as the purpose for which provisional measures can be claimed. The applicant cannot act upon his own view as correct, but act upon the assumption that his opponent may possibly be right until the final judgment is rendered. The purpose of provisional measures is sometime described as the preservation of the *status quo*. Provisional measures are

compliance of the provisional measures Orders, it could be a wise choice for the Court to hold a criterion "higher than only *prima facie*" on jurisdiction. Too fast and simple a conclusion without any consideration to the objecting grounds on jurisdiction would probably lead to great threat of derogation of the Court's dignity, due to the possible forthcoming different conclusion at a later stage. The Court, in the most recent cases, is adopting a more stringent test.

Controversy has existed on the question - is the establishment of "a *prima facie* case" another condition to the indication of provisional measures? Comparing with the municipal court's practice, the prejudgment at this stage of proceedings in international courts might probably lead to very serious or even catastrophic effects because the cases usually involve the state parties' sovereignty rights. Moreover, it is an unreasonably difficult task for the Court to decide at this stage whether a case exists, in the usually complicated inter-state disputes. Therefore, the Court has not accepted it as a condition of provisional measures.

The Court has not recognized the admissibility of the main claim as an additional condition of provisional measures, either. The investigation on the admissibility of the main claim is usually complex and closely relevant to the merits and it would "certainly prolong proceedings at the interim measures stage" and might be quite "impractical". Nevertheless, the Court is not taking it as totally irrelevant to the indication of provisional measures. The Court's practice shows that it would not reject the requests if the right claimed is manifestly not existent.

The admissibility of the request is recognized as a condition for provisional measures. The provisional measures must be designed to preserve the rights that are the subject of the main claim submitted before the Court. A link must therefore be established between the alleged rights the protection of which is the subject of the provisional measures being sought, and the subject of the principle request submitted to the Court.

Secondly, it discusses the necessity to indicate provisional measures, namely the "irreparable prejudice" and "urgency". The test of "absolute irreparability" has been abandoned. "Irreparability" is nowadays interpreted as "impossibility of full execution of the final judgment" in the Orders. Even if the infringement could be made good by appropriate means, the Court could grant the provisional measures if otherwise it would prejudice the full execution of the final judgment.

Could irreparable prejudice to human life other than the subject matter of the main claim be regarded as one of the circumstances justifying provisional measures? In the case concerning the *Land and Maritime Boundary between CAMEROON and NIGERIA*, the Court accepted that the rights at issue are the sovereignty rights over the territory and irreparable prejudice was not existed to these rights. The Court tried to ground the order on the necessity to prevent aggravation of the dispute. On the other hand, the Court tried to alternatively ground the order on establishing the "irreparable prejudice". The Court interpreted the scope of the "rights at issue in the proceedings" widely by adopting the diction of "these rights also concern persons".

From the jurisdictional point of view, the Court can only exercise judicial function within the limitation that the parties have agreed. Here the Court liberally interpreted the link that is required between the right sought to be protected by provisional measures and the subject of the main claim. The great concern on the human life is one of the important factors that influence the Court's decision.

Chapter E deals with the issue "the provisional measures and the SECURITY COUNCIL RESOLUTIONS". In *Lockerbie*, the Court was confronted with the request for provisional measures that the same subject matter was simultaneously presented before the SECURITY COUNCIL. It could be argued that the Court possesses the freedom to independently exercise its power to indicate provisional measures, even if that would contradict the Council's resolution. It should have proceeded to order the provisional measures if it considered that the circumstances so require, even if the effects of the provisional measures would be prevailed by Article 103. It is disappointing that the Court did not choose to do so. Nevertheless, even if we imagine that LIBYA had requested provisional measures to protect its rights in general international law and Article 103 had not been applicable then, the Court would still have not indicated provisional measures that contradict the Council's resolution since the enforcement of the Court's decisions depends on the Council's discretion according to Article 94(2) of the Charter. Therefore the Court's authority to indicate provisional measures independently could only work in theory. The Court's power to indicate provisional measures in particular and its judicial function in general is to some extent paralyzed by the Council's over-extension of its power under Chapter VII.

With respect to international disputes settlement, conflicting decisions usually occur just because of the overlap of jurisdiction between the organs. It is widely criticized that the SECURITY COUNCIL adopts resolutions that in nature constitute legal determinations. Chapter VII of the UN Charter in general provides the Council with the primary responsibility of maintenance of international peace. Article 39 in particular provides it with the power to determine the situation of "breach of peace" and to take necessary measures. It would be a plausible inference that the Charter permits the Council with an exceptional extension of power rather than appointing an additional judicial organ. In other words, there is an implied prerequisite for the Council to exercise the power --- it exercises the power in a manner comparable to its role as a political organ. The Council possesses the exclusive discretion on determining the situation of "breach of peace". However, when it decides measures to restore international peace, it should act within some limitations. In *Lockerbie*, the Council should not have adopted a resolution that has the effect of adjudging the right of LIBYA concerning the extradition of its accused nationals. Or at least, it could refer this legal issue to the Court and after then adopt a resolution, based on the opinion of the Court on the issue whether LIBYA possesses the right or not. Then the conflicting decisions between the two organs would have not occurred. However, this is not what the Council chose to do. The Council's practice of making resolutions adjudging the legal relations between the parties, in my view, is beyond the Council's political function.

It is the self-constraint of the SECURITY COUNCIL that could ultimately solve the problem. However, it might not be realistic in the near future. Then a tentative discussion on the incidental judicial review over the Council's action has been taken. However, the Court can only exercise incidental review to the extent that the jurisdiction conferred by the instrument overlaps with that of the SECURITY COUNCIL decision. The instances in which this could happen are very limited. Moreover, a strict requirement of proof would be exerted because the judicial review would be based on the presumption that the SECURITY COUNCIL RESOLUTION is legal and valid. The Court would act with great caution when it intends to challenge the Council's resolution. A more possible approach the Court might choose is to refer the defective resolution back to the Council and suggest it remedy it.

It is noteworthy that the Court could not review the Council's resolution at the provisional measures stage. The assertion of the Court's power of judicial review at this preliminary stage, even in an incidental manner, is doubtable because the pronouncing on the legality and validity of the Council's resolution would require detailed finding of facts and law that is impossible to achieve at this stage.

As one of the procedural mechanisms within the UN system, the provisional measures' characters and development is inevitably connected with the most fundamentals of the UN system. It therefore possesses some characteristics that are different from its counterpart in municipal law. A good example is that the Court has not recognized "a *prima facie* case" as a condition to provisional measures, considering the risk of prejudgment that usually involves sovereignty which would cause more serious or even catastrophic effects comparing to that of municipal courts and the complexity of finding "a *prima facie* case" in international disputes.

Besides the technical issues, it is even more significant that the Court's practice on provisional measures possesses some characteristics that are closely connected with the most fundamental issues in international dispute settlement. In order to find out the Court's practice on provisional measures and make some tentative prediction on its future development, it's important to always bear the wider context in mind.

The Court adapted its case law on provisional measures to the developing necessity of the international dispute settlement. For example, it is tending to exert a stricter standard as to the proof of jurisdiction, comparing to its earlier practice, considering the more frequently raised challenges to the jurisdiction from the Respondent in the later proceedings and the great significance of national sovereignty. Another example is the abandonment of the test of "absolute irreparability". Even if the infringement could be made good by appropriate means, the Court could grant the provisional measures if otherwise it would prejudice the full execution of the final judgment.

The maintenance of international peace and security is greatly inducing for the Court's indication of provisional measures, as shown in the Orders indicated to prevent the aggravation of the dispute. Accordingly the Court's practice to indicate provisional measures independently on the basis of "non-aggravation" would be inconsistent with the passive character of the Court's judicial function. It is also a shift from the Court's authority under Article 41. Moreover, it might cause some difficulties in practice.

Another example for this point is the Court's practice to indicate provisional measures to prevent irreparable prejudice to human life other than the subject matter of the main claim. Although it might be argued that the Court shall not deal with the matters that are beyond its jurisdiction. The Court, analyzing from the link between the right sought to be protected and the subject of the main claim, concluded that a direct link existed between the human life and the territorial sovereignty.

The *Lockerbie* cases show that the Court's power to indicate provisional measures is to some extent paralyzed by the Council's intrusion into the judicial functional scope. Without any institutional modification in the UN system or the Council's self-constraint, there seems to be no feasible solution to this problem. The Court does not possess the power to exert any supervisory function over the Council in the phase of provisional measures. It might follow the present practice, not to indicate provisional measures contradicting with the Council's resolutions. A more active approach it might take would be to suggest the Council remedy the defective resolution. Provisional measures constitute an integral part of the dispute settlement procedure by ensuring the full execution of the forthcoming judgment and preserving the evidence. Meanwhile, they lessen the tension and create a basis for negotiation. To this extent, they play an important role in the maintenance of international peace and security. Nevertheless, the above analysis shows that its function in practice is not as significant as expected.

**Bibliography**

A. O. Adede, The Rules of Interlocutory Injunctions Under Domestic Law and the Interim Measures of Protection in International Law, Syracuse Journal of International Law & Commentary, (1977), Vol.4, p.277.
R. P. Anand, Compulsory Jurisdiction of the INTERNATIONAL COURT OF JUSTICE, Asian Publishing House, (1961), p.85.
M. Bedjaoui, The New World and the SECURITY COUNCIL: Testing the Legality of its Acts, Martinus Nijhof, (1994), p.52-53.
A. von Bogdandy, Lawmaking by International Organizations, In: P. Wolfrum, V. Röben (eds.), Developments of International Law in Treaty Making, Springer, (2005), p.199.
D. D. Caron, The Legitimacy of the Collective Authority of the SECURITY COUNCIL, American Journal of International Law, (1993), Vol.87, p.552-588.
D. Ciobanu, Litispendence between the INTERNATIONAL COURT OF JUSTICE and the Political Organs of the UNITED NATIONS, In: Leo Gross (ed.), The Future of the INTERNATIONAL COURT OF JUSTICE, Oceana Publications, (1976), p.216-219.
L. Collins, Provisional and Protective Measures, Recueil Des Cours 1992-III, Martinus Nijhoff Publishers, (1993), p.224.
D. P. O'Connell, International Law, Vol.1, Stevens, (1965), p.13.
J. F. Dulles, War or Peace, Macmillan, (1950), p.194-195.
E. Dumbauld, Interim Measures of Protection in International Controversies, Nijhoff, (1932).
P.-M. Dupuy, Droit international public, Dalloz-Sirey, (1992), p.127.
C. Eagleton, International Government, Ronald Press, (1957), p.450.
J. B. Elkind, Interim Protection: A Functional Approach, Martinus Nijhoff Publishers, (1981).
T. J. H. Elsen, Litispendence between the INTERNATIONAL COURT OF JUSTICE and the SECURITY COUNCIL, T.M.C. Asser Institut, (1986), p.1, p.12-14.
P. A. Essoff, FINLAND v. DENMARK: A Call to Clarify the INTERNATIONAL COURT OF JUSTICE's Standards for Provisional Measures, Fordham International Law Journal, (1991/1992), Vol.15, p.839-901.
G. Fitzmaurice, The Law and Procedure of the INTERNATIONAL COURT OF JUSTICE, Grotius Publications Limited, (1986), p.496, 534, 774-777.
K. Oellers-Frahm, Multiplication of International Courts and Tribunals and Conflicting Jurisdiction – Problems and Possible Solutions, In: J. A. Frowein, C. E. Philipp, R. Wolfrum (eds.), Max Planck Yearbook of UNITED NATIONS Law, (2001), Vol.5, p.77.
T. M. Franck, Fairness in International Law and Institutions, Oxford University Press, (1995), p.230.
P. J. Goldsworthy, Interim Measures of Protection in the INTERNATIONAL COURT

OF JUSTICE, The American Journal of International Law, (1974), Vol. 68, p.270.
L. M. Goodrich, A. P. Simons, The UNITED NATIONS and the Maintenance of International Peace and Security, Brookings Institution, (1995), p.348.
E. Gordon, Legal Disputes under Article 36(2) of the Statute, in: L. Damrosch (ed.), The INTERNATIONAL COURT OF JUSTICE at a Crossroads, Transnational Publication, (1987), p.200.
D. W. Greig, The Balancing of Interests and the Granting of Interim Protection by the International Court, Australian Year Book of International Law, (1991), Vol.11, p.127.
L. Gross (ed.), The Future of the INTERNATIONAL COURT OF JUSTICE, Oceana Publishing, (1976), p.739.
Institut juridique international, Hague, The PERMANENT COURT OF INTERNATIONAL JUSTICE: Statute and Rules, (1922). (published on behalf of the Court)
Halsbury, The Laws of England, Butterworth & Co., (1911), p.219.
M. Herdegen, The 'Constitutionalisation' of the UN Security System, 27 Vanderbilt Journal of Transnational Law, (1994), Vol.27, p.135.
R. Higgins, Policy Considerations and the International Judicial Process, The International and Comparative Law Quarterly, (1968), Vol.17, p.63.
A. J. J. de Hoogh, Attribution or Delegation of (Legislative) Power by the SECURITY COUNCIL? The Case of the United Transnational Administration in East Timor (UNTAET), Yearbook of International Peace Operation, (2001), Vol.7, p.37.
F. G. Jacobs, Interim Measures in the Law and Practice of the Court of Justice of the European Communities, In: R. Bernhardt (ed.), Interim Measures Indicated by International Courts, Springer, (1994), p.50.
R. Y. Jennings, Reflections on the Term Dispute, In: Macdonald (ed.), Essays in Honour of Wang Tieya on His Eightieth Birthday, Martinus Niihoff, (1994), p.403.
H. Kelsen, The Law of the UNITED NATIONS: A Critical Analysis of its Fundamental Problems, Lawbook Exchange Ltd., (2000), p.294.
F. L. Kirgis, The SECURITY COUNCIL's First Fifty Years, American Journal of International Law, 1995, Vol.89, p.527.
E. Lauterpacht, Aspects of the Administration of International Justice, Grotius Publications, (1991), p.37,43,44,47.
E. Lauterpacht, C. J. Greenwood, International Law Reports, Gomer Press, (1994), Vol. 94, p.468-469.
H. Lauterpacht, The Development of International Law by the International Court, Grotius Publications, (1982), p.13-14.
R.S.J., Macdonald, Changing Relations between the INTERNATIONAL COURT OF JUSTICE and the SECURITY COUNCIL of the UNITED NATIONS, Canadian Yearbook of International Law, (1993), Vol.31, p.3, 21.
D. M. McRae, Use of Economic Sanctions under International Law, The Canadian Yearbook of International Law, (2001), Vol.39, p.262-276.
E. McWhinney, Judicial Settlement of International Disputes, Nijhoff, (1991), p.42.

M. H. Mendelson, Interim Measures of Protection in Cases of Contested Jurisdiction, The British Year Book of International Law, (1972-1973), Vol. 46, p.316-317.
J. G. Merrils, Interim Measures of Protection and the Substantive Jurisdiction of the International Court, Cambridge Law Journal, (1977),Vol. 36, p.101-102.
D. H. Miller, The Drafting of the Covenant, Putnam, (1928), p.3-6.
H. Mosler, Political and Justiciable Legal Disputes: Revival of an Old Controversy, In: Schwarzenberger, Cheng & Brown (eds.), Contemporary Problems of International Law: Essays in Honour of Georg Schwarzenberger on his Eightieth Birthday, Stevens and Sons, (1988), p.219.
S. D. Murphy, The SECURITY COUNCIL, Legitimacy, and the Concept of Collective Security After the Cold War, Columbia Journal of Transnational Law, (1994), Vol.32, p.201-288.
G. Nolte, The Limits of the SECURITY COUNCIL's Powers and its Functions on the international Legal System: Some Reflections, In: M. Byers (ed), The Role of Law in International Politics, Oxford University Press, (2000), p.322.
P. Palchetti, The Power of the INTERNATIONAL COURT OF JUSTICE to Indicate Provisional Measures to Prevent the Aggravation of a Dispute, Leiden Journal of International Law, (2008), Vol.21, p.630-636.
D. R. Reichert, Problems with Parallel and Duplicate Proceedings: The Litispendence Principle and International Arbitrations, Arbitration International, (1992), p.239.
M. Reisman, The Constitutional Crisis in the UNITED NATIONS, American Journal of International Law, (1993), Vol.87, p.83-100.
S. Rosenne,Provisional Measures in International Law, Oxford University Press, (2005).
- The INTERNATIONAL COURT OF JUSTICE: an essay in political and legal theory, Sijthoff, (1957), p.284.
B. Rudolf (ed.), Interim Measures Indicated by International Courts, Springer, (1994).
R. B. Russell, A History of the UNITED NATIONS Charter, Brookings Institution, (1958), p.465-466.
D. Sarroshi, The UNITED NATIONS and the Development of Collective Security, Oxford University Press, (1999), p.97.
L. Savadogo, Case Concerning Armed Activities on the Territory of the CONGO (DEMOCRATIC REPUBLIC OF THE CONGO v. UGANDA): The Court's Provisional Measures Order of 1 July 2001, British Yearbook of International Law, (2001), Vol.72, p.364.
D. Schweigman, The Authority of the SECURITY COUNCIL under Chapter VII of the UN Charter, Kluwer Law International, (2005), p.155, 217, 271, 283, 285, 301..
M. N. Shaw, International Law, Cambridge University Press, (1991), p.98-99.
- The SECURITY COUNCIL and the INTERNATIONAL COURT OF JUSTICE: Judicial

Drift and Judicial Function, The INTERNATIONAL COURT OF JUSTICE - Its Future Role after Fifty Years, A. S. Muller *et al.* (eds.), Kluwer Law International, (1997), p.226, 230-231, 235, 255-256.
K. Skubiszewski, The INTERNATIONAL COURT OF JUSTICE and the SECURITY COUNCIL, in: V. Lowe, M. Fitzmaurice (eds.), Fifty Years of the INTERNATIONAL COURT OF JUSTICE, Cambridge University Press, (1996), p.606-629.
B. Simma, H. Mosler (eds.), The Charter of the UNITED NATIONS: A Commentary, Oxford University Press, (2000), p.397.
J. Sztucki, Interim Measures in the HAGUE COURT, Kluwer Law and Taxation Publishers, (1983).
- Case Concerning Land and Maritime Boundary (CAMEROON v. NIGERIA): Provisional Measures, Order of 15 March 1996, Leiden Journal of International Law, (1997), Vol.10, p.357.
H. W. A Thirlway, The Law and Procedure of the INTERNATIONAL COURT OF JUSTICE 1960-1989. Part Twelve, British Year Book of International Law, (2001), Vol.LXXII, p.103
. - The Indication of Provisional Measures by the INTERNATIONAL COURT OF JUSTICE, In: R. Bernhardt (ed.), Interim Measures Indicated by International Court (1994), p.6.
J. S. Watson, Constitutionalism, Judicial Review and the World Court, Harvard International Law Journal, (1993), Vol.34, p.36-37.
N. D. White, The UNITED NATIONS and the Maintenance of International Peace and Security, Manchester University Press, (1990), p.69.

**Table of Cases**

**Kölner Schriften zu Recht und Staat**

Herausgegeben von
Hartmut Schiedermair und Bernhard Kempen

Band 1 Bernhard Kempen: Die deutsch-polnische Grenze nach der Friedensregelung des Zwei-plus-Vier-Vertrages. 1997.

Band 2 Hans-Georg Maaßen: Die Rechtsstellung des Asylbewerbers im Völkerrecht. Überlegungen zu den völkerrechtlichen Rahmenbedingungen einer europäischen Asylrechtsharmonisierung. 1997.

Band 3 Udo Fink: Kollektive Friedenssicherung. Kapitel VII UN-Charta in der Praxis des Sicherheitsrats der Vereinten Nationen. 1999.

Band 4 Stephan Grigolli: Sprachliche Minderheiten in Italien, insbesondere Südtirol, und in Europa. Der Gebrauch der Sprache vor Behörden und Gerichten und die Vergabe öffentlicher Stellen. 1997.

Band 5 Uta Stoy-Schnell: Das Bundesverfassungsgericht und die Corte costituzionale. Ein Vergleich der Verfassungsgerichtsbarkeiten in Deutschland und Italien. 1998.

Band 6 Christian Hillgruber: Die Aufnahme neuer Staaten in die Völkerrechtsgemeinschaft. Das völkerrechtliche Institut der Anerkennung von Neustaaten in der Praxis des 19. und 20. Jahrhunderts. 1998.

Band 7 Jochen Seitz: Planungshoheit und Grundeigentum. Die verfassungsrechtlichen Schranken der städtebaulichen Entwicklungsmaßnahmen. 1999.

Band 8 Jochen Herbst: Rechtskontrolle des UN-Sicherheitsrates. 1999.

Band 9 Kristin Möller: Die Beschaffung naturschutzrechtlicher Ausgleichsflächen im Baurecht. 1999.

Band 10 Klaus Löffelbein: Genehmigungsfreies Bauen und Nachbarrechtsschutz. Die baurechtlichen Anzeige- und Freistellungsverfahren der Länder aus nachbarlicher Sicht. 2000.

Band 11 Patrick Mittmann: Die Rechtsfortbildung durch den Gerichtshof der Europäischen Gemeinschaften und die Rechtsstellung der Mitgliedstaaten der Europäischen Union. 2000.

Band 12 Martin R. Albus: Zur Notwendigkeit eines Internationalen Umweltgerichtshofs. Zugleich eine Analyse der Staatenpraxis zum Internationalen Umwelthaftungsrecht und der Rechtsschutzmöglichkeiten bei grenzüberschreitenden Umweltbeeinträchtigungen. 2000.

Band 13 Irene Baur: Die Haftung der Europäischen Zentralbank. 2001.

Band 14 Tobias R. Ehlen: Zentralisierungsmöglichkeiten der deutschen Börsenaufsicht. 2003.

Band 15 Ulrich Steiner: Wertsicherungsklauseln. Zur Europarechtskonformität des neuen § 2 PaPkG. 2003.

Band 16 Stephanie Vogel: Der Prüfungsumfang des Bundesverfassungsgerichts bei Verfassungsbeschwerden am Beispiel der Kunstfreiheitsrechtsprechung. 2004.

Band 17 Thomas Schmidt: Deutsche Hochschulräte. Begriff, Darstellung und rechtliche Analyse. 2004.

Band 18 Kirsten Schmalenbach: Die Haftung Internationaler Organisationen im Rahmen von Militäreinsätzen und Territorialverwaltungen. 2004.

Band 19 Gunter Warg: Von Verteidigung zu kollektiver Sicherheit. Der Nato-Vertrag *auf Rädern*. 2004.

Band 20 Bernhard Kempen / Yvonne Dorf: Bodenreform 1945–1949. Eine verfassungsrechtliche Neubewertung. 2004.

Band 21 Jeanette Nolte: Die völkerrechtliche Vertragspraxis der EG und die Haftung der Mitgliedstaaten am Beispiel der Fischereipolitik. 2004.

Band 22 Rüdiger Schmid-Kühnhöfer: Die Staatlichkeit von Beihilfen. Mittel- und Transferzurechnung nach Art. 87 Abs. 1 EG-Vertrag. 2004.

Band 23 Florian Schöler: Die Reform des Europäischen Kartellverfahrensrechts durch die Verordnung (EG) Nr. 1/2003. 2004.

Band 24 Christina Maria Pelzer: Die Kompetenzen der EG im Bereich Forschung. Eine Analyse ihrer Reichweite und Grenzen vor dem Hintergrund des Art. 5 Abs. 3 GG. Dargestellt am Beispiel der Gentechnologie. 2004.

Band 25 Nikolaus Vieten: Die verfassungsrechtliche Zulässigkeit der Wiedereinführung einer Vermögensteuer. Zugleich eine Untersuchung des Halbteilungsbeschlusses des Bundesverfassungsgerichts. 2005.

Band 26 Bernhard Kempen (Hrsg.): Die rechtsstaatliche Bewältigung der demokratischen Bodenreform. 2005.

Band 27 Erik Hansalek: Die parlamentarische Kontrolle der Bundesregierung im Bereich der Nachrichtendienste. 2006.

Band 28 Thomas Günther: Zur Zulässigkeit der Errichtung privater Volksschulen als Bekenntnisschulen religiös-ethnischer Minderheiten nach Art. 7 Abs. 5 GG. Am Beispiel einer islamischen Grundschule. 2006.

Band 29 Christian Hoppe: Staatshaftung und Rechtsschutz bei Verletzung grundfreiheitlicher Schutzpflichten. 2006.

Band 30 Julia Schäfer: Die Entscheidung des ECOFIN-Rats über das Vorliegen eines übermäßigen Defizits. Eine Entscheidung zwischen Politik und Recht. 2007.

Band 31 Erika Elisabeth Orth: Ein Grundrecht auf Umweltschutz in Europa? Eine rechtsdogmatische Einordnung des Art. 37 GRC. 2007.

Band 32 Cécile Günther: Die Auslegung des Rechts auf Bildung in der europäischen Grundrechtsordnung. Eine Analyse von Schutzbereich und Reichweite – dargestellt am Beispiel des Art. 14 EU-GRCh (Art. II-74 EuVerf). 2007.

Band 33 Muna A. Yousif: Die extraterritoriale Geltung der Grundrechte bei der Ausübung deutscher Staatsgewalt im Ausland. 2007.

Band 34 Stefanie von Hoff: Die Rolle des US-Supreme Court im Prozess der Verfassungsänderung in den Vereinigten Staaten von Amerika. 2008.

Band 35 Alexander Metz: Das Recht Prominenter am eigenen Bild in Kollision mit Drittinteressen. Insbesondere vor dem Hintergrund des Falles Caroline von Hannover. 2008.

Band 36 Susanne Dyrchs: Das hybride Khmer Rouge-Tribunal. Entstehung, Entwicklung und rechtliche Grundlagen. 2008.

Band 37 Heiko F. Schmitz-Elvenich: Targeted Killing. Die völkerrechtliche Zulässigkeit der gezielten Tötung von Terroristen im Ausland. 2008.

Band 38 Stefania Slavu: Die Osterweiterung der Europäischen Union. Eine Analyse des EU-Beitritts Rumäniens. 2008.

Band 39 Thomas Krings: Der Grundrechtsberechtigte des Grundrechts aus Art. 13 GG. 2009.

Band 40 Zan He: The ICJ´s Practice on Provisional Measures. 2010.

Band 41 Anna Köhler: Private Sicherheits- und Militärunternehmen im bewaffneten Konflikt. Eine völkerrechtliche Bewertung. 2010.